A Student's Guide to History

EIGHTH EDITION

A Student's Guide to History

Jules R. Benjamin

Ithaca College

Bedford/St. Martin's

Boston ♦ New York

For Bedford/St. Martin's

History Editor: Katherine E. Kurzman
Developmental Editor: Laura Arcari
Production Editor: Karen S. Baart
Production Supervisor: Dennis J. Conroy
Director of Marketing: Karen Melton
Editorial Assistants: Jamie Farrell, Amy McConathy
Production Assistant: Thomas Crehan
Copyeditor: Lisa Wehrle
Indexer: Steve Csipke
Cover Design: Diana Coe / ko Design Studio
Cover Art: World map from *Novus Atlas* published by Willem Janszoom Blaeu and
    Iohannem Blaeu, Amsterdam, 1649. Courtesy of the Harvard Map Collection.
Composition: Pine Tree Composition, Inc.
Printing and Binding: Haddon Craftsmen, an R.R. Donnelley & Sons Company

President: Charles H. Christensen
Editorial Director: Joan E. Feinberg
Director of Editing, Design, and Production: Marcia Cohen
Managing Editor: Elizabeth M. Schaaf

Library of Congress Control Number: 00–103094

Manufactured in the United States of America.

5   4   3   2   1   0
f   e   d   c   b   a

For information, write: Bedford/St. Martin's, 75 Arlington Street, Boston, MA 02116
    (617-399-4000)

ISBN: 0–312–24765–6

Acknowledgments

About.com search results. Copyright © 1999 by Jone Johnson Lewis (womenshistory.about
    .com), licensed to About.com. Used by permission of About.com, Inc. which can be found
    on the Web at <www.about.com>. All rights reserved.
Antiwar Demonstration at the Democratic National Convention (1968). The Bettman Archive.
City Life in Ithaca, N.Y. From the collection of the DeWitt Historical Society of Tompkins
    County.
Excerpt from *The Limits of Power: The World and United States Foreign Policy, 1945–1954* by Joyce
    Kolko and Gabriel Kolko. Reprinted by permission of Joyce and Gabriel Kolko and
    HarperCollins Publishers, Inc.
Excerpt from *The Marked Men* by Aris Fakinos. Copyright © 1971 by Liveright Publishing Cor-
    poration. Originally published as *Les Derniers Barbares,* Éditions du Seuil, 1968. Reprinted
    by permission of Georges Borchardt, Inc., for the author.

*Acknowledgments and copyrights are continued at the back of the book on page 222, which constitutes an
extension of the copyright page. It is a violation of the law to reproduce these selections by any means
whatsoever without the written permission of the copyright holder.*

To Elaine, Aaron, and Adam

Preface

The first edition of this book appeared twenty-five years ago. I was motivated to write it when I discovered, as have so many others, that there was an invisible barrier between my students and the material I was teaching them. This barrier differed from one student to the next, but at its core was the students' need to learn basic skills: study, research, and writing. Although many of my students had little background knowledge in history, the skills barrier was the more serious problem and was very time consuming. If my students could not take concise notes, if they could not understand what an exam question required of them, or if they could not write clearly, then my effort to explain the meaning of the past ran up against a wall of incomprehension. Today, the situation remains much the same.

I sought to attack the skills barrier outside the classroom so that I could devote my class time to teaching history. In this effort I turned to my students — I asked them why the course material seemed so formidable and what they needed to know to demonstrate their understanding of it. The first edition of the *Guide* was a kind of collaboration: the original structure, still discernable in this eighth edition, took the form of responses to their needs. The longevity of the *Guide* attests to its ability to meet students' needs. In a quarter-century, however, some of these needs have changed. New technologies have arisen to facilitate teaching and learning. Today, writing requires skill not only with language but also with word-processing programs. Research requires knowledge not only of the organization of a college library but also of the World Wide Web. In recent editions of the *Guide* I have sought to provide students with skills appropriate to an age of digital media.

Chapter 1 discusses why people study history and how we, as historians, go about our investigations. It examines the different interpretations of history and the differing directions of research in the discipline. This chapter also describes how the study of history can prepare students for a variety of careers. Chapter 2 teaches fundamental skills about reading a history assignment, taking notes in class, and studying for exams. The chapter includes annotated examples guiding students to the main ideas of a text; a section on reading maps, charts, graphs, tables, and other nonwritten materials; and material on collaborative work and communicating online. Chapter 3 is new and focuses on writing skills. Using examples, it demonstrates clear and connected writing. It takes the reader through the steps of building an essay and provides guidance on matters of style and mechanics. Finally, examples of writing appropriate to the variety of history assignments are provided, including a sample book review. Chapters 4 and 5 deal with more complex tasks: preparing and writing a research paper. These chapters help students choose a research topic, narrow it down to a practical theme, use the library and conduct research online to gather information, organize their research, and present the results of their work. Chapters 4 and 5 also stress the importance of good writing skills and the dangers of plagiarism. The full-scale, annotated sample research paper that concludes Chapter 5 illustrates how to put together research findings and how to write footnotes or endnotes and a bibliography.

Appendix A describes the different types of information available for history research and lists hundreds of sources that can lead students to everything from a short definition of *feudalism* to a series of books on the history of medicine. Also included is a section on electronic resources available on the World Wide Web. This broad list of resources will help students with almost any assignment in almost any history course. Appendix B includes sections on local and family history research and provides lists of grammar and style manuals and common abbreviations.

New to This Edition

Each successive edition of the *Guide* has benefited from comments and suggestions from some of the hundreds of instructors who have assigned it and from some of the more than a quarter-million students who have read it over the years.

The last edition of the *Guide* was revised in ways that made it a more practical and flexible research tool. Following the recent changes in the study of history, I highlighted the latest directions in which the discipline is moving. Building on the changes of the last edition and responding to the growing influence of computers and the World Wide Web on the history classroom, I have strengthened the *Guide* in three fundamental areas. First, in response to our users' requests for more help on writing, I have completely overhauled the research and writing sections and added a new chapter on writing that covers the process of crafting an essay. This new chapter also includes material on the basics of style and mechanics. Second, in response to the needs of today's students, I have expanded and integrated my coverage of the computer as a tool for research and writing throughout. Acknowledging that many students today rely heavily on the computer, we are also offering a companion online version of the *Guide* at <www.bedfordstmartins .com/history/benjamin> for free to give students quick access to particular skills and to succinct advice on carrying out assignments while they are simultaneously working online. Lastly, I have continued to improve the *Guide* in ways that make it an even more practical and flexible reference tool. New guidelines boxes, the inclusion of new skills such as collaborative work and communicating online, a new sample book review, updated documentation models, and a greatly expanded and updated appendix of reference sources for history students make the eighth edition of the *Guide* the most complete and helpful reference guide for history students. To keep pace with the varied needs of today's history students, I have added, expanded, or amended topics in every chapter.

A chapter on writing.   In response to users' requests for the addition of material on mechanics and style, I have added a new chapter on writing that provides detailed instruction on the writing process and basic grammatical and mechanical advice. Chapter 3, "How to Write History Assignments: The Importance of Writing Skills," covers the fundamentals of good writing and includes sections on why clear writing is important, the components of clear writing, and how to build an essay. The chapter concludes with instruction on how to prepare the most common history assignments. In addition to the coverage of essay exams, book reviews, and short papers, the eighth edition now includes instruction on preparing comparative book reviews and comparative essays, and advice on comparing primary documents.

Greatly expanded and enhanced coverage of the computer as a tool for research and writing.   In this edition, I have thoroughly revised the sections dealing with online research. I have integrated advice on working with computers throughout the book and added new sections on conducting research on the World Wide Web. Other new areas include guidelines for evaluating Web sites; help on using spell- and grammar-checkers; advice on taking notes on computers and downloading materials from the Web; and an in-depth section on communicating online, including advice on using e-mail, listservs, and chatrooms, and on participating in electronic conferences and seminars.

Online version of the eighth edition.   Allowing students to consult the *Guide* while they work online, the online version of the *Guide* can be found at <www.bedfordstmartins.com/history/benjamin>. This site condenses important elements of the skills-based material from the *Guide* in an easy-to-use format for students.

New boxed guidelines.   Because of the popularity of the guidelines boxes that serve as checklists for students, I have added boxed guidelines in four areas new to the eighth edition: taking lecture notes, the components of clear writing, evaluating print and Web sources, and guidelines for peer editing.

Updated and expanded reference sources. The more than six hundred basic reference sources and guides in Appendix A, categorized by type and subject, familiarize students with research materials available in the library and online. A greatly expanded and updated section on electronic sources will help students navigate the World Wide Web with lists of search engines, indexes and directories, online archives, and databases as well as a list of specialized sites for history research. I have taken care to provide students with access to the best of the Web and to exclude sites that are unreliable or superficial.

Section on incorporating visual materials in history papers. In response to the easier access that students now have to historically significant, nonprint documents on the World Wide Web, I have expanded on the existing coverage of nonwritten materials by including advice on downloading, incorporating, and citing visual sources in research papers.

New section introducing students to group work. Because of the growing use of collaborative work in the classroom and in the workplace, I have added a new discussion of group work that includes collaborative activities online. The eighth edition also includes a new guidelines box on peer editing.

New sample book review. The new sample book review, on the *Narrative of the Life of Frederick Douglass: An American Slave,* shows students how to compose a book review.

I am always looking to improve the *Guide* and would appreciate any suggestions that you would like to share. The e-mail address for comments is <guidetohistory8@bedfordstmartins.com>.

Acknowledgments

I wish to thank the many reviewers of the manuscript: Ronald L. Hatzenbuehler, Idaho State University; Elizabeth A. Lehfeldt, Cleveland State University; Bruce Leslie, SUNY, Brockport; Carol Loats, University of Southern Colorado; Keith F. Lynip, Appalachian State University; Amy Thompson McCandless, College of Charleston; Steven Mintz, University of Houston; Paul Douglas Newman, University of Pittsburgh at Johnstown; Russ Van Wyk, University of North Carolina at Chapel Hill; Steven Jay White, Lexington Community College; William Wood, Point Loma Nazarene University. I would also like to thank my research assistant, Michael Clisham, whose work found its way into many sections of this new edition, most notably the new section on communicating online. My understanding of the World Wide Web was greatly enhanced by John Henderson, reference librarian at Ithaca College. I also want to express my great respect for those at Bedford/St. Martin's who have contributed to this edition of the *Guide*: Charles Christensen, Joan Feinberg, Katherine Kurzman, Laura Arcari, Karen Baart, Elizabeth Schaaf, Chip Turner, Amy McConathy, and Jamie Farrell. I am in their debt not only for their editorial skills but also for their commitment to this book and its mission.

Jules R. Benjamin
Ithaca College

A Note to Students

This book has been around for a long time. Since I wrote the first edition in 1975, more than a quarter of a million students have read it. Each year, students have written telling me how the book helped them to master some important part of their work in a history course. Many have offered suggestions for improving the book and some of their ideas have been incorporated into the book you are about to read. You can still write to me or the publisher. Now you can also send your comments to me via e-mail. The address is <guidetohistory8@ bedfordstmartins.com>.

I have tried to make this book useful to you regardless of the kind of history course you are taking. You may be taking world history, Western civilization, ancient history, modern history, social history, economic history, or the history of a particular region or nation. This book presents the tools you need to succeed in your history course. It also gives you skills that will open the past to you.

Each section of the book discusses a specific kind of assignment. Clear guidelines, practical examples, and concise explanations guide you through reading, studying, researching, and writing tasks. Care has been taken to organize the book in a way that makes it easy to find the answers to your questions about history assignments.

In addition to its practical purpose, I have also written this book to introduce you to the enormous world that is our heritage. This world is as fascinating as the world you live in today, or as any vision of the future. I hope to convince you that the study of history is not an idle journey into a dead past but a way to understanding and living in the present. You can use these tools to succeed not only in your history courses but in your future career. Finally, you can use them to answer important questions about your own life and your relationship to the world in which you live. This larger use is what makes the study of history really valuable.

Jules R. Benjamin
Ithaca College

Contents

4   How to Research a History Topic   *75*

CHAPTER 1

The Subject of History and How to Use It

What Historians Are Trying to Do

Since the time when human beings invented writing, they have left records of their understanding of the world and of the events in their lives and how they felt about them. By studying the records that previous generations have left, we can find out about the kind of lives they led and how they faced their problems. We can use what we learn about the experiences of people who lived before us to help solve problems we face today. Though the modern world is quite different from the societies in which our ancestors lived, the story of their accomplishments and failures is the only yardstick by which we can measure the quality of our own lives and the success of our social arrangements.

All of us look into the past from time to time. We read historical novels or books about historical events. We gaze at old photographs or listen to the stories our grandparents tell. **Historians,**[1] however, make a serious and systematic study of the past and attempt to use the knowledge they gain to help explain human nature and contemporary affairs. Professional historians spend their lives pursuing the meaning of the past for the present. To amateurs, historical research is like a hobby, but their occasional journeys into the past may contribute to the store of human knowledge and can greatly influence their own lives. Your study and research as a student qualify you as an amateur historian. Your examination of the past is part of the same search for knowledge carried on generation after generation.

[1]Terms in **boldface** are defined in the Glossary on page 217.

1

What History Can Tell You

Everything that exists in the present has come out of the past, and no matter how new and unique it seems to be, it carries some of the past with it. The latest hit by the newest group is the result of the evolution of that group's musical style and of the trends in music and society that have influenced it. Perhaps their style developed from earlier rock styles associated with the Beatles, or perhaps they are taking off from even older folk themes used by Bob Dylan. Well, Dylan was influenced by Woody Guthrie, who wrote his songs in the 1930s and whose music grew out of his contact with the heritage of American folk music from the nineteenth century, which in turn had come in great measure from earlier music in England and Scotland, some of which has its origins in the Middle Ages. Modern jazz, such as the music of Duke Ellington and Billie Holiday or the more recent music of Miles Davis, Chick Corea, and Pat Metheny, evolved from the music of black communities in the United States and the Caribbean. Enslaved black people brought the earlier forms of that music with them from Africa in the eighteenth and nineteenth centuries. So you can see that the house of the present is filled with windows into the past.

The car you ride in, although it may have been designed only a few years ago, carries within it the basic components of the "horseless carriage" of the early twentieth century. Your car works because people who knew how to make carriages, bicycles, and engines put their ideas together in a new way. The knowledge necessary to make the carriages and bicycles came, in turn, from earlier inventions. Some, like the wheel, go back into the antiquity of human history.

Everything has a history. At least part of the answer to any question about the contemporary world can come from studying the circumstances that led up to it. The problem is to find those past events, forces, arrangements, ideas, or facts that had the greatest influence on the present subject you have questions about. The more you understand about these past influences, the more you will know about the present subject to which they are related.

History and the Everyday World

Most of us are curious. Children are always asking their parents the "why" of things. When we grow up, we continue to ask questions because we retain our fascination with the mysteriousness and complexity of the world. Because everything has a history, most questions can be answered, at least in part, by historical investigation.

What are some of the things about which you are curious? Have you ever wondered why women's skirts in old movies are so long, or why French men often embrace one another whereas English men almost never do? Perhaps you have wondered how the Kennedy or Rockefeller families came to be rich, or why the Japanese attacked Pearl Harbor. Have you thought about why most of the people of southern Europe are Catholic whereas most northern Europeans are not? Many Asian peoples bow when they greet one another; many Americans shake hands. The questions could go on forever; the answers are written somewhere in the record of the past.

The record of the past is not only contained in musty volumes on library shelves; it is all around us in museums, historical preservations, and the antique furnishings and utensils contained in almost every household. Our minds are living museums because the ideas we hold (for example, democracy, freedom, equality, competitiveness) have come down to us by way of a long historical journey. Though we are usually unaware of it, the past is always with us. Because history is literally at our fingertips, we can travel back into it without difficulty.

A Brief Journey into the Past

If you have ever driven any distance, you have probably ridden over a system of very modern superhighways with high speed limits and no cross traffic or stoplights. This national highway network, begun in the 1950s, connects all the major cities of the United States and is known as the interstate system. These roads were planned by the Eisenhower Administration in 1955, and, though they are the newest highways in the country, they have a history that is half a century long.

Looking for the marks of history in the world around us is something like the task of the geologist or archeologist. However, instead of digging down into the earth to uncover the past, the historical researcher digs into the visible, everyday elements of society to find the historical roots from which they sprang. The fact that the interstate highway system built in the 1960s and 1970s had its origins in the 1950s is just, so to speak, the uppermost layer of history. If a study of the newest highways can take us back forty years, what about the historical roots of the older highways or of the country roads? How far into the past can we travel on them?

Turn off the eight-lane interstate, past the gleaming Exxon station, past the drive-up window of Burger King, past the bright signs before the multistoried Holiday Inn, and onto, say, U.S. Route 51 or 66. These are older highways, built mostly in the 1940s and 1950s. Being from an earlier period, like older strata of rock, perhaps they can tell us something of life in an earlier period of America.

When you leave the interstate system for this older road network, you first notice that the speed limit is lower and that many of the buildings are older. As you ride along at the slower pace, there are no signs saying "Downtown Freeway ½ mile" or "Indiana Turnpike — Exit 26N." They say "Lubbock 38 miles," or "Cedar Rapids 14 miles." As you approach Lubbock or Cedar Rapids, you will see motels less elaborate than the Holiday Inn. They may be small wooden cottages with fading paint and perhaps a sign that says "Star Motor Court" or "Stark's Tourist Cabins." Instead of Burger King or McDonald's, you may pass "Betty's Restaurant" or "Little River Diner." If you pay close attention to these buildings and do not become distracted by the more modern structures between them, you can take a trip into history even as you ride along. All of the older restaurants, stores, and gas stations you see were built before the large shopping centers and parking lots that separate them, and they are clues to the history of the highway on which you are riding. Places like the Star Motor Court and the Little River Diner probably were built when the road was new. Unless they have been modernized, they are relics of a previous historical period — when men named Roosevelt and Truman were president and when the cars that rode by looked like balloons with their big rounded hoods, trunks, and fenders. The diner isn't air-conditioned, and the sign over the tourist cabins proudly proclaims that they are "heated." This is the world of the 1930s and 1940s.

Now turn off the highway at State Route 104 where the sign says "Russell Springs 3 miles" or where it says "Hughesville 6 miles." Again the speed limit drops, and the bright colors fade farther away. You are on a road that may have been built in the 1920s and 1930s or earlier (in older sections of America, the country roads can go back a hundred years or more). Time has removed many of the buildings that once stood along this road, but if you look closely, the past is there ready to speak to you. The gas station here has only one set of pumps, and the station office sells bread, eggs, and kerosene. The faded advertisements on the wall display some products that you may have never heard of — NeHi Orange and Red Man Chewing Tobacco. If you see a restaurant or motel, it may be boarded up because the people who used to stop in on their way to Russell Springs or Hughesville now go another way or may no longer live in the country but in a nearby city. However, many of the homes along Route 104 are still there. They were built when only farmland straddled the road, and they may go back to a time when horses and not internal combustion engines pulled the traffic past the front door. Such relics of early technology as old washing machines and refrigerators may stand on the tilting wooden porches, and a close look behind the tall weeds beside the dirt driveway may reveal the remains of a 1936 La Salle automobile. As you stop before one of the old farmhouses, the past is all around you, and, although the place does not appear in its youthful form, a little imagination can reconstruct what life was like here on the day in 1933 when President Roosevelt closed all the banks or the day in 1918 when the Great War in Europe ended.

The line linking past to present never breaks, and the house itself has a history, as do the people who once lived in it. In this sense, every house is haunted with its own past, and a keen eye can see the signs. Enter the house and you can see the stairway that was rebuilt in 1894, and in the main bedroom upstairs the fireplace, which was put in about 1878, the year the house was built. Perhaps the old Bible on the table near the bed notes the year the family came to the United States, and the dates in the early nineteenth century when the parents of the immigrants who built the house were born.

The story could go on forever, although the evidence would become slimmer and slimmer. You could find out from county records who owned the land before the house was built, going back perhaps to the time when the people who lived on the land were American Indians. In distance you may have traveled only ten or twenty miles from the interstate highway, and it may have taken you less than an hour; but by looking for the signs of the past in the present, you have traveled more than a hundred years into history.

If you think about and study the passage of time between the old farmhouse on the country road and the gleaming service station by the interstate, you may come to understand some of the social, political, and economic forces that moved events away from the old wooden porch and sent them speeding down the interstate highway. The more you know about this process, the more you will learn about the time when the farmhouse was new and the more you will understand how the interstate highway came about, what you are doing riding on it, and into what kind of a future you may be heading.

Historians don't usually wander into history in such a casual fashion. They have to be trained in their methods of investigation and analysis. As an introduction to your own historical research and study, the next section will describe some of the tools employed by historians in their examination of the records of the past.

How Historians Work

Like you, historians are challenged by the complexity of the world, and many want to use their studies of the past to help solve the problems of the present or future. The questions that can come to mind are numberless, and serious historical investigators must choose wisely among them. They do not want to spend a lot of effort pursuing the kind of question to which history has no answer (for example, "What is the purpose of the Universe?" "Am I a lovable person?" "Who is the smartest person in the world?"). Nor do they want to struggle to achieve the solution to a problem that is not of real importance. (Historical investigation can probably tell you who wore the first pair of pants with a zipper in it, but that might not be worth knowing.) The main difficulty facing historians is not eliminating unanswerable or unimportant questions but choosing among the important ones.

A historian's choice among important questions is determined by personal values, by the concerns of those who support the historian's work, by the nature of the time in which the historian lives, or by a combination of all of these. The ways in which these influences operate are very complex, and often historians themselves are unaware of them.

When the historian has chosen his or her subject, many questions still remain. For example, does historical evidence dealing with the subject exist, and if so, where can it be found? If someone wanted to study gypsy music from medieval Europe, and that music was never written down or mentioned in historical accounts of the period, then little or nothing could be found about this subject through historical research. Even if records exist on a particular subject, the historian may be unaware of them or unable to locate them. Perhaps the records are in an unfamiliar language or are in the possession of individuals or governments that deny access to them. Sometimes locating historical evidence can be a problem.

Having determined that records *do* exist and that they can be located and used, the historian faces another and more important problem: What is the credibility or reliability of the evidence? Is it genuine? How accurate are the records, and what biases were held by those who wrote them? If sources of information are in conflict, which is correct? Or is it possible that most of the sources are in error? Historians must pick and choose among the sources they uncover, and that is not always easy to do. The historian's own biases also cloud the picture, making impartial judgment extremely difficult.

Primary and Secondary Sources of Evidence

There are two basic forms of historical **evidence:** primary and secondary. **Primary sources** (see Figures 1.1 and 1.2) record the actual words of someone who participated in or witnessed the events described or of someone who got his or her information from participants. These can be newspaper accounts, diaries, notebooks, letters, minutes, interviews, and any works written by persons who claim first-hand knowledge of an event. Another primary source is official statements by established organizations or significant personages — royal decrees, church edicts, political party platforms, laws, and speeches. Primary sources also include any official records and statistics, such as those concerning births, marriages, deaths, taxes, deeds, and court

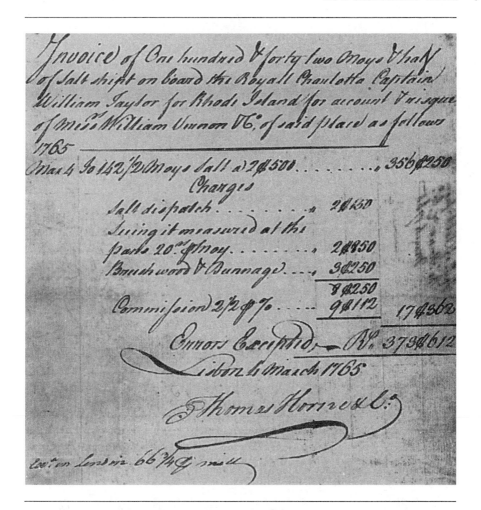

FIGURE 1.1 Example of Primary Evidence (1765)

Primary documents are often handwritten rather than printed and reflect the vocabulary and writing style of the day. Here is an invoice describing a shipment of salt carried from Lisbon, Portugal, to Providence, Rhode Island, in March 1765 "on Board the Royall Charlotta Captain William Taylor for Rhode Island for account & risque of Mr. William Vernon. . . ." The value of the cargo is written in Portuguese escudos. The document was handwritten and signed by Thomas Horne just after the salt was loaded onboard the ship. It brings us as close as we can come to the actual scene on the docks at Lisbon over two hundred years ago.

trials. Recent history has been recorded by photographs, films, and audio- and videotapes. These recordings of events as they actually

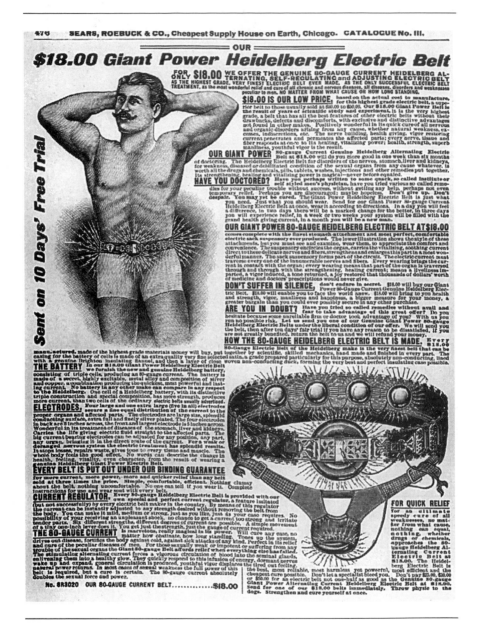

FIGURE 1.2   Example of Primary Evidence (1902)

A more recent primary document is a printed advertisement for a Heidelberg Electric Belt that appeared in the Sears, Roebuck and Company catalog of 1902. If you are doing research on some of the strange medical cures sold at that time, the claims made in this advertisement would be an important piece of primary evidence. What kind of "illness" do you think this belt was supposed to cure?

happened are also primary forms of evidence. Artifacts are another form of primary evidence. These are things made by people in the past: houses, public buildings, tools, clothing, and much more.

Secondary sources (see Figure 1.3) record the findings of someone who did not observe the event but who investigated primary evidence. Most history books and articles fall into this category, although some are actually *tertiary* (third level) evidence because they rely not on primary evidence but are themselves drawn from secondary sources.

Douglass's personal story, like American history itself, is both inspiring and terrible. Few writers have better combined experience with the music of words to make us see the deepest contradictions of American history, the tragedy and necessity of conflict between slavery and freedom in a republic. Douglass exposes the bitterness and absurdity of racism at the same time that he imagines the fullest possibilities of the natural rights tradition, the idea that people are born with equal rights in the eyes of God and that those rights can be protected under human law. Few have written more effectively about the endurance of the human spirit under oppression. And in American letters, we have no better illustration of liberation through the power of language than in Douglass's *Narrative*. With his pen, Douglass was very much a self-conscious artist, and with his voice and his activism, he was a self-conscious prophet.

Readers of the *Narrative* quickly come to realize that language, written and oratorical, had been a fascination and a weapon for Douglass during his years as a slave. When he first spoke before a meeting of New Bedford blacks against African colonization in March 1839, and when he delivered his first public speeches before a gathering of the Massachusetts Anti-Slavery Society on Nantucket Island in August 1841, he was not merely appearing as the spontaneous abolitionist miracle he was often portrayed — and portrayed himself — to be. No doubt the first effort at "speaking to white people" at the Nantucket meeting was a "severe cross," as he describes the experience in the *Narrative*.[4] But Douglass was no stranger to oratory, or to the moral arguments, sentimentalism, and evangelical zeal that characterized the antislavery movement during that era. By 1841 he had been reading abolitionist speeches, editorials, and poetry in William Lloyd Garrison's newspaper, *The Liberator*, for at least two years. And as the *Narrative* tells us in a variety of ways, Douglass had been a practicing abolitionist of a kind — out of self-interest and for his fellow bondsmen — even while he was a slave. He had read the Bible extensively, and he had discovered and modeled his ideas and style on a remarkable 1797 book, *The Columbian Orator*, by Caleb Bingham, a selection from which is reproduced in this volume.

FIGURE 1.3   Example of Secondary Evidence
This example of secondary evidence comes from David W. Blight, ed., *Narrative of the Life of Frederick Douglass, An American Slave, Written by Himself* (Bedford/St. Martin's, 1993). Douglass was an escaped slave who became a leader of the movement to end slavery in the United States. The book includes an essay, published along with Douglass's autobiography (a *primary* source), that explains the significance of the autobiography and sets it in its historical context.

When your own history **research paper** is finished, it will be secondary or tertiary evidence to anyone who may use it in the future.

The problem of determining the reliability of evidence is a serious one. Secondary and even primary sources can be fraudulent, inaccurate, or biased. Eyewitness accounts may be purposely distorted in order to avert blame or to bestow praise on a particular individual or group. Without intending to misinform, even on-the-scene judgments can be incorrect. Sometimes, the closer you are to an event, the more emotionally involved you are, and this distorts your understanding of it. We can all recall events in which we completely misunderstood the feelings, actions, and even words of another person. Historians have to weigh evidence carefully to see if those who have participated in an event understood it well enough to accurately describe it, and whether later authors understood the meaning of the primary sources they used. Official statements present another problem — that of propaganda or concealment. A government, group, or institution may make statements that it wishes others to believe but that are not true. What a group says may not be what it does. This is especially true in politics.

To check the reliability of evidence, historians use the tests of consistency and corroboration: Does the evidence contradict itself and does it disagree with evidence from other sources? Historical research always involves checking one source against another. For example, Figure 1.4 on page 11 presents two primary documents that both report the fighting at Lexington and Concord, Massachusetts, in 1775 — battles that began the Revolutionary War. As you read them, consider what additional sources would help you decide which report is more accurate. The two accounts agree on some facts but disagree on the responsibility for the fighting. Eyewitness accounts from other English soldiers and from American colonials who were there will help in determining which description is more accurate. It might turn out, for example, that parts of *each* account are correct and other parts are distorted in some way. Sometimes there is no *one* true source for the history of an event. Still, the more primary sources you read, the closer you will come to knowing the event in all its details and meanings.

The bias of a source also presents difficulties. People's attitudes toward the world influence the way they interpret events. For example, you and your parents may have different attitudes toward music, sex, religion, or politics. These differences can cause you to disagree with them about the value of a rock concert, a Sunday sermon, or the president. Historians have their own attitudes toward the subjects they are investigating, and these cause them to draw different conclusions about the character and importance of religious, political, intellectual, and other movements. Later historians must take these biases into account when weighing the reliability of evidence.

AMERICAN ACCOUNT OF THE BATTLE OF LEXINGTON:
Account by the Provincial Congress at Watertown, Massachusetts,
April 26, 1775

By the clearest depositions relative to this transaction, it will appear that on the night preceding the nineteenth of April instant, a body of the king's troops, under the command of colonel Smith, were secretly landed at Cambridge, with an apparent design to take or destroy the military and other stores, provided for the defence of this colony, and deposited at Concord — that some inhabitants of the colony, on the night aforesaid, whilst travelling peaceably on the road, between Boston and Concord, were seized and greatly abused by armed men, who appeared to be officers of general Gage's army; that the town of Lexington, by these means, was alarmed, and a company of the inhabitants mustered on the occasion — that the regular troops on their way to Concord, marched into the said town of Lexington, and the said company, on their approach, began to disperse — that, notwithstanding this, the regulars rushed on with great violence and first began hostilities, by firing on said Lexington company, whereby they killed eight, and wounded several others — that the regulars continued their fire, until those of said company, who were neither killed nor wounded, had made their escape — that colonel Smith, with the detachment then marched to Concord, where a number of provincials were again fired on by the troops, two of them killed and several wounded, before the provincials fired on them, and provincials were again fired on by the troops, produced an engagement that lasted through the day, in which many of the provincials and more of the regular troops were killed and wounded. . . .

By order,
Joseph Warren, President.

ENGLISH ACCOUNT OF THE BATTLE OF LEXINGTON:
Report of Lieutenant-Colonel Smith to Governor Gage, April 22, 1775

I think it proper to observe, that when I had got some miles on the march from Boston, I detached six light infantry companies to march with all expedition to seize the two bridges on different roads beyond Concord. On these companies' arrival at Lexington, I understand, from the report of Major Pitcairn, who was with them, and from many officers, that they found on a green close to the road a body of the country people drawn up in military order, with arms and accoutrements, and, as appeared after, loaded; and that they had posted some men in a dwelling and Meeting-house. Our troops advanced towards them, without any intention of injuring them, further than to inquire the reason of their being thus assembled, and, if not satisfactory, to have secured their arms; but they in confusion went off, principally to the left, only one of them fired before he went off, and three or four more jumped over a wall and fired from behind it among the soldiers; on which the troops returned it, and killed several of them. They likewise fired on the soldiers from the Meeting and dwelling-houses. . . . While at Concord we saw vast numbers assembling in many parts; at one of the bridges they marched down, with a very considerable body, on the light infantry posted there. On their coming pretty near, one of our men fired on them, which they returned; on which an action ensued, and some few were killed and wounded. . . . On our leaving Concord to return to Boston, they began to fire on us from behind the walls, ditches, trees, &c., which, as we marched, increased to a very great degree, and continued without intermission of five minutes altogether, for, I believe, upwards of eighteen miles . . .
I have the honor, &c.,
F. Smith, Lieutenant-Colonel 10th Foot.

FIGURE 1.4   Two Conflicting Primary Documents

Interpreting and Organizing Evidence

In analyzing the evidence, historians must find some way of *organizing* it so that they can make clear its meaning. A mass of facts and opinions concerning a subject is not a historical study. The task of the trained historian is to arrange the material so that it supports a particular conclusion. This conclusion may have been in the historian's mind at the outset, or it might be the result of investigation. If the evidence does not appear to support the conclusion, however, then the historian must either change that conclusion or seek other evidence to support it.

Once a historian is satisfied that research has uncovered sufficient evidence to support a particular conclusion, then he or she works to display the evidence in a manner that will clearly show that the conclusion drawn is a proper one. If any evidence that leads to other conclusions is uncovered, the historian has a responsibility to include it. In doing so, he or she must show how the supporting evidence is stronger than the nonsupporting evidence. There are many ways of organizing evidence in support of a conclusion. The historian's arguments in favor of a particular conclusion must be strong and convincing, and the logic of these arguments must not be faulty.

You will confront the issue faced by all historians when you conduct your own historical research, an assignment that is part of all advanced (and some beginning) history courses. (See Chapters 4 and 5.)

Changing Directions of Historical Research

When historians investigate the questions that interest them the most, they are influenced in their approach by their values and experiences, their academic training, and their beliefs about which aspects of human nature and the human environment are most important in understanding those questions. As a result, historians may focus on personal, social, political, intellectual, economic, cultural, diplomatic, ethnic, psychological, or economic aspects of their subject. Again, depending on which approach seems most helpful, they may also combine several of these research directions, and often do. For example, social historians base their research on the development of human communities and their interaction with the larger society. Cultural historians focus on attitudes and behaviors and how they change over time. Intellectual historians examine powerful ideas and how they influence beliefs. Political historians look at issues of power and how they operate in institutions such as governments, political parties, and interest groups. Diplomatic historians deal with relations between governments and nations and how they change over time. Economic historians study developments in technology, production, consumption, and the division of wealth, while historians of science and technology examine the evolution of scientific knowledge, how changes in such knowledge arise, and how its application influences society.

As the interests of historians have shifted, new approaches and questions have become important in recent years. Historians of family and private life examine the structural and emotional development of small, intimate groups and the responses of these groups to powerful forces such as wars, depressions, class and ethnic conflict, and technological change. Another area of growing interest encompasses the history of sports, the media (especially film), and other aspects of popular culture. Environmental historians examine the interaction between human communities and their habitats and the attitudes these communities have toward nature. One of the most rapidly expanding areas of research in recent decades has been women's history, an enormous topic that earlier generations of historians (most of whom were men) had ignored.

While some historians look at personal life and small groups, others, in contrast, study broad stretches of history. The field of world history takes in centuries of change across large areas of the globe. Comparative history seeks to learn the significance of an institution, political system, people, or nation by comparing its history with that of others. You can learn much about Vietnam, for example, by studying the ways in which its culture resembled or diverged from that of China.

Two older areas of historical research are reviving. Genealogy and local history have returned to importance as people in countries undergoing rapid change become concerned with holding on to or rediscovering the past of their family or neighborhood. Genealogy traces the history of a particular family. Local history, pursued with enthusiasm by residents and scholars alike, examines the evolution of a town, community, or neighborhood.

Methods of Historical Research

Certain directions of historical research have been influenced by other disciplines: family history by psychology, demography by sociology, enthnohistory by anthropology, political history by political science, and economic history by economics. While still adhering to the special focus of history — examining and explaining the past — historians welcome ideas and methods of analyzing evidence from other fields. For instance, quantitative history (called cliometrics) uses quantitative data, such as election returns, price levels, and population **statistics** of earlier periods, to re-create a picture of earlier times. Because quantitative data is uniform, it measures the same things — votes, prices, numbers of inhabitants — over time. Thus, comparisons can be made among statistics from different periods. The electoral support of a political party, the price of wheat, or the size of a town can be examined to see if it is rising or falling and at what rate.

If the uniformity of the data can be established (that is, if the numbers really *do* measure the same thing in each period), then they can be subjected to mathematical analysis. Percentages, ratios, averages, the mean, median, and mode can be obtained. If the dataset is large, the historian may subject it to more complex analyses that explore patterns within the numbers and among subgroups of them: the frequency distribution, the standard deviation, and the coefficient of variation. The more elaborate kinds of statistical analysis can determine not merely how fast prices are rising or where the majority of a party's voters reside; they also can compare different kinds of changes — party registration with price levels, population decline with employment levels — in an attempt to describe the conditions under which certain changes occur. By noting those categories of numbers (variables) that move together, the historian can begin to explore the causes of the changes under examination. Computers make this task more manageable, allowing historians to work with very large datasets and to analyze them in new ways.

The Computer and Historical Research

The computer has become an important tool for gathering historical information in all fields, not just in quantitative history. Historians use computers not only to analyze data but also to gain easier access to sources of historical information. Unpublished information residing in **archives** scattered around the world can be made available online to historians (and students) with access to computers that are part of a network like the **World Wide Web.** Primary sources that have been entered into computer databases can be read (and even printed out) by researchers anywhere. Secondary sources that are available only in special libraries can be read in this way also — provided that they have been put into computer-readable form. Already, history **databases,** containing millions of individual historical statistics, are available in many college libraries. The texts of documents, articles, and, in some cases, whole books, can be brought to your computer screen. With Web **"plug-ins,"** researchers can gain access to art, maps, photographs, recordings, and even films that once resided only in faraway archives. (For more information on using computers in your own research, see p. 81 and Appendix A, pp. 170–211.)

Philosophies of History

Historical investigation can lead to very different results depending upon the aspect of human nature or society emphasized and the kind of information obtained. Even greater differences can result from historical investigations that employ different *philosophies* of history.

A philosophy of history is an explanation not only of the most important causes of specific events but of the broadest developments in human affairs. It explains the *forces* of history, what moves them, and in what direction they are headed. The dominant philosophy of history of a particular age is that which most closely reflects the beliefs and values of that age. Most of the historians writing at that time will write from the perspective of that philosophy of history.

Perhaps the oldest philosophy of history is the **cyclical school.** According to this view, events recur periodically. The belief, in short, is that history repeats itself. The essential forces of nature and of human nature are changeless, causing past patterns of events to repeat themselves endlessly. As the saying goes, "There is nothing new under the sun." This view of history was dominant from ancient times until the rise of Christianity. The Aztecs conceived of history this way, as did the Chinese.

A central message of early Christianity was the uniqueness of the life, death, and resurrection of Jesus Christ. In societies influenced by the Christian Church — and especially in Europe in the Middle Ages — the new concept of divine intervention to overthrow the past weakened the cyclical view.[2] The resulting philosophy of history, the **providential school,** held that the course of history was determined by God. The ebb and flow of historical events represent struggles between forces of good and evil. These struggles are protracted, but the eventual victory of good is foreseen.

This particular idea of the providential school — that history is characterized not by ceaseless repetition but by direction and purpose — became an element in the thinking of the more secular age beginning with the eighteenth century. In this new age of scientific inquiry and material advancement, there arose the **progressive school,** whose central belief was that human history illustrates neither endless cycles nor divine intervention but continual progress. According to this school, the situation of humanity is constantly improving. Moreover, this improvement results not from divine providence but from the efforts of human beings themselves. Each generation builds upon the learning and improvements of those preceding it and, in doing so, reaches a higher stage of civilization. This idea of history as continual progress is still very powerful today. Currently, many variations of the progressive philosophy share the field of historical investigation.

Historiography

One final way to approach the study of history is the field of **historiography,** which is the study of changes in the methods, interpretations, and conclusions of historians over time. As historians examine secondary sources, they become aware that earlier studies of the subject they are pursuing often came to surprising conclusions. For example,

---

[2]An earlier development of this new view is found in the Old Testament.

between 1920 and 1939, most of the major histories of World War I placed principal blame for the war on Germany. The prevailing view was that German aggression against its neighbors caused the war. At the end of the war, the Treaty of Versailles required the Germans to disarm and to accept blame by paying "reparations" to the countries it fought against for the great damage the war had caused — even though Germany had suffered greatly also. Despite this general agreement, the experience of the Second World War, this one lasting from 1939 to 1945, led many scholars to rethink the origins of the first one. Historians began to ask how the Nazi movement in Germany, which had engaged in unprecedented brutality against civilians both before and during the second war, had been able to rise to power through elections. What had made so many Germans follow Hitler?

Before coming to power, the Nazi Party had repeatedly charged that Germany had to avenge itself for the war guilt placed on it by the Treaty of Versailles. Slowly, historians of World War I came to realize that the idea that Germany was alone responsible for that conflict had helped the Nazi Party to exploit the patriotism of the German people. Now they looked more closely at the world of 1914 in which the First World War had erupted. Scholars concluded that there were in fact *many* reasons for the earlier war. Germany was no longer the sole culprit. Economic and strategic competition among the major powers (Germany, England, France, Russia, and the United States) was now seen as an important factor. Intensified nationalism in all these nations — not just in Germany — had increased tensions. Also, it was now realized that a series of interlocking alliances among the great powers — which would turn a minor conflict in the Balkans into an all-European war — was another source of the explosion. A simple verdict of German guilt gave way to a complex explanation of the aims and security concerns of many nations. In this case, an attempt to understand Germany's role in World War II led to a new understanding of her role in World War I. This kind of reinterpretation or "revision" is not uncommon in history.

Here is another example: "Reconstruction" refers to the period in U.S. history just after the Civil War when the defeated South was under the political control of the victorious North. For the first time in U.S. history, black people, many of them former slaves, were allowed to be elected to and hold political office. Almost all the books written on this subject prior to the 1930s (whether by northern or southern historians) concluded that southern politics was corrupted and made ineffective during this post–Civil War period by selfish northerners and ignorant black southerners. Since the 1950s, however, scholars have come to very different conclusions. Most now believe that black people's participation in southern government was a healthy development and that the standard of politics in the South was generally equal to that of other regions of the nation at that time.

Part of the reason for this new interpretation was due to later historians' more effective use of primary sources; they looked more closely at the primary documents describing the work of the Reconstruction governments of the southern states. In addition, recent historians have compared the Reconstruction record with politics in northern and western states of the period (an example of the use of comparative history). Finally, in looking back over the older literature and by placing it in the context of the race relations that existed at that particular time, most scholars now conclude that an understanding of the racist attitudes toward African Americans does much to explain the negative conclusions of earlier historians. Historiography, then, is an example of historians using the tools of historical research to study themselves.

How You Can Use History

It is said that experience is the best teacher. Still, our learning would be very narrow if we profited only from our own experiences. Through the study of history, we make other people's experiences our own. In this way, we touch other times and places and add to our lifetime's knowledge that gained by others.

If history is the greatest teacher, what can we do with the knowledge we draw from it? In what practical ways does knowledge of the past help us to accomplish the work we do today or will do tomorrow? Perhaps you wait on customers at McDonald's or are the manager of a bank. Will knowledge acquired in history courses be of direct value to you? Probably not. You can serve burgers and fries satisfactorily without knowing that the Safavid empire of the sixteenth century was located in Persia. You can run a bank without knowledge of the philosophy of John Locke. However, while the bank manager can run the bank without *particular* historical knowledge, he or she cannot do so without writing reports explaining changes in the financial transactions of the bank over time. While the bank's computer will record the amount of money flowing into and out of the bank, it is the manager's written reports that will explain the meaning of these transactions. To write such reports, the manager must have mastered the skills of historical research. Though reports to the bank's main office deal only with the past week's or month's transactions at the branch rather than with past years or centuries, the manager must gather evidence, analyze and summarize it, and draw conclusions about it, just as the historian would do whose subject is the hundred-year history of the bank.

History is not merely a course you take in college; it is a way of thinking about the present, one that attempts to make sense of the complexity of contemporary events by examining what lies behind them. Such an examination is intellectual (its goal is to broaden understanding in general), but it can be practical as well. If business at the branch bank falls off sharply in June, what is the manager to do? Does this mean that the branch should be closed? If the manager had no records of the bank's past performance, the question could not be answered. However, all businesses look at themselves over time and employ researchers and analysts to do so. Thus the manager can examine data on the level of business done by the bank in years past. A study of that data (similar to the primary evidence of the historian) makes it clear that business always drops in June because a major depositor, a nearby factory, shuts down then for retooling. The lesson is a simple one: no business can operate intelligently without an understanding of its own history. In a sense, the office workers in business, government, and institutions operate as historical record-producers and record-keepers. When decisions about policy or future production and investment are made, these records are pulled together in research reports that examine the past experience of the firm (or department or institution) in order to judge the likely result of these decisions.

While the ability to re-create the past is an important ingredient in enabling the bank manager to do a good job, there are many careers in which knowledge of historical research techniques is an essential requirement. Government agencies, large corporations, libraries, museums, labor unions, historical parks, monuments, and restorations all take knowledge of the past so seriously that they employ staffs of historians and archivists whose sole task is to conduct research, organize records, re-create historic buildings and events, and write histories. The fields of public and corporate history, museum and archival management, and historic restoration are only some of the areas that *directly* employ the skills you acquire when studying history in school.

When you learn how to read history, how to research the past, and how to write a summary of your findings, you are mastering career skills as surely as if you were taking a course in real-estate law or restaurant management. The ability to see the present in relationship to the past is a skill needed not only by academic and public historians, archivists, historical novelists, and documentary producers; it is an essential preparation for almost any career. Understanding the past can be its own reward, but it pays off in other ways as well. In fact, people who think that history is irrelevant run the risk of history making that judgment of them.

How to Read a History Assignment, Take Notes in Class, and Prepare for Exams

How to Read a History Assignment

Reading history can be a satisfying experience, but to enjoy the landscape you must first know where you are; that is, you must have a general sense of the subject and of the manner in which it is being presented. If you begin reading before you get your bearings, you may become lost in a forest of unfamiliar facts and interpretations. Before beginning any reading assignment, look over the entire book. Read the preface or introduction. This should tell you something about the author and his or her purpose in writing the work. Then read the table of contents to get a sense of the way in which the author has organized the subject. Next, skim the chapters themselves, reading subheadings and glancing at illustrations and graphed material. If you have the time, preread sections of the book (especially the introductory and concluding chapters) rapidly before reading the full work.

After you have scouted the ground, you will be ready to read. By this time, you should be familiar with the topic of the book (what it is generally all about), the background of the author (politician, journalist, historian, eyewitness, novelist, etc.), when it was written (a hundred-year-old classic, the newest book on the subject), how it is organized (chronologically, topically), and, most important of all, its **theme** and conclusions. The theme of a book is the principal point that an author wishes to make on a subject: that the geography of Spain was a principal factor in that nation's failure to industrialize in the eighteenth and nineteenth centuries; that disagreement on moral issues between J. Robert Oppenheimer and Edward Teller delayed development of the hydrogen bomb. Most authors set out their theme in a preface or introduction. If you understand the principal point the author is trying to make, then the organization and conclusions of the work will become clear to you. The author will be organizing evidence and drawing conclusions to support the theme. By the way, if the theme is not clear or the evidence is not supportive of it, then it is not a good history of its subject no matter how many facts it contains. The ability to spot such weaknesses and describe them is part of learning history too. (For more on developing a theme, see p. 76.)

Reading a Textbook

The most common history assignment is the reading of a **textbook.** Many students hope to get by with their lecture notes, and they put off reading the text until just before the final exam. Reading the text week by week will give you the background knowledge necessary to understand the lectures and supplementary readings. In most courses the lectures embellish portions of the text, and lecturers assume that students are familiar with it. Sitting through a lecture on the economic aspects of the American Revolution will be confusing if you have not read the textbook discussion of the mercantilist theories behind many of the colonists' grievances.

Read the text chapters in close conjunction with the lectures to which they are related. If you are not sure that you understand the material, read it again. Underline (or highlight) the most prominent factual information. Also underline important generalizations, interpretations, and conclusions. Of course, don't underline most of the book. That would be a sign that you cannot tell the difference between the author's main points and the material he or she uses to tie these points together. In addition to underlining, look for passages emphasized by the author or those which you feel reflect the author's viewpoint or with which you disagree. Write your reaction or a summary of the passages in the margin. All of this will come in handy when you prepare to take a test. You will be able to reread the underlined material and your comments and obtain a quick review of the chapter's contents. Before the final, however, you may need to reread the text itself, especially if you are having difficulty in the course or wish to write an outstanding exam. (An example of an underlined and annotated textbook page is shown in Figure 2.1. on p. 21.)

Reading a Monograph

Another typical reading assignment is a **monograph** — a specialized history work on a particular subject. In addition to the procedures used in reading a textbook, you will need to pay special attention to the theme and point of view of these works. They should be read more

Civilizations in Sub-Saharan Africa

Leader of empire of Mali — Mansa Musa (1312–1337)

Under Mansa Musa (1312–1337) Mali's authority reached into the middle Niger city-states of Timbuktu, Jenné and Gao. He put Mali on the European world maps by performing a stunning gold-laden pilgrimage to Mecca, Islam's spiritual captital in the Middle East. Upon returning, Mansa Musa fostered the growth of Islam by constructing magnificent mosques in the major urban centers. With his seemingly inexhaustible supply of gold he commissioned

Growing influence of Islam

Spanish and Middle Eastern scholars and architects to transform Malian cities into great seats of Islamic learning. Leading intellectuals were sent to Morocco and Egypt for higher studies, and at Timbuktu foundations were laid for a university at the famous Sankoré mosque. For decades after Musa, Mali enjoyed a reputation in the Muslim world for high standards of public morality and scholarship as well as for law, order, and security. People and goods flowed freely, enabling the cosmopolitan cities of Timbuktu, Jenné, and Gao to flower into major market centers. Through the leadership of Sungata and Mansa Musa Islam became more deeply implanted among the elite and spread widely in the important towns.

While Mansa Musa made great advances in establishing an efficient administrative bureaucracy, he neglected to develop a formula for succession. Court intrigue and factional disputes fol-

Leader of empire of Songhay — Sunni Ali (1464–1492)

lowed the death of each Mansa. Inevitably, central authority weakened. Gao seceded in 1375 and under Sunni Ali (1464–1492) it blossomed into an expansive territorial empire called Songhay.

Important point

As in Muslim India, it was not uncommon for slaves in Africa to assume considerable administrative and military reponsibilities and on occasion usurp authority. This happened in Songhay in 1493 when a high-ranking Muslim slave, named Muhammad Touré, staged a brilliant palace coup. Lacking traditional legitimacy rooted in a pagan past, he promoted Islamic practices and found Islam an invaluable instrument for political and cultural

Expansion of Songhay under "Askia" Muhammad Touré (1493–1528)

control. Using the praise title of "Askia," Muhammad Touré (1493–1528) extended Songhay's frontiers deep into the strategic Saharan oases, across the Middle Niger to include Mali, and eastward to the emporiums of Hausaland. He then created a labyrinthine bureaucracy of ministries for the army, navy, fisheries, forests, and taxation. Songhay itself was decentralized into provinces, each ruled by a governor chosen from among the Askia's family or royal followers.

FIGURE 2.1   Example of Underlined and Annotated Textbook Page
This example is from Edward McNall Burns et al., *World Civilizations,* 6th ed. (New York: W. W. Norton), pp. 546–47.

carefully because your teacher will expect you to learn not only about the subject they deal with but about the emphasis and methods of the work. Therefore, you will need to determine the author's assumptions and values, and to understand the book's theme and conclusions. Read this kind of work not only to absorb the facts but also to analyze, question, and criticize. If you own the book, you can do your questioning and criticizing in the margins as I have shown you before in your textbook. If the book is not yours, or if you wish to have an organized set of notes about it, summarize the contents and the author's theme on index cards or on a computer file. You can then review your underlinings or index cards before the exam. (For more on taking notes, see pp. 36–41.)

Reading an Anthology

Some courses also include an anthology, a book of readings. These are usually a series of short essays (excerpts from larger works or from **primary documents**) that deal with a single subject. All of the suggestions concerning the reading of texts and history books apply here as well, but this type of assignment often calls for a particular kind of reading. Each excerpt usually discusses a different aspect or interpretation of the subject, and some are in serious disagreement. Teachers expect students to be able to assess the arguments of the various writers and on occasion to take a position in the debate. Therefore, you must read this particular kind of book with an eye to analyzing the arguments of the different excerpts or to comparing their different approaches to the subject. A good way to do this is to summarize briefly the argument or approach of each selection.

Reading a Historical Novel

Still another reading assignment is a **historical novel,** a work of fiction based upon actual occurrences and people. It is more dramatic and more personal than a text or monograph and describes the feelings of those caught up in important historical events. Reading such a novel gives you a feel for the times that it conveys and for the historical material it contains, but be cautious not to treat it as historical truth. On the other hand, if the novelist knows the historical period or event well, he or she can make it come alive in ways that scholarly works cannot.

Examples of Reading Assignments

To help you appreciate the differences among the four types of reading assignments, here are passages from each. The subject is the policy of the United States toward the Greek Civil War of the late

1940s. As you read these passages, note the different manner in which each deals with this subject.

TEXTBOOK The day before, 6 March, Truman had begun to prepare the ground. In a speech at Baylor University in Texas he explained that freedom was more important than peace and that freedom of worship and speech were dependent on freedom of enterprise. . . .

The State Department, meanwhile, was preparing a message for Truman to deliver to the full Congress. He was unhappy with the early drafts, for "I wanted no hedging in this speech. This was America's answer to the surge of expansion of Communist tyranny. It had to be clear and free of hesitation or double talk." Truman told Acheson to have the speech toughened, simplified, and expanded to cover more than just Greece and Turkey. He then made further revisions in the draft. . . .

At 1 P.M. on 12 March 1947, Truman stepped to the rostrum in the hall of the House of Representatives to address the joint session of the Congress. The speech was also carried on nationwide ratio. He asked for immediate aid for Greece and Turkey, then explained the reasoning. "I believe that it must be the policy of the United States to support free peoples who are resisting attempted subjugation by armed minorities or by outside pressures."

The statement was all-encompassing. In a single sentence, Truman had defined American policy for the next twenty years. Whenever and wherever an anti-Communist government was threatened, by indigenous insurgents, foreign invasion, or even diplomatic pressure (as with Turkey), the United States would supply political, economic, and most of all, military aid. The Truman Doctrine came close to shutting the door against any revolution, since the terms "free peoples" and "anti-Communist" were assumed to be synonymous. All the Greek government, or any dictatorship, had to do to get American aid was to claim that its opponents were Communists. And the aid would be unilateral, as Truman never mentioned the United Nations, whose commission to investigate what was actually happening in Greece had not completed its study or made a report.

— From Stephen E. Ambrose, *Rise to Globalism: American Foreign Policy Since 1938* (New York: Penguin, 1971), pp. 148 and 150.

MONOGRAPH What was really on the mind of the president and his advisers was stated less in the Truman Doctrine speech than in private memos and in Truman's March 6 address at Baylor University. Dealing with the world economic structure, the president attacked state-regulated trade, tariffs, and exchange controls — ". . . the direction in which much of the world is headed at the present time." "If this trend is not reversed," he warned, " . . . the United States will be under pressure, sooner or later, to use these same devices in the fight for markets and for raw materials. . . . It is not the American way. It is not the way to peace."[16] . . .

The question of how best to sell the new crusade perplexed the administration, not the least because Greece was a paltry excuse for a vast undertaking of which it "was only a beginning," and in the end it formulated diverse

[16]DSB, March 16, 1947, 484. See also Acheson, *Present at the Creation*, 219; Jones, *Fifteen Weeks*, 139–42. . . .

reasons as the need required.[18] The many drafts that were drawn up before the final Truman Doctrine speech was delivered to Congress on March 12 are interesting in that they reveal more accurately than the speech itself the true concerns of Washington. Members of the cabinet and other top officials who considered the matter before the twelfth understood very clearly that the United States was now defining a strategy and budget appropriate to its new global commitments — interests that the collapse of British power had made even more exclusively American — and that far greater involvement in other countries was now pending, at least on the economic level.

Quite apart from the belligerent tone of the drafts were the references to ". . . a world-wide trend away from the system of free enterprise toward state-controlled economies," which the State Department's speech writers thought "gravely threatened" American interests. No less significant was the mention of the "great natural resources" of the Middle East at stake.

— From Joyce and Gabriel Kolko, *The Limits of Power: The World and United States Foreign Policy, 1945–1954* (New York: Harper & Row, 1972), p. 341.

ANTHOLOGY (EXCERPT FROM SPEECH) The United States has received from the Greek government an urgent appeal for financial and economic assistance. Preliminary reports from the American Economic Mission now in Greece and reports from the American Ambassador in Greece corroborate the statement of the Greek Government that assistance is imperative if Greece is to survive as a free nation. . . .

At the present moment in world history nearly every nation must choose between alternative ways of life. The choice is too often not a free one.

One way of life is based upon the will of the majority, and is distinguished by free institutions, representative government, free elections, guarantees of individual liberty, freedom of speech and religion, and freedom from political oppression.

The second way of life is based upon the will of a minority forcibly imposed upon the majority. It relies upon terror and oppression, a controlled press and radio, fixed elections, and the suppression of personal freedoms.

I believe that it must be the policy of the United States to support free peoples who are resisting attempted subjugation by armed minorities or by outside pressures. . . .

It is necessary only to glance at a map to realize that the survival and integrity of the Greek nation are of grave importance in a much wider situation. If Greece should fall under the control of an armed minority, the effect upon its neighbor, Turkey, would be immediate and serious. Confusion and disorder might well spread throughout the entire Middle East.

Moreover, the disappearance of Greece as an independent state would have a profound effect upon those countries in Europe whose peoples are struggling against great difficulties to maintain their freedoms and their independence while they repair the damages of war. . . .

The free peoples of the world look to us for support in maintaining their freedoms.

[18]Acheson, *Present at the Creation*, 221.

If we falter in our leadership, we may endanger the peace of the world —
and we shall surely endanger the welfare of this Nation.

Great responsibilities have been placed upon us by the swift movement
of events.

I am confident that the Congress will face these responsibilities squarely.

— From an address delivered by President Harry Truman before a joint
session of Congress on March 12, 1947. Reprinted from Thomas G. Pater-
son, *Major Problems in American Foreign Policy,* Vol. II, Fourth Edition (Lexington: D. C. Heath, 1995), pp. 259–61.

HISTORICAL NOVEL Tzelekis was right: now it was 1949, and war was beau-
tifully organized — things were done in an orderly fashion. Various special-
ists had come in, trained in "wars of movement": The British, the Americans, with a good deal of experience in such matters. They put things in
their places, taught enemies and friends to recognize each other — you
over here, them over there. Work with a system, no fooling around! Back in
'46, you see, everything was topsy-turvy. The army was an indiscriminate
herd, no organization whatever; everyone did as he pleased, everything pell-
mell, all mixed up together slaughtering: EAM-ites, EDES-ites, X-ites — you
didn't know who was your enemy and who your friend. At night they sent
out patrols — in the morning they came back in company with the others
and cut up their captains. Other times when they fought at night with
knives and bayonets it was like mother losing child and child losing mother:
same clothes (all the rags of the world resemble each other), same appear-
ance — you came face to face with the enemy, you went at him with a dag-
ger to rip out his guts, and you saw — if you had time — that he was one of
your own men, so you let him go and went for the one beside him. And
don't forget, what mixed things up even worse was the language; since they
were all spouting Greek, who could tell them apart? . . .

Later when foreign aid began to arrive, the army got new uniforms, mu-
nitions, wireless transmitters, codes of recognition. Things were put in
order, names were given to the enemy, and the radio blared them out every
day, they were written on the walls and in the newspapers; and finally, for
the first time in their history, the Greeks began to kill each other systematically. The solution was a very simple one; and a considerable number of
people couldn't understand why they had not thought of it before.

— From Aris Fakinos, *The Marked Men* (New York: Liveright, 1971), pp.
92–93.

Note that the textbook is general in its coverage. It does not use
footnotes or quote from primary sources other than Truman's speech.
It tries to summarize the content and meaning of the event without too
much detail and without extensive proof for its conclusions. The
monograph, on the other hand, covers a small portion of the topic,
gives more detail, quotes from primary materials, and uses footnotes to
record its sources of information. The selection from the anthology is a
primary source — the Truman speech itself. Often these books are
composed of the original documents that form the basis of the histori-

cal events discussed by textbooks and monographs. Although this particular selection from a book of readings is a primary document, such works, as already noted, may also be collections of short essays or excerpts from monographs.

The section from the historical novel is very different from the first three passages. The author gives us the imaginary thoughts of some of the soldiers who fought in the Greek Civil War, far away from the formulation of foreign policy in Washington.

How to "Read" Nonwritten Materials

Interpreting Maps

History is often displayed on maps. The landscape of history is one of its most fundamental settings. The rise and fall of empires, the course of wars, the growth of cities, the development of trade routes, and much more can be traced on maps of large areas. Figure 2.2 indicates the dates on which parts of Africa came under European colonial rule. This map tells you which European countries controlled which parts of Africa and when this control was established. Analyzing the map more closely, you can see that Britain and France had the largest colonial empires in Africa and that most of Africa was free of colonial rule before the 1880s. Figure 2.3 (p. 28) indicates the dates on which the nations of Africa became independent. By comparing this map with Figure 2.2, you can determine which countries changed their names upon achieving independence. Comparing the dates on the two maps, you can figure out how long colonial rule lasted in different countries. Note also that the first wave of independence came in the 1960s and that the date for Namibian independence is 1990 — just a decade ago.

Small area maps can show the layout of villages, the outcome of battles, or the location of mines, canals, and railroads. To read a map, you must learn the *key*, which translates the symbols used on the map. A line on a map may be a road, a river, or a gas pipeline. The key tells you which it is. The *scale* of a map tells you the actual distance of the area the map represents. Maps are an important aid in understanding history because they display the physical relationship between places. Never ignore maps in a text or other reading. It is also wise to put a good map of the area you are studying near your desk so that you can see the location of places mentioned in lectures and readings. Old maps are also **primary documents.** The way that old maps describe the territories they cover can give you clues as to what was going on in the mind of the mapmaker at the time that the map was created.

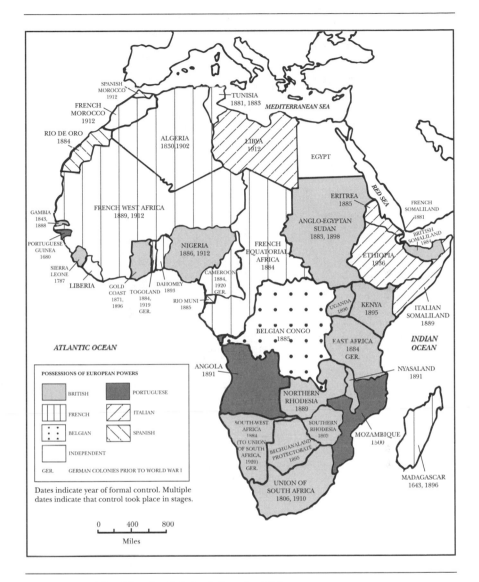

FIGURE 2.2   The March of Colonialism in Africa

Analyzing Statistical Data

In addition to maps, works in history often include statistical data arranged in **charts, graphs,** or **tables.** These data describe the amounts of something (e.g., warships, marriages, schools, bridges, deaths from smallpox) at a specific time in the past and usually compare these amounts (e.g., the number of marriages in relation to the number of schools) or trace changes in amounts over time (e.g., the number of

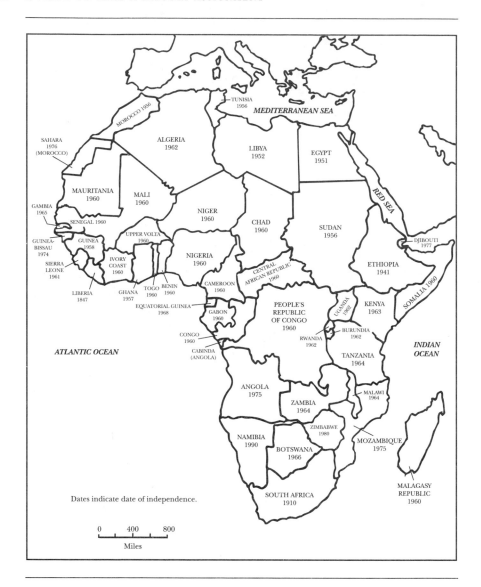

FIGURE 2.3   The March of African Independence

warships in 1820, 1830, and 1840). Figure 2.4 (on p. 29) shows a typical arrangement of statistical data with explanations as to how to read them.

The table organizes population statistics from different regions of the earth and across more than three hundred years. Reading across the lines allows you to trace the changes in population of a particular region (Europe, Africa, Asia) over time. By doing so, you can follow the population of each region at hundred-year intervals (the popula-

	1650	1750	1850	1900	1950	1980	1996
Europe	100	140	265	400	570	730	800
United States and Canada	2	2	25	80	165	252	295
Latin America	12	10	35	65	165	362	489
Africa	100	95	95	120	220	470	732
Asia	330	480	750	940	1370	2600	3430

FIGURE 2.4   **Estimated World Population**
Numbers represent millions of persons. These are rough estimates only. The figures for 1650 and 1750 in particular come from a time before it was common to conduct a periodic count (*census*) of populations. There is great debate about the size of the native populations of the Western hemisphere before 1850. (The Figure is adapted from L. S. Stavrianos, *The World since 1500: A Global History,* 4th ed. [Englewood Cliffs, N. J.: Prentice-Hall, 1982], p. 181.)

tion of Latin America in 1650, 1750, 1850, and 1950). You can note the change for each region and the rate of change. For example, the population of the United States and Canada did not increase in the hundred years between 1650 and 1750, whereas it more than doubled in the fifty years between 1900 and 1950. Reading down the chart, you can examine the population of each region during the same period in time. This allows you to compare the populations of the different regions. In 1650 the populations of Europe and Africa were the same, whereas in 1950 the European population was more than two-and-one-half times that of Africa.

More complex comparisons can be made by combining the differences between regions (reading down) and their rates of growth over time (reading across). For example, you can discover that whereas the population of Asia has grown more than that of any other region in absolute terms, its *rate* of growth from 1850 to 1980 (750 million to 2600 million, or about 350 percent) was much less than that of Latin America (35 million to 362 million, or around 1,000 percent).

Even the cold statistics of a table can provide images of the great drama of history. The decrease in African population between 1650 and 1850 may tell us something of the impact of the slave trade, and the decrease in population in Latin America between 1650 and 1750 hints at the toll taken among Native Americans by the introduction of European diseases. The large increase in the United States population between 1850 and 1900 tells us something about the history of European emigration.

The information in the table can be presented differently in order to highlight different aspects of the data. In Figure 2.5, the numbers for each region are represented as percentages of the total world population. By changing the numbers from absolute amounts to percentages, the new table facilitates the comparing of populations and population growth.

	1650	1750	1850	1900	1950	1980	1996
Europe	18.4	19.3	22.8	25.0	23.2	16.5	13.9
United States and Canada	0.2	0.1	2.3	5.1	6.7	5.7	5.1
Latin America	2.2	1.5	2.8	3.9	6.3	8.2	8.5
Africa	18.4	13.2	8.1	7.4	8.8	10.6	12.7
Asia	60.8	65.9	64.0	58.6	55.0	58.9	59.7

FIGURE 2.5 Estimated World Population
Numbers represent percentages. (The Figure is adapted from L. S. Stavrianos, *The World since 1500: A Global History,* 4th ed. [Englewood Cliffs, N. J.: Prentice-Hall, 1982], p. 181.)

Another way of presenting these population data is in the form of a graph. Note that Figure 2.6 makes more obvious the differences between numbers and thus makes comparisons easier. However, ease of comparison is traded for a loss in precision; the graph gives less specific numbers (reading along the vertical axis) than the table. A graph also requires more space to convey the same information as a table. Figure 2.6, were it to have included all of the time periods of the table, would have been very large.

The more detailed the data and their arrangement, the more historical information that can be displayed and the more intricate the comparisons that can be made. Figure 2.7 presents a table that lists the per-

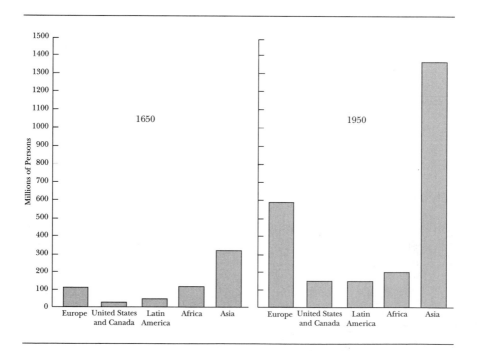

FIGURE 2.6 Estimated World Population

centage of the total vote and the number of deputies elected to the German parliament by each of the major political parties in each election from 1919 to 1933. (Note that in the parliamentary system, elections do not come at regular intervals.)

This table allows you to follow the changing fortunes of each political party. A wealth of information on German political history is contained in these figures. Between the lines one can also find pieces of the social and economic history of Germany. To choose only two examples, the strength of the Communist and Social Democratic (Socialist) parties attests to the deep dissatisfaction of many German workers with the state of the economy during the period known as the Weimar Republic. Even more striking is the tremendous growth of the National

Party	1919	1920	1924	1928	1930	1932	1933
Communist							
# of deputies	0	4	45	54	77	89	81
% of total votes		2.1	9.0	10.6	13.1	14.6	12.3
Social Democratic							
# of deputies	165	102	131	153	143	133	120
% of total votes	37.9	21.6	26.0	29.8	24.5	21.6	18.3
Democratic							
# of deputies	75	39	32	25	20	4	5
% of total votes	18.6	8.3	6.3	4.9	3.8	1.0	.8
Centrum							
# of deputies	91	64	69	62	68	75	74
% of total votes	19.7	13.6	13.6	12.1	11.8	12.5	11.7
Bavarian People's							
# of deputies	0	21	19	16	19	22	18
% of total votes		4.4	3.7	3.0	3.0	3.2	2.7
German People's							
# of deputies	19	65	51	45	30	7	2
% of total votes	4.4	13.9	10.1	8.7	4.5	1.2	1.1
National People's							
# of deputies	44	71	103	73	41	37	52
% of total votes	10.3	14.9	20.5	14.2	7.0	5.9	8.0
National Socialist							
# of deputies	0	0	14	12	107	230	288
% of total votes			3.0	2.6	18.3	37.4	43.9

FIGURE 2.7   Reichstag Elections, 1919–1933
Under the electoral system provided for in the Weimar Constitution, each party received approximately one representative for every sixty thousand popular votes cast for its candidates. Various small parties, not listed here, were underrepresented in the Reichstag. (From L. S. Stavrianos, *The World since 1500: A Global History,* 4th ed. [Englewood Cliffs, N.J.: Prentice-Hall, 1982], p. 419.)

Socialist (Nazi) Party after 1930. It was this development that brought Adolf Hitler to power in 1933. Eventually the results of that event would reverberate around the world. A table is not just numbers.

Interpreting Illustrations and Photographs

Visual material can also present historical information. However, gathering information from old paintings, drawings, and photographs can be more difficult than it may seem. You need to do more than *look* at them. First, you need to recognize the actual information that they present — what Columbus's ships looked like, how Hiroshima appeared after the explosion of the atomic bomb. Then, you need to *interpret them.* This involves an effort to understand what the artist or photographer is "saying" in the work. (This advice applies also to film and to any visual form.) When an artist draws something and when a photographer takes a picture, he or she is not simply recording a visual image but is sending a message to anyone who looks at the work. In this way, artists and photographers are like writers whose written work needs to be interpreted.

Figures 2.8 and 2.9 present two illustrations of the Spanish conquest of Mexico. Look at them and see if you can detect what they are saying.

FIGURE 2.8 **Indian Offerings to Cortés**

FIGURE 2.9   Massacre of the Aztec Indians

The first of the two is by a European artist and shows Hernán Cortés, who conquered Mexico for Spain, being offered young Indian women by a coastal tribe. The Indians seem happy to greet the Spaniards. The other was drawn by an Aztec Indian and shows Cortés's soldiers (having fought their way from the coast to the Aztec capital) massacring Indians in their main temple. Not all drawings have such obvious (and opposite) messages: the Spanish as friends of the Indians and the Spanish as murderers of the Indians. The interpretation of some visual material requires knowledge about the subject matter, the artist, the style, and the context in which it appeared. Like written descriptions of past events, art does not simply "speak for itself."

Now turn to Figure 2.10, a photograph of a clash in 1968 between Chicago police and demonstrators opposing the war in Vietnam. Like the illustrations in Figures 2.8 and 2.9, it too has information. Even a casual glance shows confusion and violence. Looking more closely, you can see the kinds of weapons used by the police and the facial expressions of some of the demonstrators. The more difficult part, again, is interpreting the photograph. Is this a scene of provocation by lawless demonstrators or an attack by the police? A careful look at the picture may help you answer this question. In any case, you need more evidence. While an (undoctored) photograph does show something

FIGURE 2.10   1968 Antiwar Demonstration at the Democratic National Convention

that actually happened, another photograph — even one of the same event — might show something very different. In most cases, the person taking the photograph has made an effort to have it say something, and you need to take this motive into account.

Not all pictures have controversial interpretations. Figure 2.11 is a photograph of a city street in Ithaca, New York, in the 1890s. There is a wealth of information here about nineteenth-century town life. Note that at this early date, the town already had electric trolleys. Note also that the horses are not pulling wagons or carriages ("buggies," as they were called) but sleighs ("cutters"). This simple fact opens up a window to farm life in winter. When roads were covered with snow and especially ice, the flat, smooth wheels of wagons could not navigate while the sharp runners of the cutter dug into the ice and gave it stability.

FIGURE 2.11   **Town Life in Ithaca, New York during the 1890s**

How to Take Notes in Class

From Class Lectures

The first rule concerning note taking is simple: pay attention. Don't sleep, doodle, talk, stare out the window, or write a letter to a friend. Some lecturers are not exactly spellbinding or fully organized in what they say, but there is no point in going to class if you are not going to listen to the lecture.

Read the text before going to class or you may be taking notes on the material in the book. If everything the instructor says is new to you, you will spend so much time writing that you won't be able to get an understanding of the theme of the lecture. If you have obtained some basic information from outside readings, you will be able to concentrate on noting points in the lecture that are new or different.

Guidelines for Taking Lecture Notes

1. Prepare for a lecture by reading all related course materials.
2. Write the course information, lecture subject, and date at the top of each page of notes.
3. Be selective — don't try to copy down everything a lecturer says.
4. Be sure to write down anything that the instructor: (1) puts on the board; (2) says is important; (3) emphasizes as he or she speaks.
5. Leave room in your notes to add additional material later if necessary.
6. Reread your notes later in the day on which they were written.
7. Underline especially important points.
8. Look up the meaning of any unfamiliar words.
9. Rewrite any parts of your notes that are poorly organized.
10. **If something important in your notes is unclear to you, ask your instructor about it.**

An instructor is most likely to prepare exam questions from material that he or she considers most important. It is therefore essential in preparing notes to determine which points in the lecture are given most prominent attention. Some instructors are very open about their preferences and clearly emphasize certain points, often writing them on the blackboard. Never fail to note something that the instructor indicates is important. Other instructors are less explicit about their biases and values, and you will have to try to figure them out. Listen closely, and make note of those interpretations and generalizations that seem to be stressed, especially when they differ from the approach in the text. You should not feel obliged to parrot your instructor's interpretations in an exam, but ignorance of them will work against you.

Your notes should be written legibly and headed by the date and subject of the lecture. They should reflect a general outline of the material covered, with emphasis on major interpretations and important facts not covered by the text. It is often best to write on every other line and to leave a large margin on at least one side of the page. This will allow you to add material later and to underline your notes and write marginal comments without cluttering the page.

If possible, reread your notes later in the day on which they were written. If your handwriting is poor or your notes are disorganized, it is best to rewrite them. Check the spelling and definitions of any unfamiliar words, and be sure that the notes are coherent. Remember, your notes are an important source of information in your studies, and if they don't make sense, you won't either.

Examples of Note Taking

To illustrate some of the essentials of good note taking, here are portions of two sets of class notes taken from the same lecture. The first example illustrates many of the common errors of note takers, and the second is an example of a well-written set of notes. The subject of the lecture was early European contact with Africa.

EXAMPLE OF POOR NOTE TAKING

Colonization of Africa — People were afraid to sail out. Afraid of sea monsters. But they liked the stories about gold in Africa. The Portuguese King Henry sailed south to find the gold mines and built a fort at Elmina.

England and France want to trade with Africa. They begin trading. Competing with Portugal. These countries got into wars. They wanted to control Africa.

China had spices. They traded with Cairo and Venice. The Asians wanted gold, but the Islams stopped all trade. They fought wars about religion for hundreds of years. Fought over Jerusalem. The Pope called for a crusade. This was in the Middle Ages.

Spices came from Asia. In Europe they were valuable because the kings used them to become rich. They also ate them.

The Portuguese wanted to explore Africa and make a way to India. Their boats couldn't get around until Bartholomew Diaz discovered the Cape of Good Hope in 1487.

Most of all, the Portuguese wanted slaves. They shipped them back from Africa. Columbus took them after he discovered America (1492). The Pope made a line in the Atlantic Ocean so the Catholics wouldn't fight. The colonies needed slaves. They sent 15 million from 1502 to the 19th century. Slaves did the hard work. They got free later after the Civil War.

Immigrants go to Africa from Europe but they don't like the hot weather and they catch diseases. The Dutch set up their own country at the Cape. Then the English conquer them.

EXAMPLE OF GOOD NOTE TAKING

Early European Contact with Africa   History 200
Why Did Europeans Come to Africa?   10/22/01
   1. Desire for gold
     — Medieval legends about gold in Africa.
     — Prince Henry (Portuguese navigator) sent men down coast of Africa to find source of gold. (Also to gain direct access to gold trade controlled by Muslims.)
     — Portuguese built forts along the coast. Their ships carried gold and ivory back to Portugal (16th century).
     — Then the other European states came (England, Holland, France, Spain) to set up their own trading posts.
     — Competed with each other for African trade. (Will talk about rivalry next week.)
   2. Wanted to trade with Asia and weaken the Muslims
     (The Muslims had created a large empire based on the religion of Islam.)
     — Religious conflict between Christianity and Islam. Fought a religious war in the 11th–12th centuries — the Crusades.
     — The Muslims had expanded their empire when Europe was weak. In 15th century they controlled North Africa and they dominated trade in the Mediterranean. They controlled the spices coming from Asia, which were in great demand in Europe. In Europe they were used to preserve meat. So valuable, sometimes used as money.
     — Portugal and Spain were ruled by Catholic monarchs. Very religious. The Catholic monarchs wanted to force the Muslims out of Europe. (They still held part of Spain.) Wanted to convert them to Christianity.
[IMPORTANT]— The Muslims controlled North Africa and Mediterranean trade. If the Portuguese and Spanish could sail to the Indian Ocean directly, they could get goods from China and the Muslims couldn't stop them. The way to Asia was the sea route around Africa.
   3. The Europeans wanted slaves
     — When the Portuguese explored West Africa (15th century), they sent back the first slaves (around 1440).
     — The Spanish conquered the New World (Mexico, Peru, etc.). (Columbus had made several trips for Queen Isabella I of Spain.)
     — In America (the name for the New World), they needed slaves. Most slaves were sent to America.
     — Native Americans died from diseases of white men. They were also killed in the wars. There was nobody to run the mines (gold and silver).
[IMPORTANT]— Sugar plantations of the Caribbean (and Brazil) needed labor. Cotton plantations in the south of U.S. also. It was hard work and nobody wanted to do it.

— 15 million (maybe as many as 40 million) slaves were brought to work the plantations starting in 1502 until mid-19th century.

Colonization of Africa
 1. Immigration (why white people didn't come)
  — They couldn't take the climate.
  — There were a lot of tropical diseases.
  — The Europeans didn't want to live in Africa, only run it.
  — Only the Dutch settlers came. They set up the Boer states in South Africa. After them came British settlers.
  — Some French settled in Algeria.
  — Some English also moved to Rhodesia.
 2. Dividing Africa
  — Whites began exploring the interior. (Will discuss exploration next week.)

Copying notes during a lecture is difficult, and even a good set of notes can be greatly improved by being rewritten. Following is a rewriting of these notes. Note how much clearer everything becomes.

REWRITTEN GOOD NOTES

Early European Contact with Africa   History 200
What Drew Europeans to Africa?   10/22/01
 Gold

There were medieval legends that there was a lot of gold in West Africa. Access to the gold was controlled by non-Christian powers (Muslims — believers in Islamic religion). Tales of gold lured the Portuguese (led by Prince Henry) to explore the coast of West Africa in the late 15th century. By the 16th century, the Portuguese had built several trading posts and forts along the West African coast and were bringing back gold, ivory, and pepper.

By the 17th century, English, Dutch, French, and Spanish ships challenged the Portuguese trading monopoly and set up their own trading posts. This was the beginning of rivalry between European countries over the wealth of Africa.

 Desire to weaken the power of the Islamic Empire (Muslims) and expand trade with Asia

Conflict between Christianity and Islam was an old religious conflict (the Crusades as an example in 11th and 12th centuries). The Muslims controlled North Africa and the Mediterranean. They also controlled the spice trade from Asia. Spices were important in Europe because they were the only known way to preserve meat.

The Catholic states of Portugal and Spain wanted to fight with the Muslims. They wanted to drive them out of Spain and challenge the large Muslim empire in Africa, the Middle East, and Asia. They hoped to convert them to Christianity. *The Muslims were strong in North Africa, but if European powers could discover a way around Africa into the Indian Ocean, they could outflank the Muslims and obtain direct access to the trade with India and Asia.*

 Slaves

Portuguese trading posts in Africa had sent a small number of slaves to Europe starting in the late 15th century. With the discovery and conquest of America at the turn of the 16th century, a new and larger slave trade began to European colonies in the New World (America).

The Native Americans died (they were killed in war and by European diseases in great numbers). There was a shortage of labor. In the 17th and 18th centuries, large sugar plantations were set up in the Caribbean and Brazil and cotton plantations in the southern United States. *The need for laborers to do the hard agricultural work led to the importing of millions of slaves from Africa.* Somewhere between 15 and 40 million Africans were sent to America as slaves between 1502 and the mid-19th century. This slave trade made Africa valuable to the European powers.

The Colonization of Africa
  Immigration
    Because of the unsatisfactory climate and tropical diseases, there was no major European immigration to Africa. The only significant white colony was set up in South Africa by the Boers (Dutch) and later the English. There were smaller European settlements in Rhodesia (English) and Algeria (French).
  Dividing up the continent
  Exploration

If you reread the poor notes now, you can easily see how little of the lecture material is recorded in them and how confusing and even erroneous a picture you get from them. What is there about the poor notes that makes them inferior?

First, they are not organized. They do not even record the title of the lecture, the course number, or the date. If these notes get out of order, they will be useless. In fact, they are almost useless anyway. They are nothing more than a series of sentences about gold, trade, spices, Portugal, and slaves. The sentences are not in any particular order, and they do not say anything important. Even the factual information does not cover the major points of the lecture. Instead, it is peripheral information about sea monsters, China, Jerusalem, Bartholomew Diaz, and Columbus, most of which the good note taker wisely omitted. By paying too much attention to trivial points, moreover, the poor note taker missed or did not have time to record the principal theme of the lecture — the relationship between European-Asian trade and the religious struggle between Islam and Christianity. The poor note taker also missed another major point — the connection between the enslavement of Africans and the need for plantation labor in the New World. Without these two points, this student cannot write a good exam on this subject.

The good notes, on the other hand, follow the organization of the lecture and touch upon the major points made in class. The notes make sense and can serve as the basis for reviewing the content of the lecture when studying for exams.

These notes have a wide margin for extra comments and the marking of important passages. (Note the sections marked "important.") The instructor had emphasized these points in class, and by making special note of them, the good student will be sure to master them.

The rewritten version, which eliminates certain unimportant or repetitious phrases and smoothes the language into connected sentences, is even better as a study guide. The greatest value of rewriting, however, is that by re-creating the lecture material in essay form, it becomes part of the note taker's own thinking. The mental effort that goes into revising lecture notes serves to impress the material and its meaning upon the mind. This makes it much easier to review the material at exam time.

From Slides and Films

Some instructors present slide lectures or show films or videotapes. Note taking in these instances involves special problems. If a lecture is accompanied by slides, you will need to include in your notes information as to what the slides illustrated (for example, the Pyramid of Cheops, the novels of Willa Cather, the assassination of John F. Kennedy, the dances of Martha Graham) and anything of importance your instructor said about the slides.

Taking notes on films or videotapes presents some unusual problems. The lighting may be dim. The greatest problem may be the film itself. In our culture, films are a medium of entertainment rather than education. Your natural response will be to sit back and relax your mind. You must fight this response and learn to probe a film as you would a lecture. If a film is essentially factual *(Walled Cities of the Middle Ages)*, note the major facts and interpretations as you would in a lecture. If a film is dramatic rather than documentary *(Ivan the Terrible, Citizen Kane)*, examine the emotional message and artistic content as well as any historical facts it describes (or claims to describe). As with the author of a book, you need to ask: What is the movie director trying to say, and what dramatic and technical devices does he or she use to say it? Your notes should record important narration and dialogue that illustrate the theme of the film. Finally, you will need to take note of pictorial elements (camera angle, sets, lighting, gestures and movements, facial expressions) because the core of a dramatic film and its impact are essentially visual. It takes practice to learn to take notes on slides and films. It will be worth the effort because photographs, films, and videotapes are used increasingly in history courses.

Classroom Participation

Classroom Discussions

Many instructors encourage class participation, and some base a portion of the final grade on it. Here are a few pointers for improving your ability to participate in class discussions.

Guidelines for Speaking in Class

1. Be familiar with the subject under discussion.
2. If a point is made that disagrees with your understanding, or if something in the lecture or discussion is confusing, formulate a clear question or statement in your mind.
3. If you don't get a chance to be recognized in class, bring up your question with the teacher when the session is over.
4. Teachers are not impressed with students who like to hear themselves talk or who ask careless questions, but if you are interested in the subject and have thought about what you want to say, never hesitate to speak up.

Giving an Oral Presentation

Some courses involve giving an oral presentation in class. Eloquence and effectiveness in public speaking cannot be mastered in a week or two, but you can make a start by taking such an assignment seriously and adequately preparing yourself in advance for it. If allowed the option, reading from a prepared text is often the safest procedure. However, this can lead to a dull presentation. It is usually better to speak from notes. This kind of presentation will be livelier and more enjoyable for the class. To do a good job, you will have to be fully familiar with your subject and pay close attention to getting your points across. You should prepare your presentation outline as you would that of a short paper. (See the section on writing short essays in Chapter 3, pp. 72–74.) Be sure that you cover all the important points and that you present them in a logical manner.

Use short phrases rather than sentences in your presentation notes. For example, if you intend to tell the class that: "Before 1848, most of the large landowners of California were Mexicans. In the decades after California was annexed by the United States, these Californios, as they were called, lost most of their lands to migrants from the eastern states," your notes need only read: "(a) Until 1848 big landowners Californios. (b) Cal. annexed in 1848. (c) Lost land to easterners." Once you are fully prepared, it is a good idea to give a dry run of your presentation before a relative, friend, or roommate. Be sure that you exhibit a knowledge of your subject because this is most likely to determine your grade. Effective public speaking is one of the most important tools of success in many fields of work, and giving a talk in class is a good opportunity to develop your skills in this area. Here are some tips to help you give your presentation.

> *Guidelines for Giving an Oral Presentation*
>
> 1. Use 3" × 5" **note cards,** each with one or (at most) two major points on it.
> 2. Write neatly and use phrases, not whole sentences.
> 3. Put a number in the corner of each note card so that they will not get out of order.
> 4. If you have a time limit, rehearse your talk beforehand so that you won't need to rush. Cut down your notes to fit the time needed to present the material clearly.
> 5. Visual aids (overhead projections, slides, or even videos) can make your presentation much more interesting. Make sure, however, that you have the resources you need well beforehand and that you know how to integrate them easily and smoothly into your verbal remarks.
> 6. Relax! Speak slowly and clearly and make eye contact with your audience every few sentences.

Group Work

Your instructor may also ask you to be part of a small group and carry out an assignment working with the members of that group. Instead of the individual oral presentation just mentioned, you may be asked to make a group presentation to the class. Conducting research and preparing a group presentation can be tricky but also very rewarding. The key to success is to clarify who in the group is to do what part of the assignment and to be sure that each member is prepared when the time comes.

Another form of group work often takes place outside the classroom. Known as **peer reviewing,** this type of work requires you to evaluate the work of another member of the class. For example, you may be asked to read and comment on the student's rough draft of an assignment. Your peer review may take the form of an informal one-on-one review in which you go through the paper with the author point by point. Some instructors may ask you to write your evaluation; others may want your review in the form of a class presentation. No matter what the format is, remember to provide *constructive* criticism that will help your classmates develop their papers. Be sure to point out the paper's strengths in addition to any weaknesses. For more on peer reviewing, see the Guidelines for Peer Editing on page 137.

Finally, a new form of group work is one in which you share your comments with other students in the class either through e-mail or through a course Web page. You can even send drafts of your work to other students or exchange peer-review drafts directly online. Using interactive computer technology also allows you to extend your learning beyond the classroom. You can talk to students at other schools in chatrooms or e-mail questions to authors of course materials. Learning to work collaboratively will be of use when you leave school and enter a working environment in which these kinds of personal and digital interactions are becoming more common.

Communicating Online

At some point in your academic career you probably have used the Web. Your professor may post his or her syllabus online or have class assignments posted there. Some students are beginning to use the Web as a means of expanding their academic experience by "talking on the Web." There are several ways of communicating with others on the Web that you can use as educational tools. The most basic tools allow you to gain better control over course material, avoid dangerous pitfalls, make connections to relevant material, and understand the larger framework of your course. At a more advanced level, these tools allow you to communicate with scholars, archivists, and Webmasters in your field, find important and underexploited resources for your research, and broaden your knowledge of the theories surrounding a particular period or aspect of history. The media of communication that you probably will find most useful and beneficial to your educational experience are: electronic mail (e-mail), list servers (**listservs**), **chatrooms,** online/electronic conferences (e-conferences), and online electronic seminars (e-seminars).

E-mail, Listservs, and Chatrooms

As you probably know, individuals with e-mail accounts can send messages to one another. The speed of interaction varies according to how quickly the participants initiate and respond to messages. Listservs are a way of managing e-mail lists of people interested in a particular topic. Instead of one-to-one or one-to-many communication — as with e-mail — listservs send out everyone's messages to everyone else on the list. Listservs are especially vauable in settings that emphasize group-oriented work. Chatrooms allow users to communicate with others who are in a specific "room." Your Internet service provider (ISP) may give you access to chatrooms. You may also find chatrooms by surfing for them on the Web. Chatroom communication may be either one-to-one or one-to-many; however, unless you are in a "private" chatroom — with just you and the recipient — your messages can be read by others who are present. While chatrooms provide users with immediate communication, unlike e-mail or listservs they do not provide users with any tangible record of the dialogue.

For educational purposes, you can use these tools to varying degrees. You may decide to pose a question to a classmate over e-mail or in a chatroom: "What was Professor Smith's advice about reading this document?" You can also work out difficult concepts in a chatroom. For example, perhaps you are dealing with a complex topic and are trying to gain control over it. You know you need to understand this material because it forms the basis for future lessons. By communicating with others, you can work through that material and master it in much the same way as you would in a study group. If you subscribe to a listserv for your class, you might post the following message:

> I understand Professor Smith's discussion of the factors that led to an anti-communist belief/paranoia in the United States during the late 1940s and early 1950s. However, I am confused about which groups expressed these fears. From the readings it appears that only the Republicans did; however, Professor Smith's lecture leads me to believe that both Republicans and Democrats did. Can anyone help me with this point?

By posting this message, you are assessing what you know and what you don't know and trying to deepen your understanding. Your message may stimulate another student's thinking on the question. A fellow classmate might respond to the posting above with the following reply:

> I think that is exactly Professor Smith's intention. As I understand it, both Republicans and Democrats expressed these fears; however, they employed different means to achieve the same ends. Because the Democrats' activities were less dramatic, it caused the Republicans to charge them with being "soft" on communism.

By replying to such a message, the student is working through the material, understanding the connections, and seeing how the material works.

Despite the advantages of these forms of communication, there are dangers as well. Most of this kind of communication is either unmediated or unedited (though some listservs do edit and filter messages). This means that anyone can say anything at anytime. Perhaps someone with whom you are corresponding tells you that the Holocaust was a Hollywood creation. While it is important to give credit to new theories, it is equally important to read electronic communication with a skeptical eye. If someone suggests something with which you are unfamiliar, it is perfectly acceptable to ask for references where you could find more information on that topic. The best advice is to know the individuals with whom you communicate, read messages critically, and don't be afraid to challenge someone if you have reason to believe that he or she is wrong.

The cooperative learning fostered through talking on the Web is of great value. Too often at the undergraduate level students look at learning from a competitive rather than a cooperative viewpoint. Some students never study or work with others. They believe that if they do so they will lose their "edge." However, historians do not work in a vacuum; historical research relies on access to the discoveries, interpretations, and analyses of others. Although seminar-type classes often rely on cooperative learning, you can have a similar experience in any class by communicating with classmates and others using the Web. By sharing information, you are not losing any competitive advantage; you are increasing and solidifying your knowledge, pointing out errors, and sharing important findings.

E-conferences and E-seminars

E-conferences and e-seminars are emerging as an important interactive means of scholarly discussion on the Web. Both deal with the presentation, discussion, and criticism of scholarly papers; however, e-conferences present several papers while e-seminars deal with only one. You may find it difficult to locate these forums on the Web. Most are either sponsored by or affiliated with universities. If you do find one, check the participation requirements. Some are only for scholars, while others allow both students and scholars to participate.

There are important things to keep in mind when joining and participating in these online scholarly activities. Both assume a high level of knowledge of the topic and therefore waste little time with introductions and background material. They assume that participants are thoroughly familiar with the material of the conference or seminar and are able to read and write on a sophisticated level.

Web Communication and Advanced Research

For students doing more advanced course work, this type of communication can help to locate important resources in your field. If you decide to tackle an obscure topic, you can use the Web to contact scholars who may make important suggestions regarding your topic. If possible, it is best to contact more than one scholar so that you have more than one interpretation of the topic. The scholars, archivists, and Webmasters with whom you would communicate are busy individuals. When contacting them, it is best to introduce yourself, describe your research, and outline your purpose for contacting them. Also be sure that you are knowledgeable in your topic, that the person you are contacting can actually help you, and that you ask specific questions.

Regardless of how you choose to "talk on the Web" it is important that you *do* talk on the Web. In so doing, you are communicating with others who can help you understand the information and whom you can help as well. You will gain a better understanding of the material for which you have questions. You will see the pitfalls to avoid by pointing out the errors in other peoples' interpretations. This experience allows you to understand an important principle of humanistic disciplines: your best work comes from dialogue among researchers.

How to Study for Exams

When a test is announced, be sure to find out what kind of an exam it will be: essay, short answer, multiple choice, and so forth. Determine what topics will be covered and what portions of the reading material and lectures deal with the topics. If you have not done all of the necessary reading, do so immediately and record the important facts and interpretations as indicated in the section on "How to Read a History Assignment" (pp. 19–26). If you have missed any lectures, obtain a copy of the lecture notes from someone who knows the rules of good note taking. Now gather together all the materials to be covered in the exam. Reread the parts of the texts that you underlined (or otherwise noted) as being important. Reread *all* of the relevant lecture notes, paying special attention to any points emphasized by the instructor. Sometimes it helps to do your rereading aloud. If an exam will cover visual materials — slides, films, maps, etc. — be sure to go over this information, even if it means watching a video a second time.

If the test is to be an **essay exam,** compose sample questions based upon the important topics and themes contained in the readings and lectures. (Many textbooks contain sample exam questions or topics for discussion at the end of each chapter.) If you do not know how to answer any portion of the sample question, go over your study materials again and look for the information needed. If you are preparing for an **objective exam** — that is, one requiring short answers — you must pay special attention to the important facts (persons, places, events, changes) in your study materials. You must be precise in order to get credit for your answer. Make a list of the outstanding people, events, and historical developments, and be sure that you can adequately identify them and explain their importance. (Again, your text may help you by providing sample short-answer questions.)

Take the time you need to prepare adequately. If tests make you nervous, the best medicine is to go into the exam confident that you know the material. Keep on studying until you have mastered your sample questions and until the material to be covered makes sense to you.

Objective and Short-Answer Exams

Objective exams call for short, factual answers. The three most common objective exams are: (1) **short answer,** (2) **identification,** and (3) **multiple choice** or true/false.

Short Answer and Identification.   Read the question carefully and don't jump to conclusions. Answer briefly (there is usually a time and space limit) and directly. Don't put anything in your answer that wastes space or time. If you are asked to identify John F. Kennedy, don't mention how he was killed (unless that is part of the question). Talk about some aspect of his presidency that was stressed in class or in course readings. When you have so little room to show what you know, answers that stray away from the core of the subject are as bad as wrong answers.

Examples of Objective Exams

Example of a Short-Answer Question

QUESTION: What were the motives that caused the European powers to explore Africa beginning in the late fifteenth century?

INCORRECT ANSWER: They wanted to dominate Africa and get all the gold for themselves. Columbus wanted to take slaves from Africa, but the Pope said it would start a war. But the war didn't start and the Europeans dominated Africa anyway because they were stronger.

CORRECT ANSWER: The wars between Christianity and Islam were an important factor. The Christian States wanted to weaken the hold of the Muslim religion on Africa and to convert the natives. They also hoped to break Muslim control of trade with Asia by finding a sea route around Africa.

(Check these two answers against the example of good note taking on pp. 38–39. These notes make clear why the second answer is satisfactory while the first one is not.)

Example of Identification Question

QUESTION: Identify the "progressive" philosophy of historical interpretation.

INCORRECT ANSWER: Historian who believed that our country was always making progress because Americans were very hardworking people.

CORRECT ANSWER: The interpretation of history that holds that human beings and their condition are continually improving as each generation builds on the foundation laid by previous ones.

(See the section on "Philosophies of History" in Chapter 1 on pp. 14–15 to find the basis for the correct answer.)

Example of Multiple-Choice Question

The British monarch at the time of the American Revolution was:

a. George II
b. Charles I
c. James II
d. George III
e. Henry I

If you look up the dates of reign of these monarchs, you will discover that George III (who was king from 1760 to 1820) was the ruler of England at the time of the American Revolution. But perhaps you already knew that.

Preparing for In-Class Essay Exams — Composing Sample Questions

Of course, the best preparation for an essay exam is to be given the question in advance. Some instructors do this (usually in the form of a **take-home exam**), but many give in-class essay exams and hand out in advance a number of possible topics or questions from which they choose in making up the exam. (For more on take-home exams, see Chapter 3, pp. 62–63.) If you face an upcoming essay exam without *any* questions presented in advance, the key to successful preparation is to come up with potential questions on your own.

As your instructor probably will have told you, the essay questions will deal with the major topics covered in the course so far. Using your texts, lecture notes, and other course materials, determine what these topics are. Then compose your own questions. For example, if the material to be covered in the exam is the reasons for the decline of the Roman Empire, list the major explanations for that decline mentioned in the course work. Among these may be civil war, military insubordination, the cost of defending distant frontiers, declining agricultural output, barbarian invasion, heavy tax burdens on the peasantry, the growth of central bureaucracy, the decline of the Senate, the cult of the Emperor, the rise of Christianity, and the rise of Islam. The exam question is likely to focus on one or more of these explanations. Be prepared to write about *each* of these factors and how they relate to one another. If the course has covered the rise of industrialization in New England, study carefully the major social and technological changes and how people responded to them. Think about the aspects of industrialization that might form the exam questions. One question might ask you to describe the ways in which factory production was different from the workshop production that it displaced. Other questions might be: How did industrialization affect family life? What were the major technological innovations behind early industrialization? How did the rise of the textile industry affect the lives of young women?

Don't prepare for an essay exam by composing questions that are too broad. If you have spent six weeks examining the decline of the Roman Empire, don't expect a broad question such as: "Discuss the decline of the Roman Empire." Don't prepare questions that are too narrow either. For example, "Who owned the biggest textile mill in New England in the 1830s?" That is a question for a short answer or an identification exam.

Writing a Good Essay Exam

Even if you have prepared properly for an essay exam, your problems are not over. You must stay calm enough to remember what you studied, you must understand the questions, you must answer them directly and fully, and you must not run out of time. None of this is easy, but here are a few pointers to follow until you gain the experience to overcome these problems. (For more on writing essay exams, see Chapter 3, pp. 62–66.)

Guidelines for Writing In-Class Essay Exams

1. When you are given the exam, don't panic. Read the entire exam slowly, including all of the instructions. Gauge the amount of time you will need to answer each question. Then choose the question you know most about to answer first.
2. Don't write the first thing that comes to your mind. Read the question slowly, and be sure you understand it.
3. Determine how you will answer the question and the central points you wish to make.
4. Write these central points or even a full outline in the margin of the exam booklet, and as you compose each sentence of your answer, make sure that it relates to one of these points.
5. Your answer must follow the question. Be as specific or general, as concrete or reflective, as the question suggests. Never allow your answer to wander away from the focus of the question. If the question asks you to "describe" or "trace" or "compare" or "explain," be sure that that is what you do.

6. Don't repeat yourself. Each sentence should add new material or advance a line of argument.

7. Where necessary, refer to the facts that support the points you are making. But the mere relation of a series of facts is not enough. You must also give evidence that you have thought about the question in broad terms.

8. Toward the end of your answer, you may wish to include your own opinion. This is fine, even desirable, but be sure that your answer as a whole supports this opinion.

9. If there is time, always reread and correct an answer after it is finished. The pressure of an exam can often cause you to write sentences that are not clear.

10. Write legibly, or your grader will be in no mood to give you the benefit of any doubts.

11. Don't write cute or plaintive notes on the exam. They seldom raise a grade and may prejudice the grader against you.

How to Write History Assignments: The Importance of Writing Skills

Why Clear Writing Is Important

The most important tasks in a history course often are the written assignments. You may be asked to write a short book review, an exam essay, or a lengthy research paper. Whatever the writing assignment, you must take the time and care to make it your best work. Every instructor has had the experience of reading a poorly written paper from a student who did not take the trouble to do his or her best. If you hand in sloppy or thoughtless work, it not only will earn you a poor grade, it will indicate that you are not aware of the importance of good writing. Writing is a task of great significance. You will be judged not only by your history instructor but by everyone else who reads your words. Your writing skills tell the reader a lot about your ability to think clearly, whether you are writing a student paper or a proposal to your boss. As this chapter emphasizes, clear thinking is the source of clear writing. Two years after graduating you may no longer remember the causes of World War I, but if you have sharpened your writing skills in history assignments, you will have acquired a skill and an asset that will last a lifetime.

Clear writing accomplishes two very important goals. First, it demonstrates that your thinking about a subject is logical. You cannot write clearly about something that you do not understand clearly. Second, clear writing is persuasive. It enables you to convey to your reader in a convincing way exactly what you want them to understand.

The Components of Clear Writing

Write Clear Sentences

Clear writing begins with clear sentences. A clear sentence leaves no doubt about the *subject* of the sentence. Consider the following examples. What are the subjects of these sentences?

EXAMPLE

On September 1, 1939, Germany was strong and Poland was weak, and so it attacked.

When Lindbergh landed his plane in Paris, everybody was very excited to see the first person to fly across the Atlantic Ocean by himself.

The subject of the first sentence, describing the outbreak of World War II, is unclear. The reader cannot tell if the subject is Germany or Poland and therefore cannot tell who attacked whom. In the second example, the subject, Charles Lindbergh, is removed from the verb that describes his great feat, making the reader slog through an unclear and confusing sentence. Now look at these revised sentences:

REVISED EXAMPLE

On September 1, 1939, Germany attacked Poland.

Charles Lindbergh *made* the first solo flight across the Atlantic Ocean.

The reader will know who (or what) is the subject of the sentence if that subject is placed as close as possible to the verb that describes what the subject is doing.

Do Not Clutter Your Sentences with Unnecessary Phrases

An additional phrase can add information to your sentence. But when phrases are used indiscriminately, they can obscure the meaning of a sentence.

EXAMPLE: Charles Lindbergh took thirty-three hours to make the first solo flight across the Atlantic.

Here a phrase has been added to the original clear sentence. It tells the reader how long the flight took. This added information does not affect the clarity of the sentence. But look what happens when several phrases are added.

EXAMPLE: Although his plane was loaded down with extra fuel, Lindbergh was still able to get off the muddy runway in New Jersey despite very bad weather that rainy morning in 1927 and the fact that several other people had been killed trying to become the first person to stay awake for the thirty-three hours it took to fly solo across the Atlantic Ocean.

In this sentence, Lindbergh's flight is surrounded by so many phrases that the main point of the sentence is lost. You should not attempt to make one sentence describe so many aspects of his first flight. If some facts are not necessary, leave them out. If they are necessary, make room for them by creating additional sentences. For example, if the weight of the fuel and the muddy runway are important but the weather conditions and the failed attempts by others are not, writing two sentences instead of one makes the additional points and makes them clearly.

REVISED EXAMPLE: Lindbergh's plane was so heavily loaded with fuel that it almost failed to get off the muddy runway in New Jersey. Once in the air, however, he was able to stay awake for the thirty-three hours it took to fly across the Atlantic.

Avoid Using the Passive Voice

The subject and verb are the core of any sentence. In the passive voice, the verb indicates that the subject is *receiving* rather than *doing*.

EXAMPLE: A vaccination against smallpox was introduced by Edward Jenner in 1796.

A clear sentence usually uses the *active voice* of the verb. This shows the subject as *initiating* rather than *receiving* an action (or thought).

REVISED EXAMPLE: In 1796, Edward Jenner introduced a vaccination against smallpox.

There are times, however, when the passive voice is acceptable, such as when you desire to place emphasis on the *receiver* of an action or thought. So while it is preferable to avoid the passive voice, you may find occasions in your writing to use it.

Use the Past Tense

When writing about historical events, use the past tense. The only exception is when you are referring to a specific written document or object (such as an old building or a work of art). Since these still exist, use the present tense to describe them.

EXAMPLE: Thomas Jefferson *wrote* the draft of the Declaration of Independence.

Since Jefferson's action took place in the past, it is correct to use the past tense in writing about the event. However, since the Declaration of Independence is a written document that still exists, you should use the present tense to write about it.

EXAMPLE: The Declaration of Independence *says* that "all men are created equal."

The effort to write clear and simple sentences forces you to think about what your subject is doing and how many points about the subject's actions (or thoughts or feelings) you need to include. The result of this effort is a series of sentences that give the reader a clear understanding of what you have written.

Link Your Sentences Together

Clear sentences need to follow one another in a connected manner. This brings us to the second element of good writing — continuity. Continuity is the *relationship* between groups of words, sentences, or paragraphs. Continuity has two elements. First, a new sentence (or paragraph) should say something *new* and *significant* about the **theme.** Second, a new sentence (or paragraph) should be connected to those around it.

Sometimes a single sentence (or paragraph) cannot do both. It takes a skilled writer to craft a sentence that advances the theme while also connecting with the surrounding sentences. It is not poor writing to separate these two tasks. In fact, it is often necessary to write a separate **linking sentence**. Such a sentence does not have to introduce new evidence about the theme. Its job is to tell the reader that you are shifting gears, moving from one point to a different but connected one. The middle sentence in the following example is a linking sentence.

EXAMPLE: Therefore, changes in printing technology made newspapers cheaper and more available. *But new technology alone does not explain rising readership.* As immigrants poured into the country from Europe, it was the new look of the newspaper, especially the use of large illustrations and photographs, that attracted these new "readers."

The linking sentence tells the reader that the paragraph (dealing with technological change) is to be followed by the introduction of a new point about the theme: how changes in the look of newspapers attracted new readers. Linking sentences usually appear toward the end of a paragraph. Sometimes it is necessary to write an entire **linking paragraph** if the shift in focus is a major one or if you are moving from one section of a long essay to another (see pp. 56–57).

Write Clear and Coherent Paragraphs

A paragraph is a series of sentences about the same point. Each of its sentences needs to be clear and each, as noted above, needs to add something to the theme or provide a link between sentences or paragraphs about the theme. Each paragraph also needs to be "coherent," that is, internally connected. A well-connected paragraph will contain sentences, each of which expands on the point being made. Keep alert for any place in your writing where you begin to repeat yourself. When a sentence does not add anything significant to what you have already said, leave it out. Keep alert also for any place where you begin to talk about a new and different point. It is here that you will need to begin a new paragraph.

Consider again the following sentences about Lindbergh's historic flight: "Lindbergh's plane was so heavily loaded with fuel that it almost failed to get off the muddy runway in New Jersey. Once in the air, however, he was able to stay awake for the thirty-three hours it took to fly across the Atlantic." Both sentences describe the famous flight. That is why they belong in the same paragraph. But suppose you are finished writing about the flight and want to talk about the wild celebration in Paris after his landing? This information probably belongs in a new paragraph.

> **EXAMPLE:**   Once Lindbergh was on the ground, his plane was mobbed by excited Parisians who lifted him onto their shoulders.

The new paragraph should then continue with its description of Lindbergh's reception in Paris until you come to a new point about him. If you want to describe the celebration for him when he returned to New York, don't add that to your paragraph about the events in Paris; start a new paragraph.

Of course, a paragraph can be short — three or four sentences — or long — seven or eight sentences. There is no rule about the correct number of sentences in a paragraph. The key to knowing when a paragraph is complete is to ask yourself: Am I moving on to a different point than the one I am making in this paragraph? If the answer is "yes," then begin a new one.

Link Your Paragraphs Together

Since each paragraph says something new, you must help the reader to see the *connection* between them. Disconnected paragraphs (like disconnected sentences) can leave the reader confused about what is coming next and why. Note the disconnection between the end of the paragraph about the flight and the sentence that begins a new paragraph in the next example.

> **EXAMPLE**
> Once in the air, however, he was able to stay awake for the thirty-three hours it took to fly across the Atlantic.
>   In 1926, Lindbergh flew mail from Chicago to St. Louis.

Unless you say something in the new paragraph to explain why you are going back to the period before the famous flight, the reader will be confused and may think that you are too. If you have a good reason for going back in time in the new paragraph, make sure that the reader understands why.

REVISED EXAMPLE

Once in the air, however, he was able to stay awake for the thirty-three hours it took to fly across the Atlantic.

    No one had expected the twenty-five-year-old Lindbergh to make it. Less than a year before the famous flight, he had been an inconspicuous pilot flying mail between Chicago and St. Louis.

By connecting your paragraphs, you make the reader understand why you are bringing up Lindbergh's earlier career. The addition of a linking sentence shows the reader why a new paragraph is necessary and what direction the writer is taking.

Guidelines for Clear Writing

1. Each sentence is clear in naming its subject.
2. Each sentence is clear about what the subject is doing (or saying, or feeling, etc.).
3. If you have several points to make about the subject, split them up into separate sentences.
4. Each sentence adds something to the theme of the essay.
5. Each sentence is connected logically to those around it.
6. Avoid the passive voice.
7. Use the past tense when writing about past historical events. Use the present tense only when writing about documents or objects (buildings, artwork, etc.) that still exist.
8. Each paragraph is clear about the point it is making.
9. When you get to a new point, start a new paragraph.
10. Prepare your reader for the transition from one paragraph to another with a phrase or sentence linking the two. (The link can be placed either at the end of one paragraph or at the beginning of the next.)
11. Each paragraph is connected logically to those around it.

Building an Essay

Clear and coherent paragraphs, held together by linking phrases or sentences, are the building blocks of essay writing. But clear and coherent paragraphs are just the foundation. To unify your points in an essay, your paper needs to have a beginning, a middle, and an end.

This section discusses how to use clear writing to prepare a writing assignment.

The Need for a Clear Beginning

The very first paragraph of an essay has a special task. In it, you should state briefly and clearly what you are going to write about. State your **theme** clearly and tell the reader briefly what central point or points you intend to make about it. Conclude your opening paragraph with a statement about why your theme is an important one. (For more on themes, see Chapter 4, pp. 76–78.) Generally you can accomplish all of this in one paragraph. However, if your paper is a long one or if your theme is complex, you might need more than one opening paragraph.

Here is an example of a well-constructed opening paragraph.

EXAMPLE OF GOOD OPENING PARAGRAPH

This paper will explore the early history of the native peoples of New Mexico. It will describe their way of life before the arrival of European explorers in the sixteenth century. The paper will examine the evidence that over a thousand years ago many tribes living in this area had developed complex communities. Although European conquest destroyed most of these communities, there are still more than a dozen of them in New Mexico today.

The theme of this paper is "the early history of the native peoples of New Mexico." The opening paragraph accomplishes several important tasks:

- The first sentence announces the theme.
- The second and third sentences tell the reader that the paper will focus on the complex way of life of these people.
- The final sentence prepares the reader for the conclusion of the paper and makes clear why the theme is worthy of study.

Now read another opening paragraph to the same paper and see if you can spot the problems in it.

EXAMPLE OF POOR OPENING PARAGRAPH

European conquerors took away the native peoples' way of life in New Mexico. Some of their villages were caves cut into hillsides; others were made of hardened clay with many rooms. They were happy for one thousand years, but all this came to an end. This paper will show you how they lived.

Instead of announcing the theme, the first sentence of this paragraph starts with the paper's *conclusion*. The writer then jumps ahead and includes specific points about the kinds of houses they lived in. The reader is left to guess that these dwellings are evidence of a complex civilization. All the reader is told about the ancient, native way of life is that the native peoples were "happy." The reader is given no idea of why the theme is important or how it will be presented. The writer's only way of telling the reader what the core of the paper will be about is vague: it will "show you how they lived." The poor organization of the introductory paragraph leaves the reader uncertain of the subject, the nature of the evidence, and the conclusion toward which the paper will be heading.

Remember, your opening paragraph summarizes the core of your paper. If you change the organization of your paper in an important way, be sure to rewrite your opening paragraph to reflect that change.

Creating a Writing Outline

Before you begin the actual writing of your paper, make a **writing outline** of the points that you intend to discuss. Your instructor may provide this outline or you may have to create it yourself. This outline should reflect your research for the essay. You may have read one article or five articles, one book or five books. You may also have watched videos or researched on the **World Wide Web.** The information in those materials will provide the main points of your outline. Tailor your outline not only to your theme but also to the assigned length of your paper. Include too many points in your outline and you will never fit them all in your paper. Include too few and your paper will be short and probably weak. Be aware that you may need to revise your outline during the research process. You may discover the need to add new points to your outline or to remove old ones. (For more on research and the outlining of papers, see Chapter 4.)

The Importance of Continuity

A written essay is a series of paragraphs. Clear writing, as we have seen, is the result of clear thinking about the theme. The essay is built by creating a series of paragraphs. Each paragraph presents something new about the theme. Each paragraph states clearly what it is adding to the theme of the essay.

Just as important as clarity is **continuity**. Each paragraph should be connected to the ones before and after by **linking sentences.**

Don't break the continuity of your essay. As you write each paragraph, ask yourself: "Does this paragraph follow from the preceding one?" "Does it add something significant to the theme of the paper?" "Do it and the following paragraphs move toward the conclusion I announced in my opening paragraph?" When you begin the next paragraph, ask the same questions. If you cannot see how the new paragraph connects with the one before it or if the content of the paragraph doesn't add anything to the theme, rewrite it so that it accomplishes these goals.

Writing a Conclusion

How do you know when to end your paper? If your instructor gives you a specific length, obviously you need to wrap up the paper once it reaches the limit allowed. But how do you know when you have written enough? You are ready to conclude your paper when you have covered all of the points in your *revised* writing outline. Now you can see the importance of preparing and revising a writing outline.

How much space should you give to your conclusion? The overall length of your paper influences the length of your conclusion. For a short essay of five to seven pages, one to two concluding paragraphs are usually sufficient. A long essay of ten to twenty pages probably will require a concluding page. Some very long papers may need a concluding section of several pages.

What should your conclusion say? Your conclusion should summarize the main points of your essay. Look at your opening paragraphs again. What did you tell the reader you intended to do? By the time you reach the concluding part of your paper, this job should have been accomplished. (If your paper has not yet accomplished this, you must ensure that your revision does.) Your conclusion is also a way of reminding the reader of the significance of what he or she has read. Finally, the conclusion is the place where you can state your own opinion about your theme (unless your instructor has told you to be as objective as possible). As with your opening paragraph, it is often necessary to rewrite your conclusion after any significant revision of the body of your paper.

Revising Your Paper

The Rough Draft.   Even a skilled writer cannot produce a finished product from scratch. Good writing, in addition to following the guidelines in this chapter, is the product of revision. Think of your writing as a multistage process. Whether you are sitting down to write a sentence, a paragraph, or an entire essay, what you are really doing is writing a **rough draft**. The goal of this rough draft is to present the most important information you have gathered (or been given) on the subject. Don't worry about writing style too much at this stage.

Before beginning to write, you should have created a writing outline. (For more on preparing a writing outline, see pp. 110–13.) Organize your rough draft according to this outline. Keep in mind, though, that the writing process is not a rigid process. If your thoughts on your topic have changed, you may need to revise your writing outline before starting to write.

The Revised Draft.   Now comes the crucial task of refining your thoughts and words to produce the revised draft. Remember, the longer the paper, the more important the jobs of organization and revision. To **revise** your paper, go over each page carefully, paragraph by paragraph, making sure that each conforms to the writing guidelines in this chapter. As you read each sentence and paragraph, ask yourself the following questions:

Is this sentence (paragraph) clear?
Have I put too many phrases in my sentences?
Have I made more than one main point in my paragraphs?
Do my sentences and paragraphs each add something significant to my theme?
Is each sentence (and paragraph) connected to the ones around it?
Do I need a linking sentence to make a transition clear?
Can the average reader follow what I am saying?

Rework each sentence and paragraph until it meets these tests. Then step away from your paper for a time (an hour, a day, or several days) to give yourself a fresh view of it when you return. For this final revision, pay special attention to organization on a broad scale. Ask yourself the following questions:

Does the introductory paragraph give an overall sense of the paper?
Do the paragraphs include all of the important information?
Does each paragraph make its contribution to advancing the theme?
Does the conclusion effectively summarize the main points I have made about my theme?

If your revised draft meets these requirements, you are done writing. If there are still problems with clarity or continuity, go through your paper again carefully to find out what your paper lacks and to revise the weak sections. (For instructions on writing and revising long research papers, see Chapter 5.)

Proofreading Your Paper

The last step in preparing a writing assignment is to **proofread** the complete paper. Read your paper carefully, looking for misspellings, missing punctuation marks, typos, and layout issues (that is, how the text looks on the page). Read slowly to catch as many small errors as you can. It may be helpful to read the paper out loud. If you can, have a friend read the paper also. Your reader may spot something you missed. Even more important, your peer reviewer can tell you if something in your paper is confusing or not easily understood. (For more on peer review, see p. 137.)

Spell- and Grammar-Checkers

Spell-checkers are a terrific help in avoiding typos and incorrect spellings, and you should always make use of them before turning in a paper. However, don't expect the spell-checker to catch all of the mis-spelled words. The spell-checker flags any word that it does not recognize, including correctly spelled words not in its electronic dictionary. It also will not catch misspelled words that it reads as other words. For example, if you write "him" when you mean to write "his," or "no" for "know," the spell-checker will not read it as a mistake. You must catch these kinds of errors yourself when you proofread your paper.

Grammar-checkers are even less reliable. When you use a grammar-checker, consider its advice as a suggestion for revision. If the grammar-checker questions the way you have said something, consider the advice given before deciding to make any changes to your original sentence, phrase, or word.

Keep in mind that you, and not your computer, are the author of your paper.

You are done! It has taken you a lot longer than you had expected. Some of the work was difficult and some tedious. For your effort, you should feel good about yourself even before you learn your grade. You have produced your best work. And with each paper to come (yes, there will be others), your "best" will get even better.

Preparing Specific Writing Assignments

Instructors assign many kinds of writing assignments: among them are essay exams, book reviews, papers that analyze historical arguments, and research papers. These papers range from a few pages in length to ten or twenty. This chapter helps you prepare the different kinds of writing assignments that you are likely to encounter in your history courses.

Writing Essay Exams

The sections in Chapter 2 on "How to Take Notes in Class" (pp. 36–41) and "How to Study for Exams" (pp. 47–51) focused on *preparing* for exams that you take in class. If necessary, refer back to these sections because they complement this one. Here the emphasis is on **essay exams** — also known as **take-home exams** — that you write outside of class. This kind of exam gives you the time to do your very best writing. The goal of any essay exam is to demonstrate to your instructor that you understand the material needed to answer the question.

When writing essay exam answers, all of the points made earlier in this chapter about clarity and continuity apply. An essay exam question requires you to write a short essay of usually two to five pages. **Documentation** (**footnotes** and a **bibliography**) is not usually required. Of course, if your instructor asks for a specific length, theme, approach, or format, you need to follow those requirements even when they differ from the information provided here.

First, note the length requirements of the exam and the due date. Obviously, you will need more time to prepare a six-page essay answer than a three-page one. If your instructor allows you access to sources (which is common), you will need to review all course material that relates to the exam question. If you have not yet outlined or taken notes on this material, do so now. Focusing on the portion of the course materials that relate to the question, make a list of the most important points. Try to find anywhere from two to six main points for each essay, depending on the length of the essay. Compose your answer by introducing and then supporting these points in logical order. As with all essays, you should have a clear, central **theme**. In this case, your theme is determined by the exam question. Be sure that your essay directly addresses the question. (See also the section on writing in-class essay exams on pp. 49–51.)

The goal of an essay exam is to demonstrate the following: (1) adequate knowledge of the subject, (2) clear thinking about the points covered, (3) clear and connected writing, and (4) clear understanding of the question. Read the following two answers to an exam question on Chinese history. Do they meet the requirements listed above?

QUESTION: Explain the origins of the Chinese Civil War of 1945–1949. How did the differing political programs of the two contenders affect the outcome of that conflict?

POOR ANSWER: The Guo Mindang (Kuomintang) had a stronger army than the Communists, but the Communists won the civil war and took over the country. Their political program, communism, was liked by the peasants because they didn't own any land and paid high taxes.

China was based on the Confucian system, which was very rigid and led to the Manchu dynasty being overthrown. The Chinese didn't like being dominated by foreigners, and Sun Zhongshan (Sun Yat-sen) founded the Guo Mindang (Kuomintang) to unite China. He believed in the Three People's Principles. At first he cooperated with the Chinese Communists, but later Jiang Jieshi (Chiang Kai-shek) tried to destroy communism because he was against it. Communism was not in favor of the wealthy people.

The Communists wanted a revolution of the peasants and gave them land. They also killed the landlords. Jiang Jieshi (Chiang Kai-shek) worried more about the Communists than about the Japanese invasion. The Japanese looked to conquer China and make it a part of their empire. Jiang Jieshi (Chiang Kai-shek) wanted to fight the Communists first.

After World War II the Chinese Communists attacked Manchuria and took over a lot of weapons. They fought the Guo Mindang (Kuomintang) army. The Guo Mindang (Kuomintang) army lost the battles, and Jiang Jieshi (Chiang Kai-shek) was chased to Taiwan, where he made a new government. The Communists set up their own country, and their capital was Beijing (Peking). That way the Communists won the Chinese Civil War.

GOOD ANSWER: The origins of the 1945–1949 Civil War can be traced back to the rise of Chinese nationalism in the late nineteenth century. Out of the confusion of the Warlord period that followed the overthrow of the Manchu dynasty in 1911, two powerful nationalist movements arose — one reformist and the other revolutionary. The reformist movement was the Guo Mindang (Kuomintang), founded by Sun Zhongshan (Sun Yat-sen). It was based on a mixture of republican, Christian, and moderate socialist ideals and inspired by opposition to foreign domination. The revolutionary movement was that of the Chinese Communist Party (CCP), founded in 1921, whose goal was a communist society but whose immediate program was to organize the working class to protect its interests and to work for the removal of foreign "imperialist" control.

Although these two movements shared certain immediate goals (suppression of the Warlords and resistance to foreign influence), they eventually fell out over such questions as land reform, relations with the Soviet Union, the role of the working class, and the internal structure of the Guo Mindang (Kuomintang). [The CCP operated within the framework of the more powerful Guo Mindang (Kuomintang) during the 1920s.]

By the 1930s, when Jiang Jieshi (Chiang Kai-shek) succeeded Sun, the CCP was forced out of the Guo Mindang (Kuomintang). By that time the CCP had turned to a program of peasant revolution inspired by Mao Zedong (Mao Tse-tung). A four-year military struggle (1930–1934) between the two movements for control of the peasantry of Jiangxi (Kiangsi) Province ended in the defeat but not destruction of the CCP.

The Japanese invasion of Manchuria (1931) and central China (1936–1938) helped salvage the fortunes of the CCP. By carrying out an active guerrilla resistance against the Japanese, in contrast to the more passive role of the Guo Mindang (Kuomintang), which was saving its army for a future battle with the Communists, the CCP gained the leading position in the nationalist cause.

In the post–World War II period, the CCP's land reform program won strong peasant support, whereas the landlord-backed Guo Mindang (Kuomintang) was faced with runaway corruption and inflation, which eroded its middle-class following. The military struggle between 1945 and 1949 led to the defeat of the demoralized Guo Mindang (Kuomintang) army and the coming to power of the CCP.

Let's see the differences between the poor and the well-written essays in regard to each of the four requirements for a well-written answer.

1. *Adequate knowledge of the subject.* The poor answer fails to indicate adequate knowledge in several ways. It is too brief, omitting many important facts. It describes the political programs of the two contending parties in the most vague terms. It refers to the CCP only as the Chinese Communists, leaving the impression that they were a loose grouping of like-minded individuals rather than a strong, well-disciplined political organization. It does not even mention the name of the most famous leader of the CCP — Mao Zedong (Mao Tse-tung). Jiang Jieshi (Chiang Kai-shek), the leader of the Guo Mindang (Kuomintang), is mentioned, but there is no mention of his political program or beliefs, other than that he was opposed to communism. Another serious defect is the lack of chronology. The answer jumps back and forth between earlier and later periods, and no dates are given for major events.

The well-written answer illustrates a good knowledge of the subject matter. The origins, philosophies, leaders, and relationship of the two contending parties are clearly described. This answer brings in related issues such as nationalism, Warlords, guerrilla warfare against Japan, corruption, and inflation, thus indicating a broader knowledge of the historical context in which the Chinese Civil War developed. The chronology is very clear, with events proceeding in proper time sequence and with all major events identified by date.

2. *Clear thinking about the points covered.* The poor answer is not organized. Note that the paragraphs do not make separate points and that each succeeding paragraph does not further develop the theme of the essay. Paragraph one is a conclusion rather than an introduction. The second paragraph goes back to the founding of the Guo Mindang (Kuomintang) but, instead of discussing the origins of the hostility between it and the CCP, merely states that hostility came into existence. The third paragraph begins by introducing the CCP (though not by name). However, it does not expand on the CCP's programs and points of conflict with the Guo Mindang (Kuomintang), but instead abruptly changes the focus of events and the time frame by introducing the Japanese invasion of China, which the last sentence of the paragraph only vaguely relates to the question. The last paragraph, instead of drawing conclusions about the causes of the Communist victory in the Civil War, merely states that it occurred.

The well-written answer, on the other hand, uses each paragraph to make a separate important point, and each succeeding paragraph further develops the theme of the essay. Paragraph one sets out the political programs of the two groups and the historical context in which the movements originated. The second paragraph explains the beginning of the conflict in the 1920s. Paragraph three discusses that conflict in relation to the Chinese peasantry during the early 1930s. The fourth paragraph discusses the development of the conflict in relation to the Japanese invasion of the late 1930s. The final paragraph summarizes the effects of the conflicts and of postwar developments on the outcome of the Civil War.

3. *Clear and connected writing.* Many sentences in the poor answer are badly constructed either because they are awkward or because what they say adds nothing to the answer. Some of the awkward phrases are "the Communists won the Civil War and *took over* the country"; "communism was *liked by* the peasants"; "China was *based on* the Confucian system"; "communism was not *in favor* of the wealthy people"; "the Japanese *looked* to conquer China"; "the Communists *set up their own country*." These phrases cause the sentences to be unclear, and they keep the student from getting his or her point across. The other major defect in sentence structure is repetitious or irrelevant sentences and phrases. These are "Jiang Jieshi (Chiang Kai-shek) tried to destroy communism *because he was against it*"; "they *fought the Guo Mindang (Kuomintang) army*"; "that way *the Communists won the Chinese Civil War*." The sentences of the well-written answer, on the other hand, are clear, and each adds new material to the essay.

4. *Clear understanding of the question.* The poor answer does not deal with the central issue of the question — the political programs of the Guo Mindang (Kuomintang) and the CCP. It notes that the Guo Mindang (Kuomintang) was founded on the Three People's Principles, but it does not explain what these were. Of the CCP, it says that there was a belief in communism (which is obvious) and peasant revolution (which is vague). These are the only references to political programs in the entire answer! It is obvious that the writer of this answer failed to understand that the central focus of the question was on political philosophy.

The well-written answer is directed to the central issue of political programs and begins on that very point. The remainder of the answer makes clear the relationship of political programs to the origins and course of the Chinese Civil War as called for in the first sentence of the question.

The Dangers of Plagiarism.   A problem that sometimes arises with take-home exams is **plagiarism**. Your instructor may allow you to **paraphrase** the sources you use in preparing your essay. Be sure, however, that you write in your own words. If you use sentences from another source, you are cheating whether you realize it or not. Most schools require instructors to penalize students severely for plagiarizing. Refer to pages 108–10 for help in avoiding plagiarism and instruction on how to paraphrase.

Writing Book Reviews

A **book review** is not a summary. Unless your instructor asks you to summarize the book's contents, spend most of your review *analyzing* its contents. Determine its theme and then describe how the theme is presented and how well it is defended. Were you persuaded by the author's arguments? If it is part of the assignment, compare the book to other course materials. Be sure that your review makes it clear that you have read and understood the book — or article, document, excerpt, or essay — and always provide the kind of analysis asked of you.

The following is an example of a book review of the *Narrative of the Life of Frederick Douglass, An American Slave, Written by Himself*, edited by David W. Blight (Bedford/St. Martin's, 1993).

Sample Book Review

Patrick P. Student

History 100

February 14, 2001

Book Review of:

David W. Blight, ed.

Narrative of the Life of Frederick Douglass,

An American Slave, Written by Himself.

Bedford/St. Martin's, 1993

This book is divided into three parts: a long introduction written by the historian David Blight, the actual Narrative written by the former slave Frederick Douglass, and a concluding section of related historical documents.

Blight's Introduction describes the reasons why Douglass wrote the story of his life as a slave. He also sets out the historical context in which the Narrative was written. For example, Blight describes the abolitionist movement in the northern United States during the 1830s, 1840s, and 1850s. He makes clear that abolitionism was a very controversial stand to take in these decades, even in the North. He also describes Douglass's important contribution to that movement. He was one of its main leaders and, some said, its most articulate orator.

Blight also explains that after Douglass's escape from slavery in 1835 the former slave lived in the North and learned about northern attitudes toward slavery. Blight points out that only a small percentage of white people in the North opposed slavery and that Douglass wanted to write about his life in a way that would convince large numbers of northerners that slavery

should be destroyed. Following this same theme,
Blight tells the reader that Douglass wanted to
picture the evils of slavery in a highly dramatic way. That is why Douglass focused his book
not only on the brutality of slave masters but
also on the psychological suffering of the
slaves, who had to endure such traumas as forced
separation from family members. As a part of his
effort to sway northern readers, Douglass emphasized the ways that slavery degraded slave owners as well as slaves.

Finally, Blight points out that Douglass's
book, first published in 1845, was a "best
seller" (p. 15), allowing Douglass to use the
book's success as a platform for his many
speeches against slavery in the United States
and in England. According to Blight, Douglass's
story was effective because "the epic character
of individuals who first <u>willed</u> their own freedom, then <u>wrote</u> the story proved irresistible to
readers in the American North and in Britain"
(p. 16). [Emphasis in the original.]

The second section contains Douglass's <u>Nar-
rative</u>. It describes his childhood, his separation from his mother, and the possibility that
his father was actually his slave master. Even
worse than the whippings he saw or endured was
what Douglass calls the "soul-killing effects of
slavery" (p. 47). For Douglass, the hopelessness
of the slaves was sometimes worse than the physical punishments.

At about the age of eight, Douglass was
sold to a master in Baltimore. It was there that
he found his first book. Though slaves were not

taught to read or write, Douglass tells us that
he taught himself enough words to read newspapers and eventually learned from reading them
the meaning of the words "slavery" and "aboli-
tion." Soon Douglass was sold again, this time
to a cruel master who whipped him regularly.
What bothered Douglass the most, however, was
that the master told him it was his Christian
duty to be an obedient slave. Douglass makes it
clear that he hated the twisting of religion to
support slavery. Finally, in 1838, his chance
came and he escaped to New York City where he
began his long career as a leader of the abolitionist movement.

The theme of Douglass's <u>Narrative</u> is that
slavery was so evil an institution that it dehu-
manized not only the slaves but the slave owners
as well. The historical context provided by
Blight (and also by the many documents in the
third section of the book) make clear how difficult it was to convince northerners that the nation itself, and not just the slaves, suffered
from slavery.

Note the important aspects of this review. The book is identified at
the top of the page. Since the book contains several parts, this feature
is pointed out first. Then the theme of the first part — the historical
context in which the *Narrative* was written and the reasons why Frederick Douglass wrote it — is described. Evidence from the Introduction is
cited to make the reader aware of the attitude toward slavery in the
North and of the small abolitionist movement there whose goal was to
end slavery. In the fifth paragraph, the review shifts to Douglass's *Narrative*. Evidence from this part of the book is cited to show the cruelty
of slavery. But the reviewer also explains the particular aspect of slavery
that Douglass found most oppressive: its dehumanizing effect on slaves
and slave masters. Because this point is unusual and very important, the
reviewer quotes briefly from the book (about the "soul-killing effect of
slavery") and then puts the page number where the quotation can be

found. The last paragraph summarizes the theme of the historical in-troduction and of the *Narrative*.

Reviews can vary widely in content to accommodate the different kinds of work they discuss. Still, a good review, like the one above, has all of the elements listed in the "Guidelines for Writing a Book Review" that appear below.

If your instructor asks for a particular kind of review, you should fol-low those directions. You might be asked to include some of the evi-dence that argues against the theme and the author's ability to present it fairly and respond to it effectively. Or you could be asked to com-ment on the author's personal or academic background and reasons for writing the book. This last point should certainly be included if there is significant disagreement among historians about the theme of the book or if the book's preface or introduction refers to such dis-agreements. With a book of this kind, your instructor may ask you to comment on the disagreement and perhaps also ask you how the book affects your views on the subject.

Unless requested by your instructor, it is usually unwise to emphasize your personal opinion in a review. If, however, you are asked to express it, don't write simply, "I liked the way the author defended women's rights." Instead say, "I was impressed by the author's use of many concrete ex-amples of actions by women to dramatize their demand for the right to vote. The day they chained themselves to the White House fence made clear how strongly they felt about their cause." Show that your opinion is the result of serious thought about the arguments made in the book.

If your assignment is a review that is longer than a few pages, you might want to quote a sentence or phrase from the book to support a point you are making. But don't use too many quotations. That is, don't fill your review with the author's words rather than your own.

Guidelines for Writing a Book Review

1. At the top of the first page, put the name of the author, the title of the work, the publisher's name, and the date of publication.
2. State the author's theme or main points.
3. Describe the evidence presented to support the theme.
4. Assess the arguments and evidence used. (Are they clear or unclear, strong or weak, convincing or unconvincing?)
5. If appropriate, describe the author's background and rea-son for writing the book.
6. If required, compare the work to related course materi-als. (Does it agree or disagree? Does it add a new perspec-tive?)
7. If expected, close with your own assessment of the book's assumptions, arguments, and conclusions.

Writing Comparative Book Reviews

Not all review assignments are concerned with only one source. A comparative book review is more difficult than a review of only one book. You must read more, of course, but you must also be able to compare the books. You need to discover what they have in common (consider theme, arguments, style, approaches to the subject, conclusions) and where they differ. The key to success in an essay of this type is to come up with a series of points of similarity or dissimilarity (or some of each) and to focus your essay on them. Don't spend too much time discussing each book separately. Build your essay around the connections between them. That is the purpose of this kind of assignment.

Comparing Essays or Articles

If your assignment is to compare essays or articles rather than books, you probably will be expected to treat them in more detail. The essays or articles will likely be on the same subject. The goals of this kind of assignment are the same as those for comparing books. What are the similarities or differences in the arguments presented? How do the authors make their points? What conclusions do they draw? The key to any comparative assignment, again, is to focus on comparing the works. Don't get bogged down with long descriptions of each one.

Comparing Primary Documents

This is a difficult task, but many instructors use this kind of assignment to judge the depth of your knowledge and your interpretive ability. Since these documents are the most direct contact we have with the past, they are filled with facts and impressions about life in a very different time and place than our own. (For more on primary documents, see pp. 6–9.) To understand them we must know a good deal about the time and place they describe and, if possible, about the people who wrote them.

Consider the following assignment: You are given a series of letters written to their families by U.S. soldiers fighting in Vietnam. Some of the letters talk about the heat and exhaustion of fighting in dense jungles or rice paddies. Some express deep hostility toward the enemy, but others contain no references to the enemy at all. Some letters are filled with questions about what is going on in the soldiers' families and hometowns and hardly even mention the war. The most surprising discovery is that a few letters mention the desire to be wounded (but not seriously) so that the letter writers can be sent home. To make sense of these letters, you need to know a lot about the ground war in Vietnam and the state of mind of the ground troops who fought there. The more you know about the historical event depicted in any set of primary documents, the more they will reveal to you.

Now you are given another group of Vietnam War letters. Unlike the first group written by "grunts" (front-line foot soldiers), these are from bomber pilots. Their war seems different. The pilots' letters don't complain about difficult living conditions. In fact, their lives on air bases or aircraft carriers seem fairly comfortable. They say that they rarely see their targets because they fly so high. Like some of the foot soldiers, the pilots do not talk about the enemy. But unlike some of the "grunts," none mentions the idea of wanting to get out of the war. In fact, their morale seems high.

If you are asked to compare the letters from these two groups of soldiers, you will be expected not only to notice the different things they write about but also to have some idea of *why* their letters are different. In this case, an understanding of the difference between the ground war and the air war and between the different types of people who fought in each is needed. Interpreting and comparing primary documents requires you to go beneath their surface. You need to understand the *context,* or historical environment, that gave rise to them.

Writing Short Essays

This kind of assignment differs from others by being longer and by requiring research and analysis of some kind. You are assigned or are expected to find on your own the materials you need to prepare your essay. Many of the skills needed here are similar to those you will need in researching and writing a lengthy research paper of the kind described in Chapters 4 and 5.

You may be asked to take a position in a historical controversy and to defend your position with historical evidence. You might be asked to compare a group of readings and draw conclusions about the differences among them. Perhaps you will be asked to write about your own life experience or that of an older relative and connect the story to important historical events. You might be asked to keep a journal in which you will write regularly about your response to ideas and subjects that arise in class discussion.

Some interpretive essays are similar to exam essays. Your instructor gives you a list of topics to choose from. Let's assume that you are taking a course in the history of journalism. You have been asked to write an essay that includes a variety of sources about the relationship between rising literacy and the growth of newspaper circulation in the United States during the nineteenth century. If you study your sources closely, you will discover that your essay cannot take the easy route: that newspaper circulation increased because more people could read. If things were that simple, your instructor would not have chosen the topic for this kind of assignment.

As you dig into your research, you come across evidence that knowing how to read doesn't automatically give a person the desire (or the money) to read a newspaper. You also learn from your sources that by the late nineteenth century, illustrations took up a large part of a newspaper page. That meant that even people who knew very few words of English might still enjoy "reading" a paper. Perhaps you are beginning to see why the question is worth writing about.

The relationship between literacy and readership is not a simple one — few things in history are. Perhaps you will conclude from your research that rising literacy and rising newspaper circulation reinforced one another; that neither was the simple cause of the other.

How do you prepare for and execute an assignment like this one? Here are some guidelines for preparing a short essay.

Guidelines for Writing Short Essays

1. Think about the topic carefully. Be sure you understand it. Ask your instructor about any aspects of the topic or question that are unclear to you.
2. Determine which materials you will need. If you have to find your own research materials, seek out those that are appropriate to the theme of the paper.
3. From these sources, take notes on any facts and explanations that seem important in giving a serious explanation of the topic.
4. Examine your notes closely and compose a theme (a principal idea or conclusion) that your paper will support.
5. Organize your paper by outlining it on paper. What evidence do you need to support your theme? Do you have enough of it or do you need to do more research? What is the best way to present the evidence?
6. Begin to flesh out a first draft. Write an introductory paragraph that states your theme and how you intend to support it. Then write a group of paragraphs for each of your main points.
7. Weave together the paragraphs so that each point follows clearly from the one before it and adds support to your argument. This is your **rough draft.**
8. Read and *revise* your draft. Be sure that each part of your paper is supported by your notes and that each adds something significant to your argument or theme. Add, delete, or change your writing where this is not the case. (If you have uncovered counterevidence — material in your notes that could be used to argue *against* a point you are making — include some of this material and then

---

> explain to your reader why you are sticking to your argument.)
>
> 9. Write your **conclusion.** This is a brief restatement of your theme or argument and a summary of the most important evidence for it. (It may also be necessary to rewrite your introductory paragraph if your theme or evidence has changed since you wrote it.)
> 10. If the assignment asks for documentation and a bibliography, be sure that you know how to create them. (For instructions on creating a bibliography, see Chapter 5, pp. 130–36.)
> 11. **Proofread** and revise your writing if necessary. Check for clarity, grammar, and spelling. If possible, have a friend read the paper and make comments.
> 12. Type the final draft neatly, following any instructions concerning form that your instructor has given.

A Note on Plagiarism: A Serious Offense

Whenever you prepare a written assignment while working from notes you have taken from books or other course materials, you must be careful how you use them. If you are not, you run the risk of using sentences or extended phrases in your paper that you copied from your notes. Even if you do this without realizing it, you have committed **plagiarism.** Unless the phrases or sentences are placed in quotation marks with their sources noted in a **footnote** or **endnote,** you have committed a very serious breach of academic honesty. Plagiarism can lead to failing a course or even to suspension. Read the section on avoiding plagiarism on page 108 to make sure you know how to avoid this danger.

How to Research
a History Topic

In basic history courses, you may be called upon to do historical research. If you take advanced courses, you certainly will be called upon to do research papers. Whether you are preparing a short essay or book review or a long class presentation or term paper, you will need to know how to gather all the necessary materials and how to organize and analyze your information. This chapter will survey sources of historical information and will explain how to use these sources most profitably. The chapter also includes sections on how to choose a topic, how to conduct research in your library and on the World Wide Web, how to record information, and how to organize your research.

What Is a Research Paper?

A **research paper** requires you to gather your own sources of information. It is one of the most creative tasks you will do as a history student. Since you choose your own material and draw your own conclusions, the product is uniquely your own. Because a lot of independent work is involved, research is often the most challenging history assignment. The skills you gain from doing this kind of a project (gathering, organizing, and interpreting evidence) are invaluable. Any professional or business career that you later pursue will call upon one or more of these skills. In years to come, you may not remember the name of the secret research program that produced the atomic bomb during World War II (the Manhattan Project) and about which you wrote a paper.

Nevertheless, you will have strengthened important skills during the research *process* that produced the paper.

Five stages of research are involved in preparing your paper: (1) choosing a topic, (2) finding the best sources of information, (3) determining what you need to record from these sources, (4) organizing your research, and (5) writing the research paper. The last step — writing the paper — is covered in the next chapter. This chapter takes you through the first four steps.

What Should I Write About?
Choosing a Topic

Some instructors assign a specific research **topic,** but most set out a range of possible topics and leave the choice to you. Choose your topic carefully. You will become bored if you have to spend weeks searching out and reading information about a subject that does not interest you. Try to select a topic about which you are genuinely curious. No matter what subject, person, or event you are interested in, it has a history. Every subject can be studied backward in time because every event was caused by events that preceded it. A history research project can be made out of almost anything. Perhaps in the neighborhood where you grew up there was a very old building and you had always wondered about when it was built and what it was used for. Finding out what the neighborhood was like when that building was new can be an exciting search.

An ideal topic is not only one about which you are curious but one about which you already know something. Perhaps you read a book about Socrates and want to know more about why he was condemned to death; or perhaps you saw a movie about the Depression and want to know what it was like to live through it. Instructors are eager to help students who show a real interest in a topic. Your instructor can assist you in selecting a subject related to your interests that also suits the particular course you are taking.

Moving from a Topic to a Theme

A **theme** is more narrow than a topic. A *topic* is the general subject that you will investigate (the influence of Islam on the Kingdom of Mali; the philosophy of Martin Luther King Jr.). A *theme* is some important point about the topic that you wish to make.[1] For the paper on

---

[1] Some instructors refer to a theme as a "thesis" and ask you to begin your paper with a "thesis statement." In this book, the same thing is accomplished by beginning your paper with a clear statement of your theme.

King, you may want to show that his famous speech at the Lincoln Memorial in 1963 expressed several elements of his religious beliefs. In that case, your theme is the connection between the speech and King's earlier religious development. This connection will be the central point of your paper and making that connection will direct your research and writing. Without a theme, you will not have a clear idea of which sources of information to investigate, what to take from them, or how to organize your paper.

The transition from a broad topic to a narrower theme is not always easy. The key is to find an aspect of your topic that can serve as the core of your paper, that fits the sources available to you, and that can be satisfactorily researched within the time available to complete the assignment. A topic such as the conquest of the Aztec Empire can produce both workable and unwieldy themes. The theme "The Correspondence of Cortés and King Ferdinand" may be feasible if it is confined to letters from Cortés about the conquest of the Aztecs. The trouble here is access to sources. Unless translations of this correspondence are available in your library or on the **World Wide Web,** you do not have the research material to explore this theme. On the other hand, the theme "The Factors that Enabled the Spanish to Defeat the Aztecs" is workable since you should not have difficulty in finding enough material on this subject. Even if resources are available, make sure that your theme is not too broad. For a topic such as European exploration of Africa, you might come up with the theme "Exploration of the Congo River." As dozens of such explorations were made over many years, this is not a proper theme — it is actually a topic. If you begin to research "Exploration of the Congo River," you will soon discover that there are too many sources and that you do not have time (or space in your paper) to do them justice.

Narrowing Your Theme

Formulating a theme that is narrow enough and yet not too narrow is tricky. It is often useful in narrowing a theme to compose questions about your topic. If your topic is Native Americans of the Western United States, ask yourself a question you would like to know the answer to. Maybe some aspect of Native American life, such as the thoughts of their medicine men or the conflict of a particular tribe with European settlers, has aroused your curiosity. You might ask yourself: "What did medicine men believe?" or "How did the Indians defend their lands?" These questions might yield themes such as "The Practice of Magic among the Cheyenne," or "Efforts of the Nez Perce to Protect their Native Lands in Oregon." For a topic about Canadian frontier communities in the nineteenth century, again, ask yourself what specific things you would like to know about them. Was the coming of the railroad of great importance to them? This might lead you to a theme: "The Canadian Pacific Railroad Comes to Winnipeg, Manitoba." (By the way, you may have noted that a theme can usually serve as a *title* for your paper.) Although composing questions is usually helpful in arriving at themes, be careful that the questions you ask are not too broad. ("Why did the Roman Empire fall?"). Questions can also be too narrow ("Who was the first person to sign the Declaration of Independence?") or too unimportant ("Why are ping pong tables green?").

If you know very little about your topic, then it is wise to learn more about it before you attempt to narrow it and produce a good theme. If your topic is the Mexican Revolution of 1910, check a brief outline history of the subject in a good historical dictionary or **encyclopedia** (for example, the *Encyclopaedia Britannica* or the *Encyclopedia of Latin America*). The description of the Mexican Revolution in these works will likely mention its principal leaders — Francisco Madero, Pancho Villa, Emiliano Zapata, and Venustiano Carranza. Perhaps your interest will now be triggered by the recollection of stories concerning Villa's daring raid on a United States border town (Columbus, New Mexico) in 1916 and how the U.S. Army under General Pershing marched into Mexico to capture him — but never did. Or perhaps you have seen the Hollywood movie *Viva Zapata,* which tells the story (not necessarily accurately) of the peasant leader Emiliano Zapata and his fight to preserve the lands of the Indian villages in his native state of Morelos. If you have ever seen photographs of Zapata (they were popular in poster form among college students in the 1960s), you know his piercing eyes and look of determination. If your interest in the Mexican Revolution is now focusing on Villa or Zapata, you should next turn to a biographical dictionary. Here you will discover that Villa's real name was Doroteo Arango and that he was a cattle thief as well as a brilliant military commander. Zapata, you will learn, led a peasant guerrilla army whose aim was to recapture the land taken from its villages by owners of expanding sugar plantations. To flesh out a paper on Villa's military career or Zapata's land reform program (some elements of which Mexican peasants are still struggling for today), turn to the **subject bibliographies** in Appendix A of this book, to the reference section of your library, or to an online reference source such as *Encyclopaedia Britannica* online. These tools will lead you to individual historical works on the Mexican Revolution, and from the book and article titles (and the descriptions of their contents if they are annotated) you will be able to determine those which may contain information on the topic you are considering.

Creating a Research Outline

A **research outline** is different from the one you will create when you *write* your paper. (See the section on preparing a **writing outline** on pp. 110–13.) A research outline helps you to investigate your theme in an organized way. It tells you which parts of your research should come first. Here is a sample research outline for investigating the topic of agrarian reform in the Mexican Revolution, which, after preliminary research, led to the theme "The Land Reform Program of Emiliano Zapata." It also includes an *estimate* (shown in italics) of the time needed for each step.

RESEARCH OUTLINE: Things I need to do before I begin. Take a tour of the library. Find out what kinds of information are kept where. Learn how to search for materials from the library's online catalog.

Task #1: [Background] Gain a general knowledge of the Mexican Revolution from a good encyclopedia, textbook, or Web site. *Approximately 1 day.*

Task #2: [Background] Learn about land reform *before* the revolution. An encyclopedia or a general history of Mexico in the 19th century. *Approximately 1 day.*

Task #3: [Information about Zapata] Life in Ananecquilco, Morelos (village and state where Zapata grew up). A **biography** of Zapata, and a book or articles examining the changes in village life in Morelos in the decades before 1910. *Approximately 3 days.*

Task #4: [Information about land reform] Books, articles, and documents (including online resources) about how the villagers lost their lands before 1910. *Approximately 3 days.*

Task #5: [Zapata's role in the effort to regain village lands] Sources that examine Zapata's early career as a village leader. *Approximately 3 days.*

Task #6: [The period of the Revolution, 1910–1920] Sources examining the role of Zapata and his followers in the revolution. *Approximately 4 days.*

Task #7: [Specific land reform programs] Books (maybe old ones available online or in your library on **microfilm** or **microfiche**) that contain **quotations** from or copies of the actual proposals by Zapata. *Approximately 2 days.*

Task #8: [The fate of the programs] Read about the final years of the revolution and of the fate of Zapata (assassinated in 1919). *Approximately 2 days.*

Not all research outlines can be this specific. The time frame, in particular, is only an estimation. It contains nineteen days of research and assumes that you spend about two or three hours each day conducting research and reading. Your particular assignment may require more or less time, depending on the length of your paper and the importance given to it by your instructor. (Remember this is only time needed for *research*. Writing your paper will, of course, take additional time.) Moreover, no outline can be followed exactly. Your own research may move back and forth among the tasks (especially the later ones) on a given day in the library. While you are gathering material on Zapata's early life, you may come across a book or a Web site about his land program.

The information you find in the library and on the World Wide Web will not be neatly divided into the tasks you have laid out. The purpose in organizing your research in a formal way, even if the actual process is much messier, is so that it will have a sense of direction that it otherwise would lack. If you don't know what kinds of sources to look for first, which to read first, and which to read later on, you may try to take notes on specific land reform proposals before you even know who Zapata was or how long the revolution lasted. Even if you cannot actually follow an outline like the one above, just making it and having it in mind as you do your research will help you. In short, don't begin serious research until you have a clear idea of what you will be looking for. You may change directions (even change your theme) after some background reading, and you can always adjust your outline. It is better to have a research outline that you change than none at all.

After conducting preliminary research to decide which aspects of your topic interest you most, narrowing your topic to a manageable theme, and creating a research outline to direct your research, you are ready to seek out sources of information. Your **library catalog** and the materials (print and digital) in Appendix A should enable you to create a list of potential sources. The next step, of course, is to find these sources. They may be in print form on the shelves of your library, they may be in microprint form (microfilm and microfiche), or they may be in electronic form such as CD-ROM databases or Web-based documents. To find these sources, you will first have to learn how to conduct research in your library and on the Web.

Conducting Research

Exploring Your Library's Resources

A college library can be an intimidating place. Don't begin your research until you are familiar with it. Take a library tour to find where and how different library resources are housed. Never hesitate to ask a librarian about the organization of the library. For example, you should know where the **stacks**[2] are — the floors where the bound books and journals are kept on shelves. You should also be able to find such areas as the **reference book** section (encyclopedias, dictionaries, **atlases,** etc.) and the microprint section (microfilms and microfiche).

Once you have a sense of the place, sit yourself down at one of the **online catalogs.** Become familiar with the library **home page.** It should tell you how to search for different kinds of material. Explore the home page carefully so that you don't overlook big pieces of the material available to you. For example, the home page should link you to a

---

[2]Some library stacks are open to students while others are not. If yours are open, wander through some of them so that you know what the inside of the library looks like.

list of the library's online databases. (For a description of online databases, see pp. 204–05.) It is often possible to jump from the home page to the **World Wide Web.** But finding information on the Web can be tricky, so it is best to begin your search in your library. (For help on conducting research online, see pp. 90–99.)

Creating a Research Bibliography

As you begin to discover useful materials in your library, make sure to copy down *exactly and fully* all of the information on each item. Your goal is to compile a **research bibliography,** a list of the sources you think will give you the information you need to describe your theme and to document the facts you use to support it. When you finally write your paper, you may not use some of the items that you list in this phase of your research. At this stage, however, cast your net broadly. (For more on creating a bibliography, see Chapter 5, pp. 130–36.)

Using the Library Catalog

The main catalog is the most important pathway into the materials you need to know about to conduct your research. In order to get what you want out of the catalog, however, you will need to know the rules for searching its contents.

Searching the Catalog by Author and Title.   You can search for books in the online catalog by author, title, or subject. The catalog will have a screen or menu that tells you which commands begin an author search, a title search, a subject search, or **keyword** search. Author and title searches are usually simple as long as you know the proper commands and spell the names or titles correctly. If you enter the author name "Chakspeere, William" (instead of "Shakespeare, William") you will not get very far. The spelling of ancient and foreign names is especially tricky. Check the spelling before you begin your search. If still uncertain, ask the reference librarian. Title searches have a few dangers also. Again, spelling is crucial. In addition, titles that *begin* with "A" or "The" can confuse the computer. The catalog's rules for title searching usually tell you which words in titles can cause trouble. Finally, be sure to get all of the words of the title just right.

While author and title searches are fairly straightforward, they require you to know in advance what person or book you are looking for. This is often not possible, especially when just beginning your research. For the most part, you will need to discover which books by which authors are related to your theme. To do this, you must search the online catalog by subject. This is a little more difficult. Unless you enter the right words, the computer will not list the materials you really need.

Searching the Catalog by Subject. Online catalogs allow you to search their contents by subject or by keyword or both. Although similar, subject and keyword searches are not the same. In a library catalog, a **subject heading** is a term (or terms) that the library profession has chosen to best describe the contents of the material included under that heading. A *keyword,* on the other hand, is a term that *you* choose because it seems to describe the kinds of sources you think you need.[3] This discussion first takes up subject headings; an examination of keywords follows.

SUBJECT HEADINGS

If you want to do the job of searching by subject heading in the most complete way, go to the official set of headings compiled by the Library of Congress. These headings are printed in the volumes, *Library of Congress Subject Headings,* usually kept in the reference section of the library or near the computer terminals. The online catalog will use these headings in its own internal organization. Another way to discover the best subject headings is to look up a book that you already know about (by author or title), and when you get it on the screen, go to "long" or "full" display. This display tells you more than the author, the title, and the location; you get the full publication data as well as the subject heading or headings under which it is placed in the catalog. Other books on your theme may be listed under this heading, so you now can use this heading to find them. Since no two computer catalogs are exactly alike, finding out how to use subject headings may require the help of a librarian. Don't be shy; a librarian's assistance can save you a great deal of time.

KEYWORDS

Another way of searching the computer catalog is by keyword. Most catalogs enable you to search in this way. Instead of trying to figure out the subject your topic is under, you ask the computer to search its records of books and other materials for certain words. If your topic is women workers in early industrial America, and you have narrowed it to the theme: "Women Workers in the Lowell, Massachusetts, Textile Mills, 1820–1850" (see the sample student paper in Chapter 5 on pp. 143–69), then your keywords are the nouns in your theme — "women," "workers," "Lowell," "textile mills." Don't search by using any of these words by themselves, for they are too general and will generate a long list of sources, most of which will not be related to your theme. Entering the word "women," for example, will get you everything in the library that has anything to do with the topic of women. Most computers

---

[3]An example of a subject heading is "Textile industry — Massachusetts — Lowell — History — 19th Century" while a keyword in the same topic area might be "women textile workers."

allow you to do complex keyword searches that combine several keywords. You can ask it, for example, to find records that mention "women" *and* "workers" or, better yet, "women workers" *and* "textile mills." (Placing the word "and" between your keywords narrows the search accordingly.) The rules for keyword searching are described in the Help (or another) menu on the computer. Again, if you need assistance with keyword searches, ask for it. Using the wrong keywords will get you a lot of material that you cannot use. Even the precise keyword can turn up unrelated items. The keyword "textile mills" may give you a useful title such as *The Textile Mills of Lowell, Massachusetts,* but it might also give you *Textile Mills in Japan During World War II.* Notice that time period is crucial in a history search. A search for "history" *and* "textile mills" or "history" *and* "women workers" should cut out most studies that are about recent developments.[4]

Don't sit at the computer monitor for long stretches trying to find that one subject heading or keyword that will give you everything you want. Once your searches have turned up a number of promising titles, print out or write down (preferably on note cards) *all* of the information on the screen that you will need for your **bibliography** (see the section on organizing a bibliography in Chapter 5, pp. 130–36) as well as the **call number** of each book. The call number indicates its location in the library stacks. (See the section on locating materials and using call numbers later in this chapter on pp. 88–89.) You will probably discover that many of the books you have listed have similar call numbers, that is, they begin with the same letters or numbers. When you get to the appropriate place in the stacks, don't look only for the specific books you found in your computer search; look at *all* of the books on nearby shelves as well. You will likely find some other works that are related to your theme.

A word of caution about using an electronic catalog. You cannot find what is not there. Not everything in the library may be included, or the electronic catalog may include only material received by the library after a certain date. Some libraries have not yet put all of their holdings online. Ask the librarian for the starting date for the catalog. Another problem is that some electronic catalogs may include material that is not in your library but in one very far away. Make sure you find out whether the material you want is on campus. Getting material from outside your library can take time. The process is called **interlibrary loan,** where your library borrows the book from another library. Don't

---

[4]The spelling of place names can make keyword searches difficult. This is especially true for place names that have changed over time. Persia became Iran; New Spain became Mexico; recently, the Soviet Union went back to its old name of Russia. Know the proper name of the place you are looking for *during the period you are focusing on.* Geographical subdivisions present problems as well. Umbria is a region of Italy; if you did not know this, you might not be able to search for it effectively. Always learn the larger geographical or political unit that your own subject is a part of.

wait until it is too late to find out that a book you really need has to be borrowed from another library.

Searching for Articles in Journals, Magazines, and Newspapers. Students often search for books but skip over other valuable sources. Books are usually easier to locate. Some computer catalogs don't even include what librarians call "nonbook" items. If, for example, you want to find journal or newspaper articles related to your theme, you need to know where to look for them. Usually nonbook items are listed in "databases" contained either on **CD-ROM** discs or on the Web. (For more on the World Wide Web, see pp. 90–99.) Like the online catalog, databases are "searchable" by title, keyword, and author. (The most useful history databases are described in Appendix A, pp. 204–05.)

Periodical articles are important nonbook sources of information. A periodical is any publication that is issued "periodically." This category of publication includes **journals** (which contain articles for students and scholars) and *magazines* and *newspapers* (which contain articles for the general reading public but can sometimes be helpful to students). Web-based or CD-ROM databases can give you access to a large number of journal articles. Others can be found in your library stacks or on microfilm or microfiche.

JOURNALS

Journals are the best periodical sources for history research. Articles in journals may contain important information related to your topic. For the theme "Women Workers in the Lowell, Massachusetts, Textile Mills, 1820–1850," you could gain useful information from an article "Letters of a Lowell Mill Girl and Friends," published in the journal *Labor History* in 1976. But how would you find out about this article and whether you can get a copy of it? In this case you need an **index** (electronic or printed) that lists journal articles by author, title, and subject.

The journal indexes of your library may be a part of the main computer catalog or may be housed on separate computers with their own databases. Most libraries also have printed copies of journal indexes. Journal indexes are also available on the World Wide Web. Wherever it is located, your library probably has an index such as *America: History and Life* that covers articles in scholarly journals. Check the subject index of this database under women workers, textile mills, and Lowell, Massachusetts. In this way, you should be able to find any journal articles it contains that are related to your topic. What you are doing is searching for journal articles in the same way you searched for books — by subject (or keyword). Of course, if you already know the author or title of the article you want, those are also search options. (There are several journal indexes for history. These are listed in Appendix A, p. 205.)

An important advantage in searching for journal articles, especially on a computer, is that the indexes are often annotated, that is, they contain brief descriptions (called "abstracts") of the contents of each article. Annotation helps you to decide whether to read the article. Certain databases allow you to print out the entire article from the computer in your library, even if the library does not have the journal in its print collection. In this way, a student at a small library can get articles instead of requesting an interlibrary loan. If you can print out a copy of an article, however, make sure that the title and annotation really sound promising. Your library may charge for such a service. Even if it is free, there is the danger that you will be tempted to print the article mainly because this is easier than going into the stacks to look for articles which you cannot print out. Seek out the articles that are most relevant for your topic, not simply those that are easiest to come by.

One final problem in searching for articles in databases or on the Web is that they usually include ones that were published only recently. At least that is the situation at this time. Databases are huge but not infinite. One of their limitations is that they only hold material published *after a certain date.* (Another less common problem is that they may *stop* at a certain date.) It is important to know the **date range** of a database. If a database has only material that is less than ten years old, you cannot find in it sources that were published or created before that date. In history research, the date range of a database is important to know; it can tell you what is *not* there and save you a lot of searching time.

Many academic journals have their own printed indexes. For example, all of the articles in the *Canadian Historical Review* will be printed in the volume *Index to the Canadian Historical Review.* Printed indexes to specific journals are kept in the stacks next to the bound volumes of the journal. Once you have looked at general journal indexes (ones that cover many journals) you will probably discover that several articles related to your topic come from a small number of journals. If this is the case, it is wise to go into the stacks and seek out the indexes to these journals. Returning to the theme "Women Workers in the Lowell, Massachusetts, Textile Mills, 1820–1850," you may have discovered that the journal *Labor History* has several articles that sound promising. If this is the case, look through the index to that journal. You will probably find other useful articles there.

Another, and quicker, way to find journal articles related to your topic is in the books and articles that you have *already* found. The **footnotes** (or **endnotes**) in these sources will include the books and articles that the author relied upon, and many of them will also be relevant to your topic. From the footnotes or endnotes, copy down any articles (and books) whose titles seem close to your topic. In fact, whenever you find a good source, check its notes (and also its bibliography) against the sources you already have and add any promising ones to your *research bibliography.* Be sure, as always, to copy down *all* of the relevant information for your own notes and bibliography. (See the sections on documenting your paper and organizing a bibliography in Chapter 5, pp. 130–36.)

MAGAZINES AND NEWSPAPERS

Current issues of popular magazines *(People, Time, National Geographic)* and newspapers rarely contain serious historical studies. However, if your library has printed or electronic copies of magazines and newspapers from the period of your topic, these can be valuable sources. For example, the *Lowell Courier* from the 1830s may very well have *contemporary* articles on women workers in the mills. This is a valuable source because it is also a **primary source.** (See the section on primary and **secondary sources** of evidence in Chapter 1, pp. 6–11.) Old issues of magazines and newspapers may be available in your library (usually on microfiche or microfilm) and can be very helpful. When you search for newspapers or magazines in your library's catalog, be sure to note the span of years that are included. If a particular magazine was published in the 1830s and 1840s, it may be useful in a paper on early textile mills. However, your library may not have issues going back that far. If your library does not have the newspaper or magazine you are looking for, try to find it on the Web.

Research in Primary Sources

One of the most interesting aspects of historical research is to read what someone who was part of a historical event or period felt and thought about the experience. The diary of a young woman crossing the West by wagon train, a newspaper article describing Babe Ruth hitting a home run, the minutes of a private meeting between President Kennedy and his advisors during the Cuban missile crisis, a recording of Bessie Smith singing the blues — each of these is as close to history as you can get and helps you to imagine what the past was like for those who lived it. If at all possible, include primary material in your research.

If a history archive (a place like a museum or historical society or a Web site where primary sources are stored and collected) has primary materials related to your topic, be sure to include some of them in your research. If your topic is less than fifty years in the past, you may be able to *interview* someone who lived through it. You can't get any closer to history than that!

Most college libraries have copies of primary materials — on microfilm, on microfiche, or on electronic databases. The World Wide Web is by far the best source for primary documents. Entire sites are dedicated to placing historical documents on the Web so that anyone, anywhere can read them and copy them. In the near future, it is likely that the Web will be the principal resource for primary documents of all kinds — print, visual, and sound. (For a list of some of these sites, see Appendix A, pp. 206–09.)

One final point about primary documents: you need to have read a lot about your topic in order to understand them. You won't know why the faces of the Italian family look so bewildered in the old photograph of immigrants arriving in America if you haven't learned about the mixture of confusion, fear, and excitement that was part of coming to the United States in the late nineteenth or early twentieth centuries. You won't know why the letters of Thomas Jefferson on the subject of slavery sound so uncertain unless you know the battle going on in his mind about the place of Africans in a republic. Use primary sources if you can, but save them until you are acquainted with your topic.

Reference Sources

Reference material is available in two places: (1) your library's section of printed reference works and electronic databases and (2) on the World Wide Web. Each year, more and more reference works (like the *Encyclopaedia Britannica* at <britannica.com>) that once existed only in print form are beginning to appear on the Web. To discover the reference sources that will give you background information and lead you to more detailed information on your topic, be sure to make use of both kinds of resources.

A very useful printed reference book or database may be just a few steps away from where you are sitting in your library. For printed bound works just ask for the reference section. You will find there hundreds of books (thousands in a large library) — dictionaries, encyclopedias, atlases, periodical and magazine indexes, and specialized **subject bibliographies.** In general, these works can help you define your terms; gather background information on a topic; and locate specific facts, dates, and biographical or statistical details. They also serve as starting points for locating additional materials. Each reference work has its own way of organizing its contents. Just as you need to learn how to conduct a Web search, so you need to learn the organizational scheme of a particular reference work. These are usually found at the beginning of each work. If you are having trouble with a printed reference source, ask the librarian for help.

There are two places to look for electronic reference sources: databases in your library and databases on the World Wide Web. Your library most likely has a number of CD-ROM databases that are useful reference tools. Be sure to ask which databases are accessible in the library. Some of these databases can also be found on the Web, but your library may have contracted for direct access to them. To find databases on the Web, ask your librarian and also see the list of electronic sources given in Appendix A on pages 204–11.

Subject Bibliographies.   The most useful reference sources are subject bibliographies. These are available in printed form in the reference section of your library and in database form on CD-ROM, also in your library, and, of course, on the Web. (You will find a large number of printed and electronic subject bibliographies listed in Appendix A.) These sources list all kinds of research material by subject. Of course, not all of the sources listed in these bibliographies will be available to you either in your library or on the Web. Still, they are the best place to begin your research for the sources you will need to examine your topic. For example, if your topic is the use of chemical weapons in the Vietnam War, the print subject bibliography *The Wars in Vietnam, Cambodia and Laos, 1945–1982: A Bibliographical Guide* may lead you to many sources on your topic. On the other hand, if your topic was the diplomacy of the Vietnam War, the Web site "Vietnam Documents" <http://www.mtholyoke.edu/acad/intrel/vietnam.htm> may be a good place to find useful material.

There is no one path to the best sources. Each has its own strengths and weaknesses. For example, Web sites may be organized so that you can search their contents the same way you search an online catalog. This is a very useful tool. On the other hand, a Web site can move and not leave a forwarding address, while a printed volume will always be on the shelf — unless someone else is using it.

Locating Library Materials and Using Call Numbers

After completing your search of the subject bibliographies, you will have a list of materials that you want to look at. If some of these are not in your library, you may be able to find them on the Web or borrow them from another library. A librarian will have to assist you in this latter task. If the materials are in your own library, the **call number** will lead you to them.

If the stacks are open to students, pay attention to the signs on the walls and at the ends of rows of shelves that tell you where a particular group of call numbers is to be found. Almost all online catalogs will tell you if a book has been taken out by someone else. If it has not been checked out and you still can't find it on the shelf, go back to the catalog and check the call number. An error of even one number in a call number can make your search all but impossible. Always be sure to copy call numbers letter by letter and number by number just as they appear in the catalog. If the number is correct, and you still can't find it, ask the librarian to help you locate it.

Browsing the Library Shelves. Most of the call numbers on the list you have created will be in groups. They will begin with similar letters and numbers. All of the books with similar call numbers will be near one another on the library's shelves. As a result, when you get to the place in the stacks where one book is located it will be surrounded by other books with very similar call numbers. Since the system of filing books by call number is related to their subject, nearby books may also be on your list. Just as important, nearby books that are not on your list may be just as close to your topic as those that are. Read the titles of the books near to the one you are seeking. If the titles seem promising, they should be added to your list.

Locating Other Historical Materials

The easiest way to go beyond the resources of your library is, of course, via the World Wide Web. However, if you are fortunate, your topic will be one on which special historical materials are available at a nearby special collections library, a museum, a historical society, the archives of an institution or corporation, or film and audiotape libraries of television and radio studios. (See the section on research in primary sources earlier in this chapter.)

Older members of your community or your own family also can be sources of historical information. People who have been leaders in local and national affairs have personal knowledge of important historical events. Perhaps you could prepare a series of questions concerning past events in which they were participants. You can write to these individuals, or perhaps speak with them. They may also have personal papers they would permit you to see. This kind of historical research is exciting and satisfying, and it may enable you to use primary historical material that no other historian has uncovered.

Elderly people are very good sources of historical material. They can tell of their years in another country or describe the America in which they grew up. They may not have been important historical figures, but they reflect the experiences of countless others and are thus the stuff of which history is made. Their recollections of how they felt and of what they and others did and said when, for example, the *Titanic* sank, when women won the right to vote, when Lindbergh flew across the Atlantic, when World War Two ended, or when the Berlin Wall came down, are priceless pieces of the historical puzzle. (See also Appendix B, "How to Research Your Family History," pp. 213–15.)

Sources for Research on the World Wide Web

Many of the computer terminals in your library and perhaps even your own computer will be connected to the **World Wide Web.** On the Web you can search for information stored in millions of computers around the world. If you know how to explore the Web, you can add a world of information to the materials available to you on the shelves of your school library.

The advantages of Web searching are numerous. The material available is immense. If you know the correct electronic path, you can reach what you are looking for in a matter of seconds. The variety is almost endless as well: books, journal articles, magazines, newspapers, primary documents, photographs, audio and video files, and so on.

Another advantage of Web searching is that you can communicate with people as well as computers. E-mail, newsgroups, and discussion groups put you in touch with other Web users who are communicating with one another. There are many history-oriented newsgroups where you can post messages, ask questions, and join conversations on history topics of interest to you. See "Electronic Discussion Lists in History" on p. 211.)

Since the pool of information is so huge, you need to navigate the Web using a variety of search tools. Knowing how to use each of these tools properly will save you a great deal of time and help assure that you come up with the most relevant and valuable material.

Using Subject Indexes and Directories

These are long lists of Web-based information sources that are arranged hierarchically by subject. That is, they start with the broadest subject and then narrow the choices offered on the screen until you reach a subject area that is close to your topic. (At present, Yahoo! is one of the most extensive and popular directories.) For example, if you are searching for information on "women textile workers in Massachusetts," you will need to begin with the first screen of the subject index containing very broad categories such as "science," "business," or "literature." If available, you would then choose the category "history." From the history page, you would further narrow your search by making links to "U.S. history," then to "19th century," then to a choice such as "labor history," or perhaps "women's history," and finally to any additional links that seem to head toward "Massachusetts" or "textile mills." If you can find either of these last two categories, all of the sources listed at that point should be very close to your topic. Unless the list is very long, check each one for historical material relevant to your topic.

The key to searching an **index** or **directory** is to choose the most promising **link** (or links) at each stage of the search. If you seem to be getting off track — for instance, heading toward "famous Massachusetts women" or "the art of textiles" — press the Back button and try a different route. One of the most useful aspects of indexes and directories is that most links are clearly labeled so that you have a good idea of the kinds of sites you are heading toward. An example of a subject index search is provided on pages 95–99. (For a list of subject indexes and directories, see p. 206.)

Using Search Engines

Search engines are more powerful search tools than indexes or directories, but they are also less precise, making search skills even more crucial. The main difficulty with search engines is that they search by word, not by subject. To search with a search engine, you type a word or phrase into the search box (say, "women textile workers") and the engine scans millions of Web pages for these words, looking especially for ones in which the words you are searching for occur more than once or are close together on the page. (Lycos and AltaVista are two current search engines that you may be familiar with.) The result, even for the fairly specific search phrase such as "women textile workers," could be hundreds (perhaps thousands) of pages that "fit" one or more of the search words. The search engine will list all of the sites where these words appear. The list usually begins with the ones that best fit the search terms.

Each search engine searches and displays its results a little differently than others. If you have a choice of engines, it is best to ask the reference librarian which is best for the kind of search you are making. Unlike the search results with indexes and directories, the list of sites that the search engine brings to your screen will have only a short title to indicate its possible relevance to your topic. This means that you will need to click on a lot of sites to see if they are useful. Once at a site, if you follow one of its links, you may discover yourself in a strange place (such as "fashions in women's clothing" because many clothes are made from textiles). You will then have to backtrack to your list of sites to try another one. As you click on promising sites, you may come up against the most frustrating part of Web searching: dead or moved links. If you are lucky, you will get a message that tells you where the new link is. If not, you will just get an error message indicating that the site you were looking for cannot be found. Then back you must go to the long list of sites your search engine came up with. As noted before, search engines cover many more Web sites than directories, but they are not as specific in what they give you. To avoid being handed thousands of sites by your search engine, type in a search term that is as specific as possible. Techniques for composing search terms that bring you a reasonable number of sites to explore and that ensure that they will be relevant to your topic are discussed in Conducting Research on the World Wide Web: A Primer on pages 93–99. (For a list of search engines, see p. 205.)

One type of search engine is easier to navigate. This is a **periodical database.** The engine searches only the data stored on a CD-ROM disc or on one site on the Web. Of course, you must choose a periodical database that contains a large number of history journals. (*America: History and Life* has already been mentioned.) Not all periodical databases will be available to you. Some are free, but you can use others only if your library has a license. Some databases contain only the title and date of the article and the name of the journal; you will have to get a copy on your own from your library or from the Web in order to read it. Other databases are **full text** and let you read the entire article or print it out for later reading. The reference librarian can help you pick the best periodical database for your topic. Searching in periodical databases should be part of any serious research effort.

Whenever you come across a Web site that has useful information, be sure to **bookmark** it; that way you can get back to it directly the next time you need it. Each site on the Web is identified by a Uniform Resource Locator or (URL). Your bookmark will store the URL. This is much better than trying to remember a long URL or even writing it down. You will also be guaranteed of finding the site again later. If you make the slightest mistake when typing the URL in the search box of the **Web browser** (for example, by leaving out a "." or a "/"), the result will be an error or a site that is useless to you.

Despite the problems inherent in conducting searches on the Web, you should always search for information on your topic using subject indexes and directories as well as search engines. In a few years, the two types of searches are likely to be combined. Some search engines already have directories within them. (For example, Yahoo! is both an engine and a directory.)

One final caution about the Web concerns the quality and reliability of what you find there. When you have finally tracked down the article (or document, picture, video, or other resource) you have been searching for and have downloaded it or printed it, you may discover that what your hard work has brought you is, well, junk. Printed materials, the kind of books and journals on the library's shelves, are written, for the most part, by people who know their subjects well, who have had their work accepted by publishers that first submitted the manuscripts to other scholars and writers, and later to editors and proofreaders. On the other hand, *anyone* can "publish" on the Web. There is much excellent and serious material available on the Web (especially **primary sources** in print, audio, and visual form), and some of it may be very helpful in your research. But nothing separates the good stuff from the bad, the serious from the silly. Web searching is less organized and less reliable than searching your library's online catalog. Be prepared to get some very strange and often unrelated material, and in huge quantity. If you find something on the Web that you want to use in your research but question its reliability, ask your instructor what he or she thinks of it. See also the section on "Evaluating Web-Based Sources," on pages 101–03.

Using Web material in your written work raises the question of how to document it, that is, how to record in your paper the exact place on the Web where you found it and when. For help with this problem, see the section on documenting Web sources on pages 129–30.

While for major research projects you cannot (and should not) do all of your research on the Web, it is important to become familiar with it. If the predictions are correct, in a few years the Web will be the principal avenue for finding just about anything or anyone. Just as computer literacy has become essential for living in a modern information environment, so Web literacy will be essential for finding your way around that environment.

Conducting Research on the World Wide Web: A Primer

There are several major obstacles to overcome when searching for useful research material on the Web. First of all, each **search engine** explores only a small portion of the Web. Moreover, each works differently, and you have to know the strengths and weaknesses of the one you are using. Sometimes you need to use more than one (or use a mega-engine that combines the searching of several engines) to find what you are looking for. Don't expect to type the name of your topic in the search line of your engine and then sit back to harvest all the information you need. Computers don't think like we do. If you ask your engine to search for the topic "education in Japan," it will dump onto your screen every site it finds that has Web pages related to Japan or to education. This could be a *very* long list. Buried within it might be a site useful to research on the history of Japanese education, but it might take you days to find it. For serious research, it is almost always advisable to use *advanced* search techniques. These techniques are usually explained on the **home page** or on the Help pages of the search engine. Be sure to read about them before you begin your search.

With advanced search techniques, you ask the engine to look for certain words and not for others, or for words in a special order, or words that appear together on the same Web page. For example, an advanced search for information on the theme "public education in Japan, 1900–1930" might look like this: "public education" AND Japan

AND history. The quotes around "public education" tell the search engine to look for Web pages that have *both* words together; the "ands" between the three segments of your search term tell the engine to return *only* those pages that mention *all three* terms. Again, be sure to take the time to learn these and other advanced search techniques. They will direct your search more specifically toward the Web pages that are closest to what you are looking for and will save you a great deal of time.

When you search with a **subject index** or **subject directory,** your task is easier because instead of coming up with search terms yourself, the directory gives them to you as a limited number of choices. In this case, the skill involved is to pick the best choice. For example, for the theme "public education in Japan, 1900–1930," don't click on the choice "Asian history" if the more specific choice of "Japanese history" is on the same page. Don't choose "current educational outcomes in Japan" rather than "Western influences on Japanese education before World War II." Remember, the index or directory may not give you easy choices; don't expect it to have a category that fits your theme exactly. The challenge is choosing the category that best matches your theme. If the category you choose leads you away from your theme, go back and try another.

When you reach a Web site that seems to fit your topic (or better yet, your theme), your next task is to search the site to see if it has relevant research material. Even a site with a promising title such as "Why Japan is Number One in Education" may contain only comparisons of student's test scores from the 1990s, clearly not the kind of material you need. In many instances, you cannot determine the usefulness of a site until you have explored it. However, if a few minutes of exploration make it clear that the site is not relevant (for instance, it is about faculty exchange programs at Japanese universities), retrace your steps and take a different route through the directory. (For more on search engines, indexes, and directories see pp. 90–92.)

Other dangers lurk in cyberspace. Each day more commercial sites are added to the Web and more commercial messages are *built into* existing Web sites. In the traditional library, you do not have to worry about an ad for an online bookseller popping up as you open the pages of a book. Numerous and distracting advertisements on a Web site usually mean that its purpose is commercial rather than educational. Still, there are some exceptions, and the best advice is to ignore the ads and focus on the text or graphics in the main frame of the page. (If you ever do your schoolwork with the television on, this should not be too difficult!)

Another difficulty with Web searching is access. As was pointed out in the discussion of **periodical databases** on page 92, some sites are available only to subscribers. This means that access to a site or to a portion of its content is controlled. If the site is not a free one, you will have access to it only if your library has a license to use it. In a predigital library you needed a library card to borrow a book, but looking at a book was free. Unfortunately, parts of the Web are not free. Still, do not be discouraged. An enormous amount of useful material on the Web is free and accessible, and the main challenge, as noted above, is finding it.

The last difficulty in using the Web has already been introduced — determining the *quality* of the information on a Web site. You may be delighted to come across an essay on "Modern Japanese Education" only to discover that it has been written by a Japanese high school student. If you have any doubts about the *quality* of the information you have downloaded or printed out, show it to your instructor. See also the section on "Evaluating Web-Based Sources" on pages 101–03.

Example of a Web Search Using Keywords

Here is an example of the steps one student took in a keyword search using a search engine. Of course, no *description* of a search is as useful as actually conducting your own search on the Web. Until you acquire a sense of what words are best for your topic and what links are most promising, don't be a timid surfer. Try one set of terms and then another just to see how different the results are. Likewise, you may find it useful to try different search engines since each will yield slightly different (and sometimes vastly different) search results. If a particular link is not a good one, press the Back button and try another. Most searches require testing a number of links before you find a good one. Once you find a good site, be sure to explore it and its links to other sites and bookmark it for future reference.

Due to the dynamic nature of the Web, a search you conduct one week using a particular search engine and set of keywords may yield different results the next week. If you tried to duplicate the example below, you would likely get somewhat different results. However, good search techniques remain the same ones discussed throughout this section. Because of the changeable nature of the Web, be sure to carefully document your sources. (For more on documenting sources, see pp. 121–36.)

Using a Search Engine to Look for Scholarly Information on the Theme "Women Textile Workers in Lowell, Massachusetts, 1820–1850." To begin your search, you will need to be familiar with the program in the computer you are using that searches the Web — its **browser.** The first page of the browser will usually be the "default" search engine or will give you the option of selecting one. A student researching the history of women textile workers in Lowell, Massachusetts, from 1820 to 1850 began her search by using the default engine, which in this case was "metacrawler." Metacrawler is a search engine that *combines* the search results of several different engines. If you have the option, it is often helpful to begin your search with such a meta-engine. (One *disadvantage* of a meta-engine is that it may not return the same list of sites on a second search *even if you use the same search terms.*)

The student's first, and most important, decision was the set of keywords she chose for the engine to search for. At the top of the screen, in the empty search box, she typed the following set of terms: +women +labor +history. (See Figure 4.1.) The plus signs between the words *on this search engine* tell the engine to look for Web pages that include *all* of those words but not necessarily in that order. (Note that she also accomplished this goal by clicking on the "all" circle under the searchbox.) Always look at any links next to the search box that explain the way the engine will read your keywords. Sometime this means linking to a search Help page. Engines can vary greatly in the meaning they give to the symbols and words (for example, +, –, AND, NOT, ALL, ANY) that connect your keywords. Finally, as any Web searcher knows, keywords that are too broad (for example, "women" or "labor") will return thousands if sites, while ones that are too narrow (such as "Lowell textile mill workers") might not return any.

After the student typed in her keywords, she pressed the Search button. Her search yielded twenty-seven possible sites for her to investigate. Some of these sites are shown in Figure 4.2. Each item on the list has a brief description of the site as well as its Web address or **URL** (Uniform Resource Locator). Clicking on the link will bring you to the Web site — if the link is a "live" one. Sometimes, however, some of the sites retrieved by a search engine will have moved to a new Web address, and the link will give you an error message. This message may tell you where the site has moved to, but sometimes you reach a dead end. In that case, try another site.

Once you have a list of sites, you need to determine which ones are

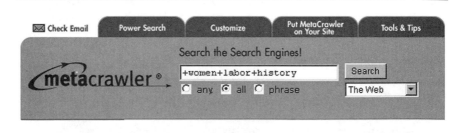

FIGURE 4.1   Example of a Search Box with Keywords
Here is the Metacrawler search box as the student researcher saw it. Note the keywords used and the plus signs used between them. The student has also selected "all," telling the search engine to look for Web pages that include all of these terms.

1. A Curriculum of United States **Labor History** for Teachers
   Infoseek: A resource of documents and lessons for use by high school United States **history** teachers.
   Google: . . . Short **History** of American **Labor**. This brief history of more. . .
   1000, http://www.kentlaw.edu/ilhs/curricul.htm (Infoseek, Google)

2. A Short **History** of American **Labor**
   Infoseek: A brief **history** of more than 100 years of the modern trade union movement in the United States.
   Google: . . . Short **History** of American **Labor**. This brief history of more. . .
   765, http://www.unionweb.org/history.htm (Infoseek, Google)

3. National Museum of **Women's History**
   National Museum of **Women's History**: Homepage of National Museum of **Women's History**, provides information about the **women** of the past, present &
   Click on this Internet Keyword to go directly to the National Museum of **Women's History** Web site.
   500, http://www.nmwh.org/ (Internet Keyword)

4. Victorian Working **Women** — Sweated **Labor**
   Essay utilizes census figures to calculate the numbers of **women** working in manual **labor** jobs in mid-nineteenth century Britain.
   500, http://www.looksmart.com/eus1/. . . /eus548999/eus558542?uniq=6432 (LookSmart)

5. Laboring woman
   Child birth captured in photographs.
   500, http://www.sugarday.com/labor.html (Direct Hit)

6. Work and **Labor** — **Women's History** — Net Links
   Work and **Labor** in **Women's History**: **women** in the workplace, definitions of **women's** work, and **women's** role and status in labor unions, from your About.com Guide to **Women's History**
   500, http://womenshistory.about.com . . . s=%2Bwomen+%2Blabor+%2Bhistory (About)

7. Triangle Shirtwaist Factory Fire — 1911
   Chronicles the devastating fire which cost the lives of 146 **women** and children. Studies **labor** conditions of the time and offers photographs.
   400, http://www.looksmart.com/eus1/. . . /eus536970/eus543107?uniq=4513 (LookSmart)

8. **Women's History** — U.S. National Parks — Net Links
   Women's History commemorated in our National Parks, from your About.com Guide
   400, http://usparks.about.com/msubw. . . s=%2Bwomen+%2Blabor+%2Bhistory (About)

9. United States **Labor** and Industrial **History** Audio Archive
   . . . U.S. **LABOR** AND INDUSTRIAL **HISTORY** WORLD WIDE WEB AUDIO ARCHIVE . . .
   300, http://www.albany.edu/history/LaborAudio/ (Google)

10. Perkins, Frances — The **Women** of the Hall
    Be introduced to Frances Perkins who served under Roosevelt's administration as Secretary of **Labor**, the first woman in the cabinet in history.
    300, http://www.looksmart.com/eus1/...8/eus76251/eus573512?uniq=3625 (LookSmart)

FIGURE 4.2 Search Results
Here is a partial list of the search results generated by the keywords "+women+labor+history" entered in the search box for the search engine Metacrawler. Note the brief description that follows each potential site.

most likely to have information about your topic. Look at Figure 4.2 to see if you can find the most promising sites. In this case, the student chose to explore the links **Work and Labor-Women's History-Net Links** (6) and **Women's History-U.S. National Parks-Net Links** (8). She chose them because the reference to net links in their titles indicated that they might lead to a wide choice of sites on women's history. She chose to ignore the link **Victorian Working Women-Sweated Labor** (4) because the description made it clear that it was about working women in England. She was also able to rule out **Triangle Shirtwaist Factory Fire-1911** (7) because it was too narrow and **Laboring woman** (5) because the description made it clear that it was about photographs of childbirth. If neither of the two promising sites worked out, her backup site was **National Museum of Women's History** (3) because, while it seemed to deal with *all* aspects of women's history (not just labor history), it was a large site and might include links that were close to her topic.

Figure 4.3 shows a page of the first site the student researcher chose to review. She is clearly getting closer to her topic since all of the links here are to some aspect of the Lowell mill girls. Of the sites in this list, two are directly on her topic: **Lowell Mill Girls** and **Mill Girls.** The

---

Lowell Mill Girls

Women's work: Young women left the farm and went to work in the mills of Lowell, Massachusetts, six days a week, twelve or more hours a day.

Lowell Mill Girls
Harriet Hanson Robinson writes of her experience as one of the factory workers in the Lowell textile mills, 1832-1848.

Lowell History
From the Lowell National Historical Park comes this history of the 19th century textile mill history.

Mill Girls
A short history of the Lowell Mill Girls, from the Lowell National Historical Park's web site. Includes reproduction of contemporary newspaper mention.

Women in the Workplace, Labor Unions
A brief history of women's labor organizing, including the 1844 organizing of women mill workers into the Lowell Female Labor Reform Association (LFLRA).

FIGURE 4.3   Lowell Mill Girls Links
This is a page reached from the link "Work and Labor — Women's History — Net Links" shown in Figure 4.2. All of these links are clearly related to the student's paper topic and are therefore excellent potential sources.

other sites probably have some material but don't look as promising as the two specifically about the mill girls.

On one of the sites shown in Figure 4.3, the student found a letter from a mill girl (a primary document) and on the other, good background material on working conditions. Both sources were the kinds that belong in a research paper. Not all searches will go so smoothly. If the sites you end up with have no serious historical material or if they lead away from your topic, press the Back button and try another link. If most of the sites in your list are off the topic, you need to change one or more of your keywords. There is no one correct search term or one correct path through the links. Be prepared for dead ends, but don't give up. Each Web search will sharpen your skills at choosing keywords and determining promising links. These skills soon will be as necessary as knowing how to read a road map or use a telephone directory.

Mining Information from Your Sources

Once you have a source in your hand, be it book, Web site download, or journal article, you need to find out if it contains the kind of information on your **topic** that you are looking for. If you chose wisely, the source should be relevant to your topic. Now you need to examine it closely to determine which parts are most useful to you. A book on Charles de Gaulle that you intend to use in your paper on "The Free French Forces in World War II" may turn out to cover only his later period as president of France. A Web download with the promising title "The Impact of World War II on France" may turn out to deal with the German occupation of France and not the Free French forces. Moreover, a source needs to be written for a scholarly audience. If the journal article you printed out from a **periodical database** is written for a high school reader, it is not likely to be of value to you. The same is true for a source that is meant to entertain rather than inform, like a video of the 1956 World Series, unless, of course, your topic is baseball history. The absence of **footnotes** and a **bibliography** in a printed source — unless it is a primary document — usually indicates that it is not meant for serious research. There is no substitute for the close examination of a source before you decide to use it in your research.

Another potential problem of any source (printed, electronic, visual, or audio) is the **bias** of the author or creator of the source. In the world of books, for example, a history of World War I by a French author is likely to have a different viewpoint from one written by a German author, especially if the books were written close to the time of the war. It is very important for you to understand the point of view from which a book was written. Many historical events and their interpretation are the centers of profound controversy. It is almost impossible for a historian to investigate one of these controversial areas without the involvement of certain biases. A particular attitude toward the topic is not necessarily bad, however. Historical problems are immensely complex, and without a sense of which things are important, the historian will not be able to choose from among those facts that can give some clear meaning to the larger questions involved. In any event, it is important for you to become familiar with the biases of the authors you read so that you will not unknowingly accept their viewpoints. If you agree with an author's bias, it is natural that you will favor his or her work in your research. But unless you understand the biases of the authors you read, and your own as well, you will not know why you agree with some authors more than others. Furthermore, you won't be able to make a logical presentation in your research paper of the varying points of view.

Evaluating Print Sources

In addition to the problem of bias discussed previously (p. 99), you will need to evaluate other aspects of printed works so that you can use them most effectively. You should always begin by looking at the table of contents. A quick look will show you how broadly the topic is covered and will let you know if all or only parts of the work deal with your topic.

If the book has one, read the preface. In it the author may explain why he or she wrote the book and identify the audience for which it was intended. The intended audience is a good indicator of whether a source will be useful. For instance, a book written for high schoolers will likely be too low level.

Print sources may also contain an introduction. Sometimes this replaces a preface, sometimes it follows it. Here the author usually explains the background of the book, the kinds of questions it addresses, and perhaps some of the conclusions. The introduction will give you an overview of the topics discussed and can help you evaluate the usefulness of a work. You should also read the concluding chapter or section of the work to see if the author has addressed aspects of the topic that you will need for your paper. It will also tell you something about the author's bias.

Consider also the date of publication. Is the book a new or an old work? Does that fact matter to your research? The older the book, the less it will reflect recent scholarship. Nevertheless, an old book may be a classic or may itself be a primary document useful to your research.

Take a look at the bibliography. Here the author lists all the sources examined in preparing the book. Do these indicate background material that is relevant to your topic? Do they seem like serious sources? Are they the kind that you should use in research? If so, the book may be valuable. Indeed, the bibliography may be a source of other books on your topic.

Finally, consider the body of the work. This, of course, is the book itself. Once you have decided that it is a serious and useful source, you must read it with comprehension. You need to note whether it is a primary or a secondary source. As a **primary source,** you must place it in its historical context. As a **secondary source,** you should note whether it is based on primary sources or only on other secondary sources. Finally, you must grasp the author's **theme,** arguments, and conclusions. Your notes on these subjects will determine your ability to use the book effectively in your own paper.

Guidelines for Evaluating Print Sources

1. What information is given about the author? Is the author a serious or scholarly writer?
2. Read the table of contents, preface, and other introductory materials. Take a look at the conclusion or any concluding chapters. These sections will give you an overview of the subject matter of the work. Do all or only parts of the work deal with your topic? Who is the intended audience? Is it written for historians or for a general audience? Is the level appropriate for your research?
3. What is the date of publication? If the book is old, it will not reflect recent scholarship. Does this fact matter to your research? Remember that older works may be classic works or primary sources that are valuable to your research.
4. Is the work a primary or secondary source? If it is a secondary source, does it use primary sources as evidence? You may find it useful to consult the primary sources directly.
5. Consider the bibliography. Do the sources listed indicate serious works that are relevant to your topic? You may find it helpful to consult directly other sources listed in the bibliography.

Evaluating Web-Based Sources

If you have downloaded or printed out text from the Web, many of the guidelines for evaluating print sources apply. This is especially true for the issue of bias. Web documents, however, have some special characteristics.

Of course, the quality of the Web site is determined by the quality of the material on it. A well-maintained, regularly updated university, library, museum, or government site usually contains reliable information. However, not all material linked to a site has been evaluated by the Webmaster — the person who maintains the site. Often a site will have links that lead to less serious sites. Make sure that the site you get material from is as serious as the site through which you found it. If you go offsite, know the kind of territory into which you have moved. (You will also need the **URL** of the new site to document your source.)

The currency of a site can tell you much about its possible relevancy. A site that hasn't been updated in a long time will not contain very recent materials. It will also likely contain dead links. Determining the date of a Web document can be difficult. Often the author places this date, or the latest "update of the document," in a prominent location. Other times, it cannot be found. Do some exploring, but if you cannot tell the date the document was created, note that fact so that if you use it you can alert your reader to the problem. (Since the documentation of a Web-based source includes the date on which it was retrieved, you should not lead the reader to assume that the retrieval date and the creation date are the same.)

Web documents, just like printed works, may be primary or secondary sources. This fact is usually, but not always, made clear. A Web document can be a copy of a primary document. It may also be a "new" document created by its author for the Web without the use of other sources. Many Web documents, however, are secondary sources placed on the Web to make the information widely available. These documents should have all of the hallmarks of a printed secondary source: author, date of publication, footnotes, and bibliography. If you cannot tell who the author is or whether the source is primary or secondary, you should hesitate to use the document in your research. If you do use it, explain the problems about its source to your reader.

When citing Web sources, you will need to record the page numbers, but sometimes page numbers on a Web document can be confusing. If a printed document has been reformatted to fit the needs of the Web, the original page numbers may be lost. At other times, the "pages" of the electronic document are different from the pages of the original, but the latter are included in the Web version. It is best to record the original page numbers for your research.

Another difficulty with Web documents is that they can be removed from the site where you found them. A well-maintained site should be a stable site, one where things just don't disappear without notice. But be aware of such a possibility. Some Web sites regularly change their content, usually to make way for newer content. This should not be a serious problem with historical sources on the Web, but be sure to note the date on which you took something from the Web.

It is more difficult to evaluate the quality of sources on the Web as opposed to those in print because the Web has millions of potential authors. That is one of its strengths. For researchers, it can also be one of its weaknesses. Be sure to do your Web research in stable, scholarly sites, and the problems noted here will be greatly reduced. Here are some questions that you should ask of any Web site that you are reviewing.

Guidelines for Evaluating Web Sites

1. Who or what is the sponsor of the site? This should be indicated in its URL and also somewhere on the **home page.** Is the sponsor a university or public library (that's good!) or an individual who has created the site as a hobby (not always good)? If it is an individual's site, what information is posted about the author and the author's credentials?

2. Does the sponsor of the site have a bias that has influenced the kind of material on the site? Is there a variety of views expressed on the site?

3. What is the intended audience for the site? Are its contents meant to serve students, faculty, or other professinals? Is it designed for research? Or is it filled with commercial links and advertisements or links to sites that are concerned with entertainment rather than research?

4. Does the site contain links to historical sources? That is, can you get (download or print out) from it the kind of material you would find in a good library? The best sites are often those that give you access to sources in libraries or archives.

5. How current is the site? Has it been kept up to date? (Look for this information on the home page.) A site that has not been updated since, say, 1995, may not have important recent material. Are most of the links live? A site with many dead links has not been well maintained.

6. If the site is a promising one, are the materials there relevant to your topic and theme? Does the material on the site include the information you need to document it in your work? Does the information support or go against the material you have already uncovered? If it is very different from what your research has already uncovered, pay special attention to the preceding guidelines.

7. If you have any questions about the relevance or reliability of a site, check with your instructor.

How to Read Your Sources

Reading scholarly books, journal articles, and Web documents may seem easy, but, unless you have had experience in reading serious historical studies, you may have problems. First of all, some of the vocabulary may be new to you. A work on the French Revolution will contain such words as "Jacobin," "Thermidor," and "Girondin." A study of the atom bomb will talk about implosion and fission and such places as Tinian and Eniwetok. It is best to have a good dictionary handy. Another problem will be the academic or scholarly style of writing often found in specialized works. The best thing to do is to read difficult sentences slowly and look up any words unfamiliar to you. As you become familiar with your topic, you will learn the meanings of the terms used by scholars. The way to get through the complex prose and vocabulary is to have a good command of English grammar and a familiarity with the subject being discussed. It is also best to ease into your topic gradually by reading the least specialized works first.

As you become familiar with the style and terminology used in a work, your main task will be to understand the points the author is trying to establish. All good works of history do more than just lay out a series of historical events and then combine them to form an understandable story of what occurred. Good historians want to prove a point, to show that a series of historical events means one thing rather than another. A history of the rise of Adolf Hitler won't merely tell you that the National Socialist Party, which he led, increased the number of its representatives in the German Reichstag (parliament) from 12 to 107 in the election of 1930. It will attempt to describe the conditions that led to such an outcome and to explain the impact of the election on later events. Perhaps the author will discuss unemployment, German nationalism, the cartelization of German industry, the Treaty of Versailles, the growth of the German Communist Party, anti-Semitism, the structure of the German family, the philosophy of Nietzsche, or the insecurity of the lower middle class. The author will probably deal with some of these more extensively than others, and will attempt to show how the emphasized factors offer a better explanation of the subject than any others. Although almost all historians will agree on the number of National Socialist members of the 1930 Reichstag, each will construct the causes and effects of that fact in different ways — sometimes in *very* different ways. If you wish to understand a particular author's interpretation of an event, you must know how the author arrived at that interpretation and what significance he or she believes it to have. Only a careful reading of the entire work and close attention to its main arguments can give you such knowledge. Remember, history works are a selection of certain facts and interpretations constructed to explain a particular writer's understanding of a historical subject. If your own research relies heavily on a particular book, you will need to know its theme and bias.

How to Take Notes from Your Sources

The first rule in note taking is to know in advance what you are looking for. In order to avoid either taking note after note that you will never need or failing to note things that you will, you should have a clear understanding of your theme and the kind of evidence you are seeking. This is especially difficult at the outset of your research when your understanding of your theme is still somewhat vague. It is thus important to define the scope and content of your research as quickly as possible or your research and note taking will wander, and valuable time will be lost.

As you go through a source, you will find portions that you will want to refer to in your own research paper. You will want to note the author's general idea or perhaps even record the actual words used. While overreliance on quotations can be a weakness, if you feel that a quote is necessary, be careful to copy the words exactly. Be sure that the meaning of the words you quote is clear and that you have not altered the author's point by quoting it out of context. If you wish to use a quotation, say, to show that Robert E. Lee was a good military strategist, a quotation such as "Lee was more admired by the average soldier than any other commanding officer" doesn't make that point because it refers to his popularity, not his generalship. Moreover, if the following sentence in the book is "However, his strategic decisions were not usually equal to those of Union army commanders," then you have actually altered the author's point by taking it out of its original context. Make sure you understand the author's meaning before you use a quotation. Again, be sure not to overquote. Do not quote more material than is necessary to convey the desired point clearly and accurately. Finally, never quote something simply because you find it difficult to express in your own words. You will have to compose the idea in your own words when you write your paper, and it is best to think about the meaning of your research material now.

The most important points made by an author usually cannot be summed up in easily quotable form. When you want to record general arguments and conclusions, it is best to write your own paraphrase or summary of particular points. If the author has spent several pages relating the decline in trade between Spain and Mexico to the Wars of Mexican Independence, you may want to summarize the findings by noting that the author feels that the diminishing economic tie between colony and mother country was one of the major factors leading to Mexican independence. If you wish to note the evidence itself, you may want to paraphrase the author's description of the decline in trade with several sentences of your own that include the main factors of this decline.

Whether you are quoting an author's exact words or summarizing a point, the rules of note taking are the same. As you read, it is best to have a pile of index cards beside you (4" × 6" or 5" × 8"). When you come to something you want to note, write the author's name, the book title, and the page number or numbers at the top of the card. If you are taking notes on a journal or newspaper article, you will need to record such information as date, volume number, section, and page number. The exact page numbers are essential because you will have to use them when you write your footnotes. If your quote or paraphrase covers more than one page from your source, be sure to make that fact clear on your note card. Also, it is essential to place each paraphrase or quotation on a separate card so that you can arrange them by period or subject or topic when you prepare your paper. Placing a brief topic heading in the corner of each card will make such arrangement easier. (See Figure 4.4.)

If you are quoting, be sure to use quotation marks and to copy the quotation word for word. If you are quoting something that the author has quoted, you must be sure to point this out when you use the material and to identify the original source. Be sure to include in your note an introduction to the quoted material in your own words, stating who said it (if other than the author) and in what context. This will ensure that you use it properly in your paper. If a quotation is very long and if there are parts that relate to matters other than the one you are referring to, then you may omit portions of the original quote by inserting **ellipses** — three periods (. . .) — in the quoted material.[5] For example, if the quotation reads "Feudalism, despite later idealizations of it, was maintained by an oppressive social order," you may want to leave out "despite later idealizations of it," and quote the sentence as "Feudalism . . . was maintained by an oppressive social order." However, never omit anything if doing so would change the meaning of the material. If the sentence had read "Feudalism in its later stages in Moravia was maintained by an oppressive social order," the entire sentence would have to be quoted, or its meaning would be seriously altered.

To give a clearer sense of what note taking involves, there are two sample note cards in Figure 4.4. The first contains a quotation from a book and the second a paraphrasing of several paragraphs from a journal article.

Taking Notes on a Computer.   If you can bring your sources to your computer or, better yet, bring your laptop computer to your sources, you have another note-taking option. You can create your notes in your word processing program and use the power of the computer to orga-

---

[5]If the portion omitted is the end of a sentence, this is indicated by inserting four periods — three to indicate omission and the fourth to indicate the end of the original sentence. In this case, the closing quotation mark appears after the fourth period.

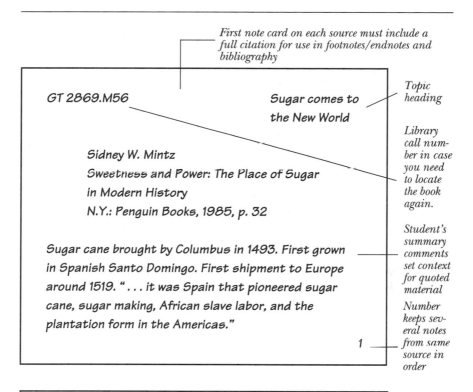

First note card on each source must include a full citation for use in footnotes/endnotes and bibliography

GT 2869.M56 .... Sugar comes to
the New World

Topic heading

Library call number in case you need to locate the book again.

Sidney W. Mintz
Sweetness and Power: The Place of Sugar
in Modern History
N.Y.: Penguin Books, 1985, p. 32

Sugar cane brought by Columbus in 1493. First grown
in Spanish Santo Domingo. First shipment to Europe
around 1519. "... it was Spain that pioneered sugar
cane, sugar making, African slave labor, and the
plantation form in the Americas."

1

Student's summary comments set context for quoted material

Number keeps several notes from same source in order

E171.J87

Michael A. Bellesiles
"The Origins of Gun Culture in the United
States, 1760–1865"
The Journal of American History 83
(1996): 425–55

Not widely used before 1865

Author argues that guns were not as important
before the Civil War as they became later. "Judging
from the popular literature of the day, the public
seemed completely uninterested in firearms." (439)
"Even western magazines showed a decided coolness
toward hunting and militarism. ..." (440)

1

Quotations from different pages must be identified separately

FIGURE 4.4　**Sample Note Cards**

nize them. For example, you can code your notes and the files you put them in with a term or terms that will allow you to bring them together by using the Search function of your word processing program. Be sure you know your program very well, especially if it does not have special tools for creating and organizing notes. Even a simple program can be useful if you create a series of folders for the major aspects of your paper and type your notes into files within them. Be careful though; name each file with a word or two that refers to its content. In this way, if you later change the organization of your paper, you will have a clue as to which files need to be moved to new folders. Also, when you begin to write your paper, be careful to save the text files and folders under names that cannot be confused with those you created for your notes. Still, like the electronic revolution in general, some day almost all research notes will be made this way. If you are fortunate enough to have the hardware and software, learn how to use them to their fullest potentials.

Photocopying and Downloading Sources off the Web

As technology has improved, it has become possible to print the electronic sources you uncover on **CD-ROMs** or the Web. These complement the older system in which you took the book or article from the library shelf over to the copy machine. Whenever you come across a source of modest length (such as an article) and you feel that it may be very important in your research, photocopying it may be better than note taking. It will save time, but don't fool yourself; at some point you will have to read and take notes on all those copied pages. The same is true of downloaded or printed out computer files. Don't copy or print out anything without reading enough of it to know that it contains material central to your theme.

Avoiding Plagiarism

The only thing worse than misquoting from your sources is plagiarizing from them. Plagiarism is easy to fall into. Because of your inexperience with your subject, it will be tempting to use the more sophisticated language of the historians you are reading. In most cases, their expertise will enable them to make their point clearly, and it is easy to get into the habit of using their words instead of your own. Don't fall into this trap. First of all, your instructor is also a historian and can tell the difference between the language of someone who has spent years researching a topic and that of the average history student. Second, and more important, thinking is learning. If you substitute the simple task of copying for the more difficult but rewarding one of thinking about something and then putting it into your own words, then you are doing yourself a disservice. Finally, plagiarism is dishonest and is considered a very serious violation of college rules. The penalty can be severe, sometimes leading to suspension.

When taking notes, *never* copy the author's words unless you intend to quote them in your paper. In that case, be sure to put very clear quotation marks on your note card at the beginning and end of each word-for-word passage. In all other instances, summarize the author's ideas and information *in your own words.* Of course, proper names, dates, statistics, and other very specific facts need to be recorded just as they appear in the material you are using. Even here, you must be careful. If the source says: "George Washington, a great patriot, a great general and our greatest president, was born in 1732," you can put the date of his birth in your paper without quotation, but you cannot say he was "a great patriot, a great general and our greatest president" *or anything very close to this* without plagiarizing.

There will always be some resemblance between the points that you make in your paper and those that were in your research sources. This is even necessary if you are to correctly interpret your sources. *However, all the words in your paper (except for quoted material) must be your own.*

The Art of Paraphrasing

To help you avoid plagiarism, here is a passage from J. Joseph Hutchmaker and Warren I. Sussman, eds., *Wilson's Diplomacy: An International Symposium* (Cambridge, Mass.: Schenckman, 1973), p. 13, followed by two paraphrasings. Paraphrase A constitutes plagiarism, but B does not. The subject is the diplomacy of Woodrow Wilson. Here is the original text:

> Wilson took personal responsibility for the conduct of the important diplomacy of the United States chiefly because he believed that it was wise, right, and necessary for him to do so. Believing as he did that the people had temporarily vested their sovereignty in foreign affairs in him, he could not delegate responsibility in this field to any individual. His scholarly training and self-disciplined habits of work made him so much more efficient than his advisors that he must have thought that the most economical way of doing important diplomatic business was for him to do it himself. Experience in dealing with subordinates who sometimes tried to defeat his purposes also led him to conclude that it was the safest method, for he, and not his subordinates, bore the responsibility to the American people and to history for the consequences of his policies.

> **PARAPHRASE A:** Wilson took personal responsibility for conducting diplomacy because he believed it was right for him to do so. Believing that the people had vested their sovereignty in foreign affairs in him, he couldn't delegate this responsibility. His scholarly training and self-discipline made him more efficient than his advisers. He thought that the most economical

way of doing important business was to do it himself. Experience in dealing with subordinates who sometimes tried to defeat his purposes led him to conclude that it was the safest method because he bore responsibility to the American people for the consequences.

PARAPHRASE B: Wilson felt personally responsible for major diplomacy because he believed that the voters had entrusted him with such matters. He was more capable than his advisors in this area. He, and not his advisors, was responsible to the people.

Paraphrase A is too close to the original. Rather than recording the main points of the passage, it repeats many phrases word for word. Not only is it time consuming to take such lengthy notes, but the identical and almost identical phrases, if used as your own, would constitute plagiarism. Paraphrase B records only the principal point of the passage — that Wilson decided major foreign policy issues on his own because he felt personally responsible to the people in such matters. It does not copy the phraseology of the original. In this way, you save time, protect yourself from the danger of plagiarism, and still are able to use the central idea of the passage. Paraphrasing that reduces your readings to their essential points and uses your own words is not easy at first. But mastering this technique will prevent plagiarism and produce a finished paper that is truly yours.

Organizing Your Research

During the process of research you are aided by your **research outline** (discussed on pp. 78–80) which helps you to determine what sources to seek first and when to read them. When your reading is finished (or almost finished), it is time to arrange all those notes and note cards so that you can create a paper out of them. It is time to prepare a **writing** (as opposed to a *research*) **outline.** Take a good look at your note cards and especially at the headings that you placed in the corners of the cards. It is from among these headings that you should find the major parts of your theme.

Preparing a Writing Outline

If your topic is the conflict between Israel and its Arab neighbors, and you have narrowed it to the theme, "Origins of the 1947 Partition of Palestine," several major points should have appeared in your reading and should be reflected in your notes and in the headings to your note cards. The claims of three parties (Arab, Israeli, British) were no doubt mentioned in many of your readings. As a result, you should have notes concerning Arab nationalism, Zionism, and British colonial policy. These three perspectives are natural sections of your paper, each with a place in the writing outline. The shifting state of opinion within the United Nations (the body that would vote on the partition of Palestine) and the role of the United States (the most important power outside the region) should have appeared in your research and in your notes as well. This suggests two more possible sections for your paper. If your notes reflect what your research uncovered about your theme, you should have more notes, say, on the British decision to withdraw from Palestine than you do, say, on the Balfour Declaration of 1917. That declaration should be *mentioned* in your paper, but the British decision to withdraw is much closer to your theme and thus deserves a section rather than a mention. That is why, as noted above, British colonial policy should be an important part of your writing outline. Be guided by your notes. If your research has been broad and thorough and your notes contain material closely related to your theme, you will end up with more notes on some points than others.

Once you have a general plan for the *parts* of your paper, the next question is: In what *order* should you include them in your paper? If your theme is "The Impact of the Great Depression on African Americans," you may decide to deal with the theme chronologically and separate your paper into sections dealing with the period before 1929, the Hoover years, the early New Deal, and the late New Deal. Or perhaps you want to cover the subject topically, setting up separate sections on African American reactions to economic discrimination, the National Association for the Advancement of Colored People, the U.S. Communist Party, organized labor, and New Deal legislation. Or perhaps you will want to consider the ideas of important African American leaders and writers of the day, setting up sections dealing with E. Franklin Frazier, Richard Wright, Ralph Bunche, W. E. B. Du Bois, A. Philip Randolph, Langston Hughes, Zora Neale Hurston, and Claude McKay.

A *chronological* approach begins with events that predate those that are the main focus of the paper. It then moves, step by step, through stages that group together spans of time. These spans may be in years, decades, or — for a very broad theme — centuries. Each time span is later than the one preceding it, and they generally do not overlap.

Time spans do not have to be the same length. It is best to use larger time units when discussing events that occurred long before the main events covered in the paper and to use smaller units when covering the period closest to the main events. A different rule applies to the length of each *section* of the paper: those portions dealing with periods removed from central events should be briefer than those portions close in time to such events.

A common problem with chronological organization is determining how far back in time to begin. Do you start ten or a hundred years before the time of the main events of the paper? A similar problem is determining where to stop. Do you stop with the main events themselves, or do you add short sections covering later periods as well? There is no hard and fast rule, but it is wise not to cover too much ground. That is, don't start too long before or end too long after the principal events of your topic. A paper covering a long period of time can be very unwieldy, and is best handled by another form of organization.

A *topical* form of organization is suited for more general themes — those that deal with ideas, social systems, or other complex phenomena that involve a mixture of political, social, economic, cultural, and intellectual backgrounds. In this form of organization, the task is not so much to build a historical sequence leading up to a particular event, but to weave a fabric composed of the many separate lines of historical development that form the background to the main topic. In some cases, the same topic can be organized by either method.

To give you an idea of how the same theme might be organized by each of the two methods, here are sample outlines of each kind. The student's research dealt with the topic of the United States and Vietnam and was narrowed to the theme "How Did the United States Become Involved in the War in Vietnam?"

CHRONOLOGICAL ORGANIZATION

Japanese invasion of Indochina turns U.S. attention to the area. (1940–1941)

U.S. policy toward Southeast Asia in W. W. II (1942–1945)
Strategy against Japan
Aid for anti-Japanese guerrillas in Vietnam
The U.S. military and the Viet Minh

U.S. attitude toward the return of French control (1945–1949)
Defeat of Japan
Creation of a government by the Viet Minh under Ho Chi Minh
Tensions between U.S. and French goals in Vietnam

Impact of the Cold War (1949–1954)
The "fall" of China and its impact on U.S. policy
Need for French involvement in NATO
War in Korea and the "containment" of Communism

Geneva Conference and the creation of the Republic of South Vietnam (1954–1960)
France defeated by the Viet Minh
The Geneva Conference
The roles in the conference of: France, China, the Soviet Union, and the United States
The United States and the government of Ngo Dinh Diem
The failure of reform efforts in the South
The rise of insurgency in the South
Aid from the North

United States defends the South from "aggression" from the North (1960–1963)
The role of U.S. advisors

Instability in the government of South Vietnam
The overthrow of Diem's government

Growing U.S. military involvement to prevent the defeat of the Saigon government (1963–1968)
U.S. ground troops sent to Vietnam
The escalation of the air war

Conclusion (1968–)
Military stalemate in Vietnam
Growing domestic opposition to the war
The decision to withdraw from Vietnam
The lessons to be learned

Note that the sections are in almost perfect chronological order. Don't expect to write your paper in fixed time compartments, however. There are bound to be sections that run into each other. In fact, to tie your paper together, some overlap between sections is necessary. (See the section on organizing your paper in Chapter 5, pp. 116–17.)

TOPICAL ORGANIZATION

Anticommunism in America
The Red Scare after World War I
The New Deal and the debate over American "socialism"
The cultural bases of anticommunism

The Cold War and resurgence of anticommunism in the United States
The Soviet Union as a threat to the American "way of life"
The "loss" of China — the domestic political debate
Stalemate in Korea — the domestic political debate

U.S. interests in Southeast Asia
Strategic positions and economic investments
The "domino theory"

Debate over U.S. involvement in Vietnam
The debate within the U.S. government
The debate in Congress
The debate in the universities
Conclusion
The forces that drew the United States into Vietnam
Contemporary judgments about U.S. involvement in Vietnam

This paper covers some of the same ground as the chronologically organized one. Nevertheless, this particular organization leads to a different paper from the first one. In the final analysis, the outline that you create will reflect the nature of your interest in your theme, the kind of research materials you have uncovered, and the way they have influenced your thinking. (For another example of organizing a paper see the outline on pp. 141–42 for the sample student paper .)

Organizing Your Notes

The note cards or computer files and the kinds of information they contain have helped you to create a writing outline (at least a tentative one) for your paper. Now that the outline is done, go back to your notes and decide which section of the paper they are most relevant to. For example, the notes concerning the impact of the Korean war on U.S. involvement in Vietnam, which you took from a book about the Cold War in Asia, should become the basis for the section in the chronologically organized paper named "War in Korea and the 'containment' of Communism," or the section in the topically organized paper named "Stalemate in Korea — the domestic political debate." Mark each group of notes (usually in the upper right-hand corner) with the name of the section of the outline to which they are most directly related. Some groups of notes will not neatly fit in just one section; in that case, mark two or more section headings in the corner. If you cannot find any place in your outline where certain notes go, then something is wrong. Either don't use this group of notes, because they are not dealt with in the outline, or change the outline to accommodate them.

Make sure that you have enough information on each section of your outline to do it justice. If, looking at your notes, you see a mismatch between a section of the outline and the notes needed to support it, you must alter or eliminate that section or, more likely, reread the relevant sources and take notes more directly connected with the point you want to cover in your outline. Notes and outlines are rarely in perfect harmony at the outset. Be sure you have the notes you need. Don't wait until the paper is half written to discover that an important part lacks the kind of documentation it should have.

Budgeting Your Research Time

If you are writing, say, a fifteen- to thirty-page paper, expect to read about a dozen sources. This is not a firm figure, however, and your teacher and the subject you choose are the best guides to the proper amount of research. If you read too few sources, your work will be shallow and perhaps unsatisfactory. If you read too many, you will not complete your work in the allotted time. It is best to make a tentative bibliography early in your research and discuss its adequacy in terms of topicality, authoritativeness, and length with your instructor. In addition, discuss with your teacher the outline for your paper.

If you have never written a long research paper before, you may be unsure as to how much time to allow for each aspect of your research and writing. Only experience will tell you the best budget of time for your particular work habits, but here are some general rules.

For a paper of fifteen to thirty pages due at the end of a fifteen-week semester, you should allow approximately 10 percent of your time (one to two weeks) for choosing a topic and theme, preparing a tentative bibliography, and familiarizing yourself with the general contours of your topic; about 60 percent (seven to eight weeks) for reading the available research materials and taking notes from them; about 10 percent (another week) for thinking and talking about what you have read and organizing your notes; and about 20 percent (two to four weeks) for writing and typing the preliminary and final drafts.

If your term is much shorter than fifteen weeks, or if your assignment must be finished before the end of the semester, you will need to shorten your budget accordingly. Remember that by the end of the term, exams will dominate your attention, and a paper due the final week of classes is best finished at least a week before that time so as not to conflict with studying for finals.

How to Write
a Research Paper

Preparing to Write

Why Your Paper Needs a Theme

Before you begin to write, you need to have narrowed your **topic** to a **theme,** to have fully researched that theme, and to have organized your research according to your **writing outline.** (See pp. 110–13.)

As you prepare to write, keep the limitations of your theme and of your research in mind. Be sure to confine your writing to these limits. Avoid the temptation to go beyond your theme, or you may end up back at the broad *topic* with which you started. Let your theme guide your paper. Don't attempt to record in your paper *everything* on which you took notes. Just because you have read something doesn't mean that it belongs in your paper. Look carefully at your outline. It should have excluded peripheral material that turned up in your notes. As you write, ask yourself, "Does what I am writing belong in my paper? Is it part of my outline?" If the material isn't in your outline, then don't write about it. (Or, if necessary, change your outline to include it.) Then ask yourself, "Does what I am saying belong in *this* part of my paper, or should it be in some other part?" Be sure that your notes are organized according to your outline or you will be putting material in the wrong place, and your paper will not be logically developed.

Your Writing Outline

By the time you begin to write, your writing outline may look different than it did when you first put it together. There is nothing wrong with that. The effort to match research to your outline usually leads either to further research (if you don't have documentation for part of the outline) or to expansion of the outline (if you find important documentation for a relevant point that was not originally included). If you discover that your sources make an important point that you had not intended to cover, you must make room for it in your outline so that it appears in your paper. Another reason for changing an outline is finding material that differs strongly with one of the points you had intended to make. Always make room in your paper for *counterevidence,* that is, for points made by authors that disagree with part (or all) of your interpretation of the theme. Having done so, be sure to explain why you believe the evidence in support of your interpretation is stronger. You should not claim that your ideas are the *only* correct ones. You should show, however, that there is solid evidence for your interpretation.

If you have not already done so, review your notes now and arrange them according to the section of your outline (and the section of your paper) that they most directly refer to. Now, finally, you are prepared to write. The goal of your writing should be to: (1) introduce your theme clearly and briefly, (2) describe it in a series of well-documented parts, and (3) draw clear and brief conclusions concerning what you have said about your theme.

Writing the Text

Chapter 3 discusses the importance of writing skills. As you prepare your paper, you may find it helpful to review the material in Chapter 3 on the components of clear writing and building an essay.

The Rough Draft

Your first draft will change, perhaps many times, so don't worry too much about the exact wording when you write it. Your introductory paragraph (or two) will certainly have to be rewritten after the **rough draft** is done, but it is still a good place to start. By setting out in your introduction the points that you wish to make in the paper, you will make it easier to confine your writing to statements that develop your theme. For example, a paper on the independence of Texas that concerns the theme "The Role of Sam Houston in Texan Independence" needs to focus tightly on Houston's role. By saying in your introduction that this is your goal (and why it is worth writing about), you will keep yourself on track. Of course, other people will appear in your paper (the Mexican general Antonio López de Santa Anna, for example), but a clear focus on Houston in your draft introduction will keep you from writing a long section of your paper on Santa Anna or having too much to say about the defense of the Alamo (Houston was not there). While these subjects should be mentioned in your paper, only the parts that directly bear upon the issue of Houston's leadership should be included. Always use the test of relevance to the theme as you write your paper.

How long should each section of your paper be? There is no correct length, of course, but each section should be long enough to make the point you want to cover in it. As you write the rough draft of each section, keep in mind the information you want to include. Develop each section from the notes that support it, but don't feel obliged to use all of these notes. When you have made the point you intended to make — stop. In addition, you need to write a connecting sentence — either at the end of one section or at the beginning of the next — that introduces the next point you intend to make. Now you are prepared to repeat the process in the next section of your paper, and in the next, until you reach your conclusion.

Keep the overall length of the paper in mind as well. If your paper is limited to twenty-five pages and your outline has seven points to it, don't start out with a section six pages long. Of course, sections may be of unequal length; some points are more important than others or take more space to document. Here is a very general guide: for a paper of twenty-five to thirty pages, it is best to have no more than six to eight sections. You will need at least two, and perhaps as many as four pages, to make the points you wish to cover in each section. You also need to leave a few pages at the end for your conclusion, endnotes (unless you use footnotes, which also lengthen your text), and bibliography. Keep your overall limit in mind, or you can end up with too many (or too few) pages.

The last section of your paper is, of course, the **conclusion.** It is usually wise *not* to include it in your rough draft. If you change your paper in subsequent drafts, your conclusion would then need a complete rewriting. Still, it is worth pointing out here that the goal of your conclusion is to summarize briefly the points you have made concerning your theme. In the paper about Sam Houston's leadership, for example, you would briefly refer to the evidence, both positive and negative, that you presented about him.

The conclusion is also the place for any opinions you may have formed as a result of your research and writing. Unless you are asked to write an opinion piece, don't load your paper with personal comments. Instructors will likely consider this a weakness. Still, unless told not to, you may include some personal remarks in your conclusion. After all, if your topic is worth writing about it *should* leave you with plenty to think about. Should you decide to say something of your own, however, make your remarks clear. Take the trouble to set down your own thoughts as carefully as you did those of the authors whose works you read.

Clear Writing: A Matter of Continuity

As you write the rough draft of each section keep in mind the information you wish to include and the points you wish to make. If your theme is "German Aid to the Forces of General Franco in the Spanish Civil War," then the section that deals with the reasons behind the German support might begin by briefly describing the circumstances surrounding Franco's appeal to Hitler in 1936. The main body of the section would explain in some detail Hitler's reasons for giving aid (for example, strategic and economic considerations, ideological and diplomatic factors) and would conclude by relating these reasons to the subject of later sections, such as the actual aid given and its effect on the course of the war. Your principal concerns as you construct each section of your paper should be: Does this section follow logically from the one preceding it; does it adequately support and develop the central theme; and does it establish the necessary background for the section that follows?

As each section mirrors the overall structure of the paper by containing an introduction, a main body, and a transition to the next section, so each paragraph of which the section is composed contains a similar structure. A well-constructed paragraph begins with a sentence that introduces the information to be developed and concludes with a sentence that leads to the next paragraph. If each paragraph is developed in this way, and if sentences explaining the relationship between paragraphs are included where necessary, then the paper as a whole becomes a tightly knit series of related statements rather than a random group of facts that do not seem to move in any clear direction. The key to tight construction is for each sentence to have two components: it must be related to the one preceding it, and it must continue the development of the theme to which it is related.

The best way to ensure that there are no gaps in logic between your sentences is to construct each paragraph from the viewpoint of the average person who might read your paper. Very often, a disconnected set of sentences may seem clear to you because as you write them you unconsciously fill in the gaps with your own knowledge. Your reader most likely does not have this knowledge and has to depend entirely on the words you write. If these are not enough to make your point clearly, you must be more explicit. Refer back to Chapter 3 for detailed help on writing.

Quotations: When and How to Use Them

Good general rules are: don't quote too often, don't quote too much, and rely on your own words unless there is a good reason for quoting those of your source. Unless it is necessary to use the *very same* words found in a source to make a point that is crucial to your argument, don't use a quotation. However, if your source has said something highly controversial, you may want to make it clear to the reader that you have not misinterpreted it. In this case a direct quotation may be useful. If you do quote, be sure to include enough of the original statement to make its meaning clear. On the other hand, don't make a quote any longer than is necessary. Finally, set off quoted words with quotation marks at the beginning and end. (A common error is forgetting one set of quotation marks.)

Quotation Form. In most cases a paraphrase or summary of your source, properly footnoted, is sufficient. If you need to quote, however, here is how you should do it.

If a quotation is brief, taking up no more than two or three lines of your paper, then it should be written as a part of the text and surrounded by quotation marks. You should introduce the quotation by clearly identifying the speaker. The reader will always want to know who is speaking and in what context. Don't say: *The strikers were "a dangerous mob."* Say: *According to D. H. Dyson, the plant manager, the strikers were "a dangerous mob."* If you do not wish to quote a whole statement, it is necessary to indicate those parts that you are leaving out by inserting **ellipses** (three periods ". . .") wherever words are missing. (See the example that follows.)

If your quotation is very long, it must be separated from the sentences that precede and follow it. It should be indented ten or more spaces and appear in single-spaced type. Do not surround it with quotation marks.

SHORT QUOTATION EXAMPLE: The early settlers were not hostile to the Native Americans. As pointed out by the Claxton *Banner* in 1836: "Our Sioux neighbors, despite their fierce reputation, are a friendly and peaceable people."[1]

SHORT QUOTATION EXAMPLE WITH OMISSION: As pointed out by the Claxton *Banner* in 1836: "Our Sioux neighbors . . . are a friendly and peaceable people."[1]

LONG QUOTATION EXAMPLE: The early settlers were not hostile to the Native Americans. As pointed out by the Claxton *Banner* in 1836:

> Our Sioux neighbors, despite their fierce reputation, are a friendly and peaceable people. No livestock have been disturbed, and the outermost cabins are unmolested. We trust in God that our two peoples may live in harmony in this territory.[1]

Remember that all quotations must be footnoted.

Incorporating Visual Materials into Your Paper

Illustrating important points in your paper with visual material such as maps, charts, tables, drawings, and photographs can strengthen its arguments. Computers also make it easier to integrate visuals into your text. You can create your own charts and tables on your computer or download pictures and photographs to illustrate an important point about your theme. Be sure not to "pad" your paper with visuals, however. Ask your instructor about the quantity that is appropriate. You can either place the visuals on or near the page with the text they illustrate or you can put all visual material at the end of the paper in an appendix. If you use an appendix, you need to place a footnote in the text that directs your reader to the page where the corresponding image is located. If your visuals are within the body of the paper, make sure that they are cleanly separated (perhaps by a top and bottom line) from the surrounding text. Even more important is formatting them so that they end up where you want them when your paper is printed out. Each visual, regardless of its position (within text or in an appendix), should have a title just above or below it that makes it clear what it refers to. Finally, except for visuals that you create, be sure to note at the bottom of each where you found it. Doing this is as necessary as documenting printed sources with footnotes. (For more on documenting sources, see the following section.)

Documenting Your Paper: Citing Your Sources

Documentation means telling your reader where the material in your paper comes from; documentation says to the reader, in effect, "here is the source for the information." Documentation usually takes the form of **footnotes** or **endnotes,** but it can also include illustrations, diagrams, photographs, or any special material that you place in your paper to support your theme.

When and How to Use Footnotes and Endnotes

Footnotes are forms of documentation that appear at the foot of the page while endnotes appear at the end of the paper. (A sample endnote page can be found on p. 163.) They both include the same information. If your instructor has no preference, you can choose to put your documentation in either place, but you must be consistent throughout the paper. You must number your notes consecutively. (When **proofreading** be sure that the number in the text matches the number in the note.) As both footnotes and endnotes have the same form, the following discussion that describes how to write them will, for convenience, use the word "footnotes" to refer to both types.

If you quote from or closely summarize your research sources, you must tell your reader where the original information can be found. In this way, the reader can check the accuracy of your quotes and statements, judge the **bias** and credibility of your sources, or carry out research of his or her own. On occasion, you may also want to use footnotes to make comments that qualify or supplement statements in your paper.

The question that troubles students the most is: Which of the statements that I make in my paper need footnotes? There are only a few hard and fast rules to guide you. However, three types of statements *must* be footnoted: (1) direct quotations, (2) controversial facts or opinions, and (3) statements that directly support the main points made in your paper. Another group of statements — those which summarize important points from your sources — should be footnoted and *must* be if they are used to sustain an important part of your argument. Finally, statistics are almost always footnoted.

Some clarification concerning rules 2 (controversial points) and 3 (support for main points) may be helpful here. Controversial facts or opinions are those on which your sources disagree or which will surprise your reader. Suppose, in your theme "Treatment of Slaves on Mississippi Plantations," you write that some slaveowners were kind to their slaves. This statement may surprise the reader and thus must be footnoted. Researching "European Discoverers of America" you find that all sources agree that Vikings visited the New World long before Columbus. However, if most people believe that Columbus was the first European to see the New World, then it is necessary to show the reader the source of your information with a footnote. Finally, statements of fact or opinion that directly support main points should be footnoted. If your theme concerns the Protestant Reformation, and you treat nationalism as a major factor in the break with Catholicism, then your references in the text to nationalist forces should be footnoted. On the other hand, if you treat the wealth of the Catholic Church as a very minor factor, then your references to that need not be footnoted.

The number of footnotes to use is another thorny problem. Some papers have more factual or controversial material than others and thus need more footnotes. As a rule of thumb, if your paper has quite a few pages without any footnotes, then you are probably not documenting as much as you should. On the other hand, if you are writing five or more footnotes per page, you may be overdoing it. There is no such thing as the *right* number of footnotes, but a twenty-five-page paper might contain anywhere from fifteen to seventy-five footnotes, depending on the subject.

One final point about what to footnote. Using a footnote does not give you permission to plagiarize. (For more on plagiarism, see Chapter 4, p. 108.) You should not use sentences or even phrases from your research sources. Your ideas may come from your sources, but the words must be your own.

How to Write Footnotes

When you decide that a footnote is necessary, place a number at the end of the sentence that contains the information to be documented. Occasionally, you may want to footnote two different things in the same sentence. In this case, place each number right after the word or phrase you want to footnote. Some writers place the number at the end of a paragraph rather than at the end of a sentence. This is proper only if the footnote refers to the material in the paragraph as a whole. If you are footnoting specific facts or quotations, the number should appear right after the facts or quoted material. If you are footnoting a general idea or opinion, place the number at the end of the paragraph or paragraphs that discuss it. All footnote numbers in the text should be in superscript — that is, a half-line above the line of type. The number should not be put in parentheses and should be inserted after any punctuation (except a dash).

Footnote Form. Here are examples of footnotes showing the different forms required for citing different kinds of sources. Unless your instructor tells you to use a different form, follow the examples below.

Books

1. BASIC FORMAT FOR A BOOK (FIRST REFERENCE)

The *first time* you refer to a book, list all of the information as in the example:

> 1. Michael Norman, Greater Share of Honor (New York: St. Martin's Press, 2000), 64.

A first reference to a book should include:

1. Author's full name, followed by a comma.
2. Book title in full, underlined or italicized.
3. Publication information (enclosed in parentheses and followed by a comma): place of publication, followed by a colon; name of publisher followed by a comma; date of publication.
4. Page number(s) cited, followed by a period.

2. BOOK (SECOND REFERENCE)

A second or later reference *to the same book* need only use the author's last name and the page number.

> 2. Norman, 102.

If, however, you cite more than one book (or article, etc.) by the *same author,* any second or later reference must include a shortened form of the title in order to make clear to the reader *which* of the works you are citing.

> 3. Norman, Greater Share of Honor, 68.

Some book footnotes are more complex. If a book has *several authors,* if it has a *translator* or *editor,* or was published in *several volumes* or *editions,* then the footnote has to include such information as in the following examples.

3. TWO OR THREE AUTHORS

When there are two authors, both are listed. If there are three authors, include all three separated by commas.

3. Catherine Clinton and Christine A. Lunadini, The Columbia Guide to Women in the Nineteenth Century (New
York: Columbia University Press, 2000), 48.

4. FOUR OR MORE AUTHORS

If there are more than three authors, the footnote includes the
name of the one listed first on the title page followed by "et al." ("and
others").

4. Charlotte V. Brown et al., The Humanities (Boston:
Houghton Mifflin, 2000), 309.

5. CORPORATE AUTHOR

5. Congressional Quarterly, Congressional Quarterly's
Guide to Congress, 5th ed. (Washington, D.C.: Congressional Quarterly, 1999), 122.

6. UNKNOWN AUTHOR

6. The Life and Death of a Polish Shtetl (Lincoln: University of Nebraska Press, 2000), 84.

7. TRANSLATION

7. Wislawa Szymborska, View with a Grain of Sand,
Stanislaw Baranczak and Clare Cavanagh, trans. (New York:
Harcourt Brace, 1995), 109.

8. EDITORS

In an edited work without an author, the editor's name, followed
by "ed.," appears where the author's name normally would.

8. T. Douglass Price, ed., Europe's First Farmers
(Chicago: University of Chicago Press, 2000), 98.

9. EDITION OTHER THAN THE FIRST

If you are using a later edition of a work, the edition is placed after
the title.

9. David Kobrin, The Black Minority in Early New York,
2d ed. (New York: Center for Thanatology, Research and
Education, 2000), 101.

10. MULTIVOLUME WORK

If there is more than one volume to the work, the number of the specific volume used comes first, followed by the general title and the publication information.

> 10. Bernard Bailyn, <u>Federalist and Antifederalist Speeches, Articles, and Letters during the Struggle over Ratification</u>, vol. 2 of <u>The Debate on the Constitution</u> (New York: The Library of America, 1993), 714.

11. WORK IN AN ANTHOLOGY

> 11. Jeremy Black, "Military Power and the Fate of the Continents," in <u>War and the World</u> (New Haven: Yale University Press, 2000), 186.

12. ENCYCLOPEDIA OR DICTIONARY

With well-known reference books, facts of publication are usually omitted. However, you must cite the edition if it is not the first. When a work is arranged alphabetically, the item is preceded by *s.v.,* meaning *sub vero,* "under the word."

> 12. <u>The Columbia Dictionary of Quotations</u>, s.v. "Lincoln, Gettysburg Address."

Periodicals

13. JOURNAL ARTICLE (FIRST REFERENCE)

The first time you cite an article, include all of the information as in the example:

> 13. Stephen Goode, "Rethinking Good History," <u>Insight on the News</u> 1 (2000): 25.

A first reference to an article should include:

1. Author's full name followed by comma.
2. Title of article followed by comma, all in quotation marks.
3. Title of the journal (or magazine), underlined or in italics.
4. Volume number of the journal and, in parentheses, the year of the volume, followed by a colon.
5. Page number(s) cited, followed by a period.

14. JOURNAL ARTICLE (SECOND REFERENCE)

The second and any later reference to the *same article* is in shortened form as in the example:

14. Goode, 27.

If you cite more than one article (or book, etc.) *by the same author* a second or later reference must include a short title. For example, if you cite two (or more) articles by Goode, the second and later references must make clear to the reader *which* article by Goode you are referring to, as in the example:

15. Goode, "Rethinking Good History," 28.

Some journal article footnotes are more complex.

15. ARTICLE IN A MAGAZINE

Reference to a popular magazine requires author, title of article, title of magazine, date, but no volume number or page number.

15. Patricia J. Williams, "Remembering in Black and White," The Nation, 28 February 2000.

16. ARTICLE IN A JOURNAL PAGINATED BY VOLUME

16. E. Lawrence Abel, "And the Generals Sang," Civil War Times 39 (2000): 45.

17. ARTICLE IN A JOURNAL PAGINATED BY ISSUE

17. Daniel Horodsky, "How U.S. Merchant Marines Fared During WWII," Insight on the News 16, no. 1 (2000): 46.

18. ARTICLE IN A NEWSPAPER

Reference to a newspaper article requires year, month, *and* day (and edition if more than one) as well as author, title, name of paper, and section if appropriate.

18. Richard Norton Smith, "Founding Fathers in the Dock," The Wall Street Journal, 22 February 2000, sec. A, p. 40.

19. UNKNOWN AUTHOR

If the magazine or newspaper article has no author, the citation begins with the name of the article.

19. "Rebel Yell: South Carolina and the Confederate Flag," The Nation, 14 February 2000, 4.

20. EDITORIAL

20. Editorial, "TRB From Washington: A Century of Insight," The New Republic, 3 January 2000, 17.

21. LETTER TO THE EDITOR

21. Letters, Paul J. Herr, Foreign Affairs, April 2000, 180.

22. BOOK OR FILM REVIEW

22. David E. Long, "The Great Ulysses," review of Ulysses S. Grant: Triumph Over Adversity, 1822-1865, by Brooks Simpson, Civil War Times, May 2000, 10.

Other Sources

23. MATERIAL FROM AN INFORMATION SERVICE OR DATABASE

23. Muskingum College, "Content-Specific Learning Strategies for History." Learning Strategies Database, <http://www.muskingum.edu/~cal/database/history.html> (1999).

24. GOVERNMENT PUBLICATION

24. U.S. Department of State, Foreign Relations Volume XVII, Arab-Israeli Dispute, 1964-1967 (Washington, D.C.: GPO, 2000), 25.

25. PAMPHLET

25. Dennis Grimmestad, Britta Bloomberg, and Pat Nunnally, Preserving Minnesota: Planning for Historic Properties into a New Century (St. Paul: Minnesota Historical Society, 1991).

26. DISSERTATION

26. Frank Byrne, "Becoming Bourgeois: Merchant Culture in the Antebellum and Confederate South" (Ph.D. diss., The Ohio State University, 2000), 15.

27. ABSTRACT OF A DISSERTATION

27. David Charles Ingerman, "America, Russia and the Romance of Economic Development" (Ph.D. diss., University of California, Berkeley, 1999), abstract in America Since 1607 678 (1999): 308t.

28. COMPUTER SOFTWARE

28. The American Pageant CD-ROM, Windows 3.1 Ver., IBM, Lexington, Mass.

29. VIDEO

29. In the Barracks, dir. Hellmut Kirst (New York: The Scholar's Bookshelf, 1999), videocassette.

30. SOUND RECORDING

30. Martin Luther King Jr., Martin Luther King at Zion Hill (Los Angeles: Duotone Records, 1962), sound cassette.

31. SLIDES

31. Mary Stofflet, American Women Artists: The Twentieth Century (New York: Harper and Row, 1979), slides.

32. LECTURE OR PUBLIC ADDRESS

32. Winnie Mandela, "The Origins of Conflict and the Journey to Peace" (paper presented at Woodrow Wilson Symposium at the Johns Hopkins University, Baltimore, Maryland, 7 April 1996).

33. INTERVIEW

33. Herman J. Viola, "Viola Records the View of the American Indian," interview by Stephen Goode, Insight on the News (3 January 2000), 37.

Internet Resources

34. WEB SITE

34. Carole Fink, "The World Transformed," n.d., <http://www.ihr.sas.ac.uk/welcome.html> (14 January 2000).

35. GOPHER SITE

35. "Korean War's Forgotten Regiments," 1999, <gopher://gopher.lis.unt.edu:2025/htdocs> (15 February 2000).

36. FTP SITE

36. Sandra M. Wittman, "The Lesson of the Vietnam War,"
13 March 2000, <ftp.ftp.servecc.oakton.edu/~wittman/
warlinks.htm> (6 March 2000).

37. E-MAIL MESSAGE

37. Phillip Herald, "Re: Questions on the Civil War,"
6 April 2000, personal e-mail (7 April 2000).

38. LISTSERV MESSAGE

38. Joseph Keller, "The 20th-Century Middle East,"
1 April 2000, <B-Huron@h-net.msu.edu> (5 April 2000).

39. NEWSGROUP MESSAGE

39. T. J. Buchlian, "Re: Historical Fiction," 6 April
2000, <http://x31deja.com> (8 April 2000).

40. SYNCHRONOUS COMMUNICATION (MOOS, MUDS, IRCS)

40. The Mud Connector, "Ancient Empires," 21 October
1999, <http://www.mudconnect.com> (6 April 2000).

Organizing a Bibliography

A bibliography is an alphabetical listing of the sources you have used
in writing your paper. It must include *all* of the sources that appear in
your footnotes or endnotes. However, do not include all of the sources
you looked at in the course of your research. If your bibliography is
long (say, more than twenty items) you should separate it into several
categories: (1) primary sources and documents, (2) books, (3) articles,
(4) nonprinted sources (tables, pictures, Internet pages, etc.). The list
is alphabetized according to the last name of the author. If a work has
no author (or editor or translator), alphabetize it according to the first
word (except for "A," "An," "The") of the title. Begin each entry at the
left margin and indent any additional lines five spaces. Each item in a
bibliography is single-spaced with double-spacing between items. If a
work has more than one author, alphabetize according to the last
name of the first author mentioned on the title page of the book or article. That name should be followed by *all* of the others, though these
with first names first. (A sample bibliography can be found on p. 167.)

Bibliography Form.   Here are examples of bibliography entries
showing the different forms required for citing different kinds of

Directory to Bibliography Documentation Models

BOOKS

1. Basic Format for a Book, *131*
2. Two or Three Authors, *132*
3. Four or More Authors, *132*
4. Corporate Author, *132*
5. Unknown Author, *132*
6. Translation, *132*
7. Editors, *132*
8. Edition Other than the First, *132*
9. Multivolume Work, *132*
10. Work in an Anthology, *133*
11. Encyclopedia or Dictionary, *133*

PERIODICALS

12. Journal Article, *133*
13. Article in a Magazine, *133*
14. Article in a Journal Paginated by Volume, *133*
15. Article in a Journal Paginated by Issue, *133*
16. Article in a Newspaper, *133*
17. Unknown Author, *134*
18. Editorial, *134*
19. Letter to the Editor, *134*
20. Book or Film Review, *134*

OTHER SOURCES

21. Material from an Information Service or Database, *134*
22. Government Publication, *134*
23. Pamphlet, *134*
24. Dissertation, *134*
25. Abstract of a Dissertation, *135*
26. Computer Software, *135*
27. Video, *135*
28. Sound Recording, *135*
29. Slides, *135*
30. Lecture or Public Address, *135*
31. Interview, *135*

INTERNET RESOURCES

32. Web Site, *135*
33. Gopher Site, *136*
34. FTP Site, *136*
35. E-mail Message, *136*
36. Listserv Message, *136*
37. Newsgroup Message, *136*
38. Synchronous Communication (MOOs, MUDs, IRCs), *136*

sources. Unless your instructor gives you different instructions, follow the examples below.

Books

1. BASIC FORMAT FOR A BOOK

```
Norman, Michael. Greater Share of Honor. New York:
     St. Martin's Press, 2000.
```

An entry in a bibliography for a book should include:

1. Author, last name first, followed by a period.
2. Title of work underlined or in italics, followed by a period.
3. Place of publication, followed by a colon.
4. Publisher, followed by a comma.
5. Date of publication, followed by a period.

If you include more than one source by the same author, use three hyphens instead of repeating the name.

2. TWO OR THREE AUTHORS

Clinton, Catherine, and Christine A. Lunadini. The
    Columbia Guide to Women in the Nineteenth Century.
    New York: Columbia University Press, 2000.

3. FOUR OR MORE AUTHORS

Brown, Charlotte V., et al. The Humanities. Boston:
    Houghton Mifflin, 2000.

4. CORPORATE AUTHOR

Congressional Quarterly. Congressional Quarterly's Guide
    to Congress. 5th ed. Washington, D.C.: Congressional
    Quarterly, 1999.

5. UNKNOWN AUTHOR

The Life and Death of a Polish Shtetl. Lincoln: Univer-
    sity of Nebraska Press, 2000.

6. TRANSLATION

Szymborska, Wislawa. View with a Grain of Sand. Trans-
    lated by Stanislaw Baranczak and Clare Cavanagh. New
    York: Harcourt Brace, 1995.

7. EDITORS

Price, T. Douglass, ed. Europe's First Farmers. Chicago:
    University of Chicago Press, 2000.

8. EDITION OTHER THAN THE FIRST

Kobrin, David. The Black Minority in Early New York.
    2nd ed. New York: Center for Thanatology, Research
    and Education, 2000.

9. MULTIVOLUME WORK

Bailyn, Bernard. Federalist and Antifederalist Speeches,
    Articles, and Letters during the Struggle over Rati-
    fication. Vol. 2 of The Debate on the Constitution.
    New York: The Library of America, 1993.

10. WORK IN AN ANTHOLOGY

```
Black, Jeremy. "Military Power and the Fate of the Con-
     tinents." In War and the World. New Haven: Yale Uni-
     versity Press, 2000.
```

11. ENCYCLOPEDIA OR DICTIONARY

Well-known reference works usually are not cited in bibliographies.

Periodicals

12. JOURNAL ARTICLE

```
Goode, Stephen. "Rethinking Good History." Insight on the
News 1 (2000): 25-26.
```

An entry in a bibliography for a journal article should include:

1. Author, last name first, followed by a period.
2. Title of article followed by a period.
3. Title of the journal (or magazine), underlined, or in italics.
4. Volume number of the journal and, in parentheses, the year of the volume, followed by a colon.
5. Pages on which the article begins and ends, followed by a period.

13. ARTICLE IN A MAGAZINE

Remember, the pages encompassing the entire article are listed in the bibliographic entry. The specific page or pages are cited in the note.

```
Williams, Patricia J. "Remembering in Black and White."
     The Nation, 28 February 2000, 9-11.
```

14. ARTICLE IN A JOURNAL PAGINATED BY VOLUME

```
Abel, Lawrence E. "And the Generals Sang." Civil War
     Times 39 (2000): 45-50.
```

15. ARTICLE IN A JOURNAL PAGINATED BY ISSUE

```
Horodsky, Daniel. "How US Merchant Marines Fared During
     WWII." Insight on the News 16, no. 1 (2000): 46-49.
```

16. ARTICLE IN A NEWSPAPER

News items from daily papers are not listed separately in a bibliography. Instead, the name of the paper with the run of dates should be listed in a general alphabetical list or a section devoted to newspapers.

17. UNKNOWN AUTHOR

"Rebel Yell: South Carolina and the Confederate Flag."
    The Nation, 14 February 2000, 4.

18. EDITORIAL

Editorial. "TRB from Washington: A Century of Insight."
    The New Republic, 3 January 2000, 17.

19. LETTER TO THE EDITOR

Letters. Paul J. Herr. Foreign Affairs, April 2000, 180.

20. BOOK OR FILM REVIEW

Long, David E. "The Great Ulysses." Review of Ulysses S.
    Grant: Triumph over Adversity, 1822-1865, by Brooks
    Simpson. Civil War Times, May 2000, 10-13.

Other Sources

21. MATERIAL FROM AN INFORMATION SERVICE OR DATABASE

Muskingum College. "Content-Specific Learning Strategies
    for History." Learning Strategies Database.
    <http://www.muskingum.edu/~cal/database/history
    .html> (1999).

22. GOVERNMENT PUBLICATION

U.S. Department of State. Foreign Relations Volume XVII
    Arab-Israeli Dispute, 1964-1967. Washington, D.C.:
    GPO, 2000, 25.

23. PAMPHLET

Grimmestad, Dennis, Britta Bloomberg, and Pat Nunnally.
    Preserving Minnesota: Planning for Historic Proper-
    ties into a New Century. St. Paul: Minnesota Histor-
    ical Society, 1991.

24. DISSERTATION

Byrne, Frank. "Becoming Bourgeois: Merchant Culture in
    the Antebellum and Confederate South." Ph.D. diss.,
    The Ohio State University, 2000.

25. ABSTRACT OF A DISSERTATION

Ingerman, David Charles. "America, Russia and the Romance
of Economic Development." Ph.D. diss., University of
California, Berkeley, 1999. Abstract in America
since 1607 678 (1999): 308t.

26. COMPUTER SOFTWARE

The American Pageant CD-ROM. Windows 3.1 Ver., IBM,
Lexington, Mass.

27. VIDEO

In the Barracks. Dir. Hellmut Kirst. New York: The
Scholar's Bookshelf, 1999. Videocassette.

28. SOUND RECORDING

King, Martin Luther Jr. Martin Luther King at Zion Hill.
Los Angeles: Duotone Records, 1962. Sound cassette.

29. SLIDES

Stofflet, Mary. American Women Artists: The Twentieth
Century. New York: Harper and Row, 1979. Slides.

30. LECTURE OR PUBLIC ADDRESS

Mandela, Winnie. "The Origins of Conflict and the Journey
to Peace." Paper presented at Woodrow Wilson Symposium at the Johns Hopkins University, Baltimore,
Maryland, 7 April 1996.

31. INTERVIEW

Viola, Herman J. "Viola Records the View of the American
Indian." Interview by Stephen Goode. Insight on the
News, 3 January 2000, 37.

Internet Resources

32. WEB SITE

Fink, Carole. "The World Transformed." N.d.
<http://www.ihr.sas.ac.uk/welcome.html> (14 January
2000).

33. GOPHER SITE

"Korean War's Forgotten Regiments." 1999. <gopher://
     gopher.lis.unt.edu:2025/htdocs> (15 February 2000).

34. FTP SITE

"The Lesson of the Vietnam War." 13 March 2000.
     <ftp.ftp.servecc.oakton.edu/~wittman/warlinks.htm>
     (6 March 2000).

35. E-MAIL MESSAGE

Herald, Phillip. "Re: Questions on the Civil War."
     6 April 2000. Personal e-mail (7 April 2000).

36. LISTSERV MESSAGE

Keller, Joseph. "The 20th-Century Middle East." 1 April
     2000. <B-Huron@h-net.msu.edu> (5 April 2000).

37. NEWSGROUP MESSAGE

Buchlian, T. J. "Re: Historical Fiction." 6 April 2000.
     <http://x31deja.com> (8 April 2000).

38. SYNCHRONOUS COMMUNICATION (MOOS, MUDS, IRCS)

The Mud Connector. "Ancient Empires." <http://www.
     mudconnect.com> (21 October 1999).

Revising and Rewriting

Leave time in your writing schedule for revising your paper. Before writing your final draft, put the paper aside for a day or two (another reason to leave time) and then reread it. This way, you will gain a fresh perspective and may detect weaknesses that you hadn't noticed before.

A **rough draft** always needs smoothing out. As you reread your paper, ask these questions: (1) Does the paper have thematic unity, and do its parts clearly follow one another? (2) Is there adequate support for the major claims and interpretations? (3) Are the points made clearly and convincingly?

While you examine the overall structure of the paper for defects, you also need to look closely at the language itself. If you have repeated yourself, eliminate the repetition; if you have included material that is unrelated to your theme, discard it. Check the connections between paragraphs to see if the reader can follow your argument. Make sure that you have accomplished what you set out to do in your introduction and that your **conclusion** makes it clear that you have done so. Go over the footnotes or endnotes and the bibliography to check style and accuracy.

Finally, examine your writing for errors in spelling and grammar. **Proofread** carefully and slowly. At normal reading speed your eyes can go right by major errors. You are so familiar with your paper that you may not see what is on the page. Reading your paper aloud will help you catch unclear phrases. Showing it to a friend will let you know where your readers might have problems.

Sometimes reading a draft of another student's paper is part of the work for the course. If you are asked to **peer edit** the work of a classmate, here are some things to keep in mind. If your instructor gives specific guidelines for this assignment, follow them. What you read here are just some suggestions to get you started.

Guidelines for Peer Editing

1. Don't be overly critical. Your goal is to assist your classmate in seeing the strengths and weaknesses in her/his draft. Your ability to do this comes from your "outsider" status. You have not been submerged in the research and are able to take a fresh look at the essay.
2. Pay special attention to the theme of the essay. Is it stated in clear terms?
3. Does the body of the paper provide important evidence to support the theme?
4. Are the points made in support of the theme well organized and are they clear to you as a reader?
5. Are the paper's conclusions justified by its arguments and **documentation?**
6. Whether your comments to your classmate are written or oral, be supportive. Give the writer the kind of help you hope to get from your own peer reviewer.

Word Processing: Advantages and Dangers

Word processing programs are similar, but each has its own peculiarities. You need to become familiar with the program that you intend to use. The advantages of word processing are apparent only if you are not constantly at war with the program. Take the time to learn the basic commands: how to move around the screen, to delete, to move blocks, to save, to print, etc. There is no need to be afraid of a computer, but big chunks of what you have written can disappear if you don't know how to save what you write or if you forget to do so regularly. It can be costly to learn a program *after* you have begun to use it.

Know the basics of your keyboard and of your printer also. Don't tackle a twenty-five page paper on a machine that is new to you. Warm up with smaller projects first. If you are faced with a new machine or program just before beginning a big project, take some time to learn your way around.

One thing that word processing programs cannot do for you is type. If you are a weak typist, *take your time.* You may hit the wrong letters so often that constant deleting and rewriting slows you to the pace of the old typewriter. Worse yet, your stumbling fingers may hit a control or function key and do real damage to your draft. If you cannot type without looking at the keyboard, don't type more than a sentence without reading it on the screen! Don't be intimidated, but be sure to type at a speed that you can handle.

Changing what you have written either because it is wrong or because you think of a better way of saying it is the greatest advantage of composing with a computer. Read each sentence as it appears on the screen. Does it make sense? Does it say what you want it to say? Will your reader understand it? Does it take your theme another step along the way? If not, revise it; don't wait until you have written more. If you wait, you will only entangle your weak sentence with others. When you go back to change the weak one, you will probably have to change surrounding sentences also so that they are connected to one another in a clear way.

The same advice for sentences holds true for paragraphs. Don't write too many paragraphs without rereading to see if they make sense together. Remember, you can only see one screen at a time. This can give you a tunnel-like vision of your paper. The paragraph on the screen may read well, but the one that just scrolled off the top of the screen may not be logically connected. Every few paragraphs, scroll back to earlier paragraphs (or even earlier pages) to ensure that whole sections of your paper hold together. If you lose a sense of the structure of any part of your paper, print it out and read it on the printed page. Don't let big pieces of your writing go by without rereading them — *and saving them.*

When you have finished a draft, print it out and read it as a whole. Mark any changes in red and save them on disk right away. If you don't do this, you may lose track of which changes you have and have not made. On the other hand, since rewriting is so easy on a computer, what is on your disk can quickly jump ahead of what you have printed. Be vigilant or your "final" hard copy may not reflect all the changes that are on the disk.

Use Spell- and Grammar-Checkers with Caution.   It is a good idea to run these checking programs every time you finish a section of your paper. However, they are *not* replacements for your own *proofreading* of your work. They only catch spelling errors that are not other words — write "no" when you mean "know" and it will satisfy the checker every time. Also, most grammar-checkers will balk at some words and phrases that are just fine. Since only you know what you mean to say, only your eyes and brain can spot all of the spelling and grammar problems. Print out and read over carefully each page of your work.

Formatting Your Paper.   You also need to pay attention to the format of your paper — how it looks to the reader. Your instructor may require a special format. If not, here are some guidelines for formatting your paper.

Guidelines for Formatting Your Paper

1. Always set at least one-inch margins when you type.
2. Print out your text double-spaced. (Long quotes and foot-notes or endnotes can be single-spaced.)
3. Make sure that all pages are numbered consecutively.
4. Prepare a separate title page that includes at least: your name, the name of the course and instructor, the date, and the title of your paper.

Example of a Research Paper

As a final aid in preparing your **research paper,** this chapter ends with a full-scale example. The examination of the research paper begins with a discussion of how the **topic** and **theme** were chosen and then moves on to the **writing outline** that the student developed. Finally, there is the paper itself, including **endnotes** and a **bibliography,** all of which follow the rules and suggestions made earlier in this chapter.

Several aspects of the sample research paper are designed to aid students. Annotations in the margin help you to see what the text is trying to accomplish. Also in the margin are a series of subtitles to the paper. Note how each one represents a stage in the unfolding story and is related to part of the writing outline. Finally, a comment in the margin of each endnote tells you what point in the paper is being supported. As you read the paper, ask yourself about the point the author is making and how she is accomplishing the goal. Pay special attention to the way in which the parts are put together and how each section adds strength to the effort to describe and support the theme. Read through the end-notes also to determine why a citation is full or shortened and to see the form used for writing them. Note also the form of the bibliography. If anything is unclear, refer back to the earlier sections of the *Guide* on writing (Chapter 3) and research papers (Chapter 5).

There are two important ways in which this sample research paper can help you. First, you can read the paper as a whole *before* you write your own. This will give you a clearer sense of what your paper should look like, how it should be developed, and the kind of **documentation** it should have. Second, you can refer to the paper *while* you are writing your own in order to answer specific questions you may have about such issues as the introduction, continuity between paragraphs, the form of quotations and endnotes (or footnotes), the bibliography, and the conclusion.

How the Theme Was Chosen

The theme chosen for this paper would fit a variety of courses: Pre–Civil War U.S. History, American Labor History, Women's History, and the History of Industrialization, among others. Within the framework of one of these courses, the student became curious about the lives of workers in the earliest factories. This led to a *topic* about industrialization in New England where the student had grown up. Preliminary research indicated that textiles were the first goods to be made in factories, so the topic was narrowed to workers in that industry. When the student discovered that many of the earliest workers were young women who were the same age as she was, she decided to look at their lives in particular. The largest number of these women worked in mills in Lowell, Massachusetts, so that town was chosen. (The student's research also made it clear that there were numerous sources that discussed Lowell mill workers.) The time period to be covered was the one during which women workers were the principal workforce in Lowell. Finally, the student discovered from preliminary research that in the early nineteenth century there was great concern about the impact of industrial work on American society and especially on women. All of this narrowing led to the theme "Wage Slavery or True Independence: Women Workers in the Lowell, Massachusetts, Textile Mills, 1820–1850." (See the section on coming up with a theme for your paper in Chapter 4, pp. 76–77.)

The Writing Outline for the Theme

The writing outline was created from the student's **research outline** and subsequent research notes. (See the section on creating a research outline in Chapter 4, pp. 78–80.) The research phase had made clear that several important aspects of the theme had to be examined in the paper. Several sources gave detailed accounts of the experiences of the women workers, showing both positive and negative aspects of their working lives. It became clear that this subject should have an important place in the paper. Sections 4, 5, and 6 of the outline focus on this subject. Section 4 talks about work life, section 5 social life, and section 6 the women's response to changes in the mills. Having decided on the importance of the work experience, it became necessary to give the reader an understanding of how these women came to be mill workers in the first place. Section 3 examines this subject. Showing how the women came to be mill workers required an explanation to the reader of where the mills themselves came from. This is necessary because the mills represent the first stage of industrialization in America, one of the points of the theme. Sections 1 and 2 deal with industrialization. Section 7 covers the end of the period during which women workers predominated in textile work. The other two sections, of course, are the introduction and conclusion.

The subheadings within each section are divisions of the larger subject and determine the order in which a section will be developed. For example, section 4, "Life in a mill town," examines, in order, adjusting to life in a mill town, a typical workday, the work itself, the pay received, and the mill-owned boarding houses where the girls lived. Look at each part of the outline to see the function it serves and how the whole of the outline fully covers the important parts of the theme. Try to be sure that your own outline sets the stage for writing the paper the way this one does.

SAMPLE WRITING OUTLINE

Wage Slavery or True Independence:
Women Workers in the Lowell, Massachusetts,
Textile Mills, 1820–1850

Introduction
1. Attitudes toward industrialization in the United States
    a. Prejudice against industry by Americans
    b. Early industrialization in England
2. The origins of the textile industry in eastern Massachusetts
    a. The preindustrial economy in America
    b. Slater-type mills
    c. Plans for a textile mill in Lowell, Massachusetts
3. Recruiting women workers
    a. The choice of a female workforce
    b. Overcoming the prejudice against women working outside the home
    c. Building a "moral" community
    d. Why young women chose to work in the mills
4. Life in a mill town
    a. Adjusting to life in the mills
    b. Typical workday

    c. Nature of work

    d. Rate of pay

    e. The boarding house

  5. Social life

    a. Leisure hours

    b. Female companionship

    c. The *Lowell Offering*

  6. Women workers' resistance to factory discipline

    a. "Turnouts"

    b. Slavery or independence?

  7. Declining conditions of work in the Lowell mills

    a. End of paternalism

    b. The coming of the Irish workers

Conclusion

    a. Young women's experience of early industrialization

Turning Research into Writing

Pay attention to the marginal comments that run down the sides of the pages of this sample paper. Compare them to the writing outline that you have just read. Note that each major section of the outline has a corresponding place in the paper itself. When you finish reading the paper, look at the marginal comments down the sides of the pages that contain the endnotes. Here you will see that each of the main points made in the paper is documented. That is, each point has one or more accompanying notes that tell the reader where the information came from. (See the section on documenting sources on pp. 121–36.)

Wage Slavery or True Independence:

Women Workers in the Lowell, Massachusetts,

Textile Mills, 1820-1850

Unless your instructor has a special format, your title page should look something like this one. Whatever layout you choose (don't get carried away with exotic ones) be sure to include: paper title, course name and number (and section, if necessary), instructor name, your name, and the date.

American History 200,

Section 4

Professor Jones

Jane Q. Student

December 8, 2001

1

Introduction.

This paper will examine the development of the textile industry in Lowell, Massachusetts, and the young women who served as its principal workforce between 1820 and 1850. It will attempt to show how these women came to accept what was for them an unusual form of labor and how they

Statement of theme.

shaped it to serve their own purposes. Such a story helps to explain much about early industrialization in America and particularly about the role of women in the early factory system. The paper also addresses the issue of whether these women workers were mere laborers exploited by the mill owners or were actively engaged in expanding the constricted opportunities for women.

Attitudes toward industrialization in the United States.

Until the early nineteenth century, the vast majority of Americans grew up in farm families. As the industrial revolution spread across England, rural Americans felt certain that the dark and dreary factory towns that were beginning to dot the English countryside would not arise in America. News coming from England contained reports that a permanent class of exploited workers was being created there. America, with its commitment to opportunity, would not, people were sure, experience such a fate. New England had been in the forefront of the struggle against British rule. Rural people in that region were especially proud of their independence and suspicious of anything that seemed

Superscript numbers refer to endnotes.

to copy the ways of the English.[1]

2

New Englanders watched the rise of industrialization in England with concern. Changes in production there were most noticeable in the making of cloth. As late as the 1760s, English textile merchants were still making cloth by the age-old "putting out" system. They bought raw wool and hired women to spin it at home. When the wool had been spun into yarn, the merchant then sent it to weavers who also worked in their homes. In that decade, however, new machinery (the carding cylinder, spinning jenny, and most important, the water frame) was developed that made possible the shift of spinning and weaving from homes to what were called "factories." By 1800, many such factories had been established in England, usually employing children to do most of the work. Many of these children were orphans or "paupers" from families so poor that they could not even afford to feed them. Conditions in these factories were very bad, and stories of these dark and dangerous mills (some accurate, some exaggerated) filtered back to America reinforcing the prejudice against England and industry.[2]

The economy of New England early in the nineteenth century was tied to commerce and agriculture, not industry. The wealth of New England merchants had been made in foreign trade, and few of them saw the need to turn to other pursuits. Some worried that the development of American manufactures would cut down on the need to import foreign goods. Until the War of 1812, which cut the United States off from

3

trade in English goods, most wealthy merchants in the Northeast were content to stay in the business that had made their riches.[3] Moreover, where would American factory workers come from? England had a large class of peasants who served as a pool of potential factory labor. In America, however, when land wore out or harvests were poor, Yankee farmers could move west to the vast territories being taken from Native Americans.

The origins of the textile industry in eastern Massachusetts.

While great changes in the production of textiles were taking place in England, most New Englanders still spun yarn at home and some also wove their own cloth. In most cases they were simply making clothes for their families. Much of this work was done by women. A spinning wheel was a possession of almost every household.[4] Despite their anti-industrial prejudice, however, New England farmers witnessed, in the first two decades of the nineteenth century, a slow shift in the way cloth was made in America. Home production gradually gave way to "putting out" and that system was eventually replaced by factory production. Why did this change occur?

Unlike most merchants in America, a few, like Samuel Slater and Francis Cabot Lowell, were impressed by the mechanization of English textile production and began to think about an American textile industry. Men like these noted the massive increase in productivity in the English textile industry. At first, Slater, and others who followed his lead, built small mills

4

in rural villages and employed not children as
in England but whole families. The building of
Slater-type mills did not directly challenge the
New England way of living. Most villages already contained small mills run by water power
(streams pushing paddle wheels) that ground corn
or wheat. Since the textile mills hired whole
families who already lived in the villages, family and village life was not greatly altered.[5]

One new development in textile production,
however, did raise troublesome questions about
the impact of industrialization on America's
rural way of life. This change came from a new
type of mill. The first of its type was built in
Waltham, Massachusetts, in 1813 by Francis Lowell and a small group of wealthy Boston merchants.[6] Three years earlier, Lowell had returned from a long trip to England. The British
government would not allow the plans for the new
power looms to be taken out of the country, but
Lowell had paid close attention to their construction on his many tours of English mills and
returned to America with enough knowledge in his
head to eventually reproduce a machine compar-
able to the English power loom.[7]

In Waltham, Francis Lowell built a large
mill that carried out both the spinning and
weaving processes. In fact, every step of the
production process was done in a series of connected steps. Waltham was not a village with a
textile mill in it, it was a "mill town" in
which the factory dominated the economic life of
a rapidly growing city. Most significantly, Low-

*Transition sen-
tence introduces
discussion of new
type of mill.*

5

ell's system of production brought important changes in the lives of his workers. He hired them as individuals, not as families, and many came from great distances to live and work in the new mill town. When Lowell died in 1817, the small group of Boston businessmen who had invested in his mill at Waltham spread the new factory system to other places. Their biggest investment was in the small village of East Chelmsford about twenty-seven miles from Boston and lying along the swift-flowing Concord and Merrimack Rivers. There they built what was soon the biggest mill town in the nation with more than a dozen large integrated mills based upon mechanical looms. In honor of their friend, they called the new town Lowell.[8]

The growth of Lowell between 1821 and 1840 was unprecedented.[9] A rapidly developing textile industry like the one at Lowell needed larger and larger numbers of people to work the mechanical looms and other machines in their factories. Given the prejudice against factory work in New England, how could large numbers of natives be drawn to work in the mills? It was a question that had been carefully pondered by the wealthy men who built the big textile mills at Lowell, Massachusetts.

Recruiting women workers.

The mill owners, aware of the negative view of English mill towns, decided to confront the problem by creating a planned community where workers would live in solid, clean housing rather than slums. Their source of workers would

6

also be different. The rapidly running rivers
that ran their mills were not near the major
coastal cities. No large pool of potential laborers lived near their new town. The mill owners
had to find a large group of people whose labor
was not absolutely necessary to the farm economy. The solution to their labor problem came in
the form of hundreds (later thousands) of young
women who lived on the farms of the region.[10]

Several developments in the social and economic history of New England tended to make this
group of workers available. Population growth
was making it more and more difficult for farmers to find land close by for their sons (and
their sons' families). Generations of the same
family had hoped to live near one another. By
the 1820s, however, many farms in New England,
especially those on the less productive land of
Maine and New Hampshire, had run out of good
land and had to find sources of income outside
of agriculture. While some farmers went west to
find more fertile land and a less harsh climate,
others sent their sons to work on neighboring
farms, or as apprentices to craftsmen (shoemak-
ers, blacksmiths, or leather workers). Extra
cash was something that most farm families were
in great need of.[11]

Another factor helped set the stage for the
successful industrialization of textile production. This one was within the structure of the
family itself and worked in favor of producing a
new group of workers for the mills. The position
of women (wives and, especially, daughters) in

the family was an inferior one. While adult, property-holding males were citizens with full civil rights, the same was not true for women <u>of any age</u>. The father of the family had the legal right to control most aspects of the lives of his wife and daughters. His wife could own no property. Her signature on a document meant nothing as only her husband could transact business. Daughters had even less independence. They were bound by social conventions to obey their fathers and rarely were able to earn money of their own. In fact, even travel away from home was unusual. The idea that a woman's place was in the home was not merely a powerful concept, it was, with rare exceptions, a rule binding a woman's behavior. While the work of daughters and wives was important to the family economy (it literally could not have functioned without their labor at field work, food preparation, cleaning, washing, etc.) they gained no independent income or freedom as a result. Indeed, so strong was the belief that daughters' lives would be bound by decisions made by their fathers, older brothers, and, eventually, their husbands, that many could not imagine for themselves a life of active, public involvement of the kind expected of men. For some women, however, their inferior position in family and society gave them an incentive to take hold of any opportunity to weaken their bonds of inferiority.[12]

Women's motives were economic as well as social. Very few opportunities for employment outside the home existed; teaching in a local

school was one of the most common, but that was
very poorly paid and lasted for only a few
months a year. The new mill work was steady
work, and it paid more than any alternative
available to women.[13] The young girls could thus
contribute to their family's welfare by sending
home a portion of their pay. This economic motive added to their desire to move outside the
traditional sphere of the family. For many of
them, the chance to live away from home and with
other young women like themselves offered an independence that was otherwise impossible.[14]

Hiring young women, of course, ran up
against strong Yankee resistance. As noted
above, fathers rarely allowed their daughters to
leave home when they were young. According to
the prejudices of the period, young women were
unprepared for a life among adult, male
strangers. Their "innocence" and "purity" had to
be protected by their family. The goal held out
for these girls (almost the only respectable
one) was eventual marriage. To prepare for that,
they had to learn wifely duties and practical
household skills. God-fearing New England fathers were very reluctant to let their daughters
leave the farm to live and work among strangers
in a faraway town.[15]

To confront this prejudice, the mill owners
created boarding houses around the mills where
groups of girls would live and take their meals
under the care of a boarding housekeeper who was
usually an older woman, perhaps a widow. Strict
boarding house rules were laid down by the com-

9

pany; rules that served the company's purposes
but also reassured parents that their daughters'
behavior would still be monitored even though
they were away from home. For example, the young
women could not have visitors in the late
evening. (See the reproduction of boarding house
regulations on page 10.) Moreover, the girls
would never grow into a permanent working
class--something that no one wished to see--as
it was expected that they would return to their
homes for visits and after a year or two would
go back to their villages. While they stayed in
Lowell, their reputations (and thus their opportunity for marriage) would be protected by the
town fathers.[16]

The mill owners did not advertise for help.
They sent recruiters into the countryside to explain the special nature of Lowell and to soothe
parents' fears. Because of the farmers' need for
extra income, and the women's desire for independence, this effort was often successful.[17]
Over the years, thousands of young women took
the long trip by stagecoach or wagon from their
rural homes to mill towns like Lowell.

Life in a mill town.

Upon first arriving in Lowell, the young
girls were naturally nervous. They had not lived
away from home or ever worked in a factory. They
were not used to the atmosphere of a city. The
boarding house was new also. Living with a
strange woman (and probably her family) who
might or might not be a caring mother-substi-
tute, also required adjustment. The girls shared

10

*Visual documenta-
tion of boarding
house life.*

REGULATIONS

FOR THE

BOARDING HOUSES

OF THE

MIDDLESEX COMPANY.

THE tenants of the Boarding Houses are not to board, or permit any part of their houses to be occupied by any person except those in the employ of the Company.

They will be considered answerable for any improper conduct in their houses, and are not to permit their boarders to have company at unseasonable hours.

The doors must be closed at ten o'clock in the evening, and no one admitted after that time without some reasonable excuse.

The keepers of the Boarding Houses must give an account of the number, names, and employment of their boarders, when required; and report the names of such as are guilty of any improper conduct, or are not in the regular habit of attending public worship.

The buildings and yards about them must be kept clean and in good order, and if they are injured otherwise than from ordinary use, all necessary repairs will be made, and charged to the occupant.

It is indispensable that all persons in the employ of the Middlesex Company should be vaccinated who have not been, as also the families with whom they board; which will be done at the expense of the Company.

SAMUEL LAWRENCE, Agent.

JOEL TAYLOR, PRINTER, Daily Courier Office.

Figure 1. Rules for boarding houses where mill girls stayed. (Source: Merrimack Valley Textile Museum.)

the home with a dozen or more other girls and usually roomed with three or four of them. Most were homesick for a time. While all this was happening, of course, the girls had to make the difficult adjustment to the rigorous rules and long hours at the mill.[18]

Mill work was not only an opportunity, like so much of early factory labor, it was hard work. The typical workday began at five a.m. and did not end until seven in the evening, or later. Thus the women worked an average of twelve hours a day. They were given only thirty minutes for lunch and forty-five for dinner. Since they took their meals at the boarding house, the thirty minutes for lunch had to in-clude a quick walk (perhaps a run) to and from the house, leaving only fifteen or twenty min-utes for the meal.[19] The mills operated six days a week so that the only day off was Sunday, part of which was usually spent at church. Thus free time was confined to two or three hours in the evening (boarding house rules required them to go to bed at ten) and to Sunday afternoon.[20] For many, however, this was still more leisure (and more freedom) than they would have had at home.

Despite a workday which, including meals, took up fourteen hours, most of the young women did not find the work very strenuous or particu-larly dangerous. As the mill owners had claimed, Lowell did not resemble the grimy, packed mill towns of England.[21] Still, the work was tedious and confining--doing the same operation over and

12

over again and under the watchful eye of the
overseer. In the ideal plan for Lowell, the
overseer was to take the place of the absent father (just as the boarding-house widow was to be
the substitute mother), someone responsible for
seeing to the safety and welfare of the girls on
the job. Of course, the overseer was also hired
by the company to ensure that the mill ran
smoothly and efficiently. He saw to it that the
women worked steadily and recorded their hours
of labor; any possibility of time off required
his approval.[22]

The young women earned an average of three
to four dollars a week from which their board of
$1.25 a week was deducted.[23] At that time there
were no other jobs open to women that paid as
well. As noted above, rural school teachers
earned less than one dollar a week and taught
for only three months of the year.[24] Three or
four dollars a week was enough to pay their
board, send badly needed money home and still
have enough left over for new clothes once in a
while. Many women workers even established savings accounts, and some eventually left work
with several hundred dollars, something that
they could never have done at home.[25]

In Lowell the women became part of a grow-   *Social life.*
ing city that had shops, social events, and ca-
maraderie that were absent in their rural villages and farms. While most felt responsible to
send part of their earnings home, enough was
left over to give them consumer choices unavail-

13

able to their rural sisters, cousins, and
friends. Also, unlike farm and family chores,
mill work offered free time on Sundays and in
the evenings.[26]

Even though their free time was very limited, the women engaged in a wide variety of activities. In the evening they wrote letters
home, entertained visitors (though there was
little privacy), repaired their clothing, and
talked among themselves. They could go out to
the shops, especially clothing shops. The mill
girls at Lowell prided themselves on a wardrobe
that, at least on Sunday, was not inferior to
that of the wives of prosperous citizens.[27]
One of the most surprising uses of their free
time was the number of meetings attended by mill
girls. There were evening courses that enabled
the young women to extend their education beyond
the few years of schooling they had received in
the countryside. They could also attend lectures
by prominent speakers. It was not unusual for
the audience for serious presentations to be
composed mostly of mill girls. In their spare
time, they also read novels and essays. So
strong was the girls' interest in reading that
many mills put up signs "No reading in the
mills."[28] Perhaps the most unusual pursuit of at
least some mill girls was writing. Determined to
challenge the idea that mill girls were mindless
drones of the factory and that they had not the
refinement necessary to make them good wives,
about seventy-five mill girls and women
contributed in the 1840s to a series of publica-

14

tions that featured stories and essays by the workers themselves. Indeed, much of the editorial work was done by these women as well.[29]

The most well-known of these publications was the Lowell Offering. The Offering stayed away from sensitive issues concerning working conditions, and the mill owners certainly benefited from the reputation for seriousness that it earned their workers. Still, the women controlled the content of the publication and wrote on subjects (family, courtship, fashion, morality, nature, etc.) that interested them.[30] A few of the Offering writers even went on to literary careers, not the kind of future that most people expected of factory workers. Charles Dickens toured the mills in 1842 and later said of the girls' writing that: "Of the merits of the Lowell Offering, as a literary production, I will only observe . . . that it will compare advantageously with a great many English annuals."[31]

Example of a quotation with ellipsis. Short quotations are integrated into the text.

Though the Offering was a sign that something unusual was happening in this factory town, the women still worked in an industry that caused them hardship. In the early years, the owners had tried to keep up the image of the factory as a pleasant place. Buildings had many windows and much sunlight. The town had large green spaces and the atmosphere of a country village.[32] As time went on, however, the mill companies became more interested in profits and less concerned about their role as protectors of their young workers.

15

By the 1830s, tensions in the mills had
begun to rise. Factory owners, observing a decline in the price of their cloth and the growth
of unsold inventories, decided to lower their
workers' wages.[33] When the reduction was announced in February 1834, the women workers cir-

Women workers' resistance to factory discipline.

culated petitions among themselves pledging to
stop work ("turn out") if wages were lowered.[34]
When the leader of the petition drive at one
mill was fired, many of the women protested.
They left work and marched to the other mills to
call out their workers. It is estimated that
one-sixth of all women mill workers walked out
as a result. The strikers wrote another petition
stating that "we will not go back into the mills
to work until our wages are continued . . . as
they have been."[35] While the "turn out" was
brief and did not achieve its purpose, it did
demonstrate the attitude of many of the women
workers. They did not accept the owners' view
that they were minors under their benevolent
care. The petitions prepared by the strikers indicate that they thought of themselves as the
equal of their employers. The sense of independence gained by factory work and cash wages led
them to reject the idea that they were mere factory hands. Petitions referred to their "unques-
tionable rights," and to "the spirit of our pa-
triotic ancestors, who preferred privation to
bondage. . . ." One petition ended "we are free,
we would remain in possession of what kind prov-

Example of a quotation with emphasis added.

idence has bestowed upon us, and remain daughters of free men still."[36] This language indi-

16

cates that the women did not think of themselves
as laborers complaining about low wages. They
were free citizens of a republic and deserved
respect as such. Since many of the young women
had older relatives who had fought in the Revolutionary War, they felt that they were protect-
ing not only their jobs but also their indepe-
dence. While it is true that the strike failed
and that these women did not really have the
"independence" they were so proud of, this issue
was so important to them that many left the
mills and went home when it became clear that
mill work required a lessening of their status.
They had accepted mill work because life away
from home and good wages gave them greater freedom. When mill work came to seem more like
"slavery" (a comparison that also appeared in
the petitions) than independence, many changed
their minds. In 1836, a similar effort to lower
wages led to an even larger "turn out."[37] The
willingness of these young women to challenge
the authority of the mill owners is a sign that
their new lives had given them a feeling of mutual strength.[38]

Economic recession in the late 1830s and
early 1840s led to the layoff of hundreds of
the women workers. Many of the mills were forced
to part-time schedules. In the 1840s and 1850s,
the mill owners tried to maintain profits despite increased competition and lessened demand.
They did so by intensifying the work process.
The speed of the machinery was increased as was

*Declining condi-
tions of work in
the Lowell mills.*

17

the number of machines tended by each worker.
Paternalism was discarded. To save money the
companies stopped building boarding houses.[39]
The look of Lowell changed as well. Mill buildings took up more of the green space that had
been part of the original plan.

By 1850, Lowell did indeed look something
like an English mill town. By then, however, the
need to pacify the fears of potential workers
and their families was gone. Terrible famine in
Ireland in 1845 and 1846 had caused a large number of Irish to immigrate to the United
States.[40] As conditions in the mills declined,
more and more young Yankee women left the mills
for home or other work. Their places were
rapidly taken up by the very poor Irish for whom
work of any kind in America was an opportunity,
and who did not have the option of returning to
their homes. Slowly, Lowell had become just another industrial city. It was dirty and over-
crowded, and its mills were beginning to look
run-down.

Conclusion.   By 1850, an era had passed. By then most of
the mill workers were recruited from newly
arrived immigrants with backgrounds very different from those of the young New England women.
During the period from the 1820s to the 1840s,
however, young women from rural New England made
up the majority of the textile workers in the
area. At that time, an unusual era in the development of industrialization took place. Large
textile mills with complex production systems

18

were operated largely by young women who did not
think of themselves as workers but as free citizens of a republic earning an independent existence for a few years before returning to their
homes. These women gave the mill owners the workforce that was needed to make the U.S. textile
industry large and profitable. Many fortunes
were made for investors living in Boston and
other major cities.[41] But the farmers' daughters
profited as well. Not only did they earn more
money than earlier generations of women had been
able to, they did so outside the home.

A great debate had raged during the 1830s
and 1840s about the impact of industrialization
on American life. Because of the general belief
that women were weak, it was presumed that they
would be taken advantage of as workers, especially as they were away from the protection of
the male members of their families. Further, it
was feared that mill work would "defeminize"
them and that young men would not marry them because they had not been brought up in an environment of modesty, deference to their fathers
and brothers, and daily practice in domestic
tasks such as cleaning, sewing, and cooking.[42]
Seen from a longer perspective, however, the
women showed these fears to be unfounded. Even
more importantly, as effective workers they un-
dermined the stereotype of women as frail and as
thriving only in a domestic environment. While
these young women helped make possible the industrialization of New England, at the same time
they expanded their opportunities. Many women

*Restatement of
theme.*

19

reformers and radicals in later years, as they
raised the banner for equal rights for women in
more and more areas of life, referred back to
the example of the independent mill girls of the
1830s and 1840s who resisted pressures from
their employers, gained both freedom and matu-
rity by living and working on their own, and
showed an intense desire for independence and
learning.[43] Great fortunes were made from the
textile mills of that era, but within those
mills a generation of young women gained something even more precious--a sense of self-
respect.

20

Endnotes

1. Caroline F. Ware, The Early New England Cotton Manufacture (Boston: Houghton Mifflin Co., 1931), 4-8; Barbara M. Tucker, Samuel Slater and the Origins of the American Textile Industry: 1790-1860 (Ithaca: Cornell University Press, 1984), 38-41; Robert F. Dalzell, Enterprising Elite: The Boston Associates and the World They Made (Cambridge: Harvard University Press, 1987), 12-13; Jonathan Prude, The Coming of Industrial Order: Town and Factory Life in Rural Massachusetts, 1810-1860 (Cambridge: Cambridge University Press, 1983), 6-12; Allan Kulikoff, "The Transition to Capitalism in Rural America," William and Mary Quarterly 46 (1989): 129-30, 141-42.

2. Tucker, Slater, 33-40.

3. Dalzell, 41-42; Ware, 3-8, 62.

4. Thomas Dublin, Women at Work: The Transformation of Work and Community in Lowell, Massachusetts, 1826-1860 (New York: Columbia University Press, 1979), 14; Adrienne D. Hood, "The Gender Division of Labor in the Production of Textiles in Eighteenth-Century Rural Pennsylvania," Journal of Social History 27, spring 1994, <http://www.searchbank.com/infotrac/session/4/0/82904/3?xrn_7> (9 September 1996).

5. Tucker, Slater, 79, 85, 99-100, 111; Barbara M. Tucker, "The Family and Industrial Discipline in Ante-Bellum New England," Labor History 21 (winter 1979-80): 56-60.

6. Dalzell, 26-30; Tucker, Slater, 111-16.

Endnotes begin on a new page.

1. American attitudes toward industrialization in England and mill work in general.

2. The rise of industrialization in England.

3. The origins of industrialization in America.

4. Home spinning in America.

Example of citation from the Internet.

5. Slater-type mills and family production.

6. The creation of Waltham mills.

21

7. H.C. Lowell and power loom.

7. Dalzell, 5-6.

8. The founding of Lowell.

8. Tucker, 116-17.

9. The growth of Lowell.

9. Dublin, 19-21, 133-35.

10. The owners' choice of a female workforce.

10. Dublin, 26, 76; Benita Eisler, ed., The Lowell Offering: Writings by New England Mill Women (1840-1845) (Philadelphia: J.B. Lippincott Co., 1977), 15-16.

11. Problems of the farm economy.

11. Christopher Clark, "The Household Economy: Market Exchange and the Rise of Capitalism in the Connecticut Valley, 1800-1860," Journal of Social History 13 (winter 1979): 175-76; Gail Fowler Mohanty, "Handloom Outwork and Outwork Weaving in Rural Rhode Island, 1810-1821," American Studies 30 (fall 1989): 42-43, 48-49.

12. The inferior position of women.

12. Eisler, 16, 19, 62; Barbara Welter, "The Cult of True Womanhood," American Quarterly 18 (1966): 155, 162-65.

13. Limited opportunities for women in New England.

13. Eisler, 16, 193; Clark, 178-79; Dalzell, 33.

14. Women's desire for independence.

14. Dublin, 40; Tucker, Slater, 255-56; Harriet H. Robinson, Loom and Spindle (1898; reprinted in Women of Lowell, New York: Arno Press, 1974), 194; Eisler, 61-63, 81-82.

15. Early nineteenth-century rural attitudes toward women.

Example of a film citation.

15. On the influence of patriarchy see Tucker, Slater, 25-26; Robinson, 61; Welter, 152, 170-71. Also see Sins of Our Mothers, 58 min., WGBH/WNET/KLET/PBS, 1988, videocassette.

16. Early Lowell paternalism.

16. Dublin, 77-79; Eisler, 19-24.

17. The method of recruiting women workers.

17. Eisler, 18-19. On the decline of New England agriculture see Clark, 176; Ware, 14.

18. Getting used to town life and the boarding house.

18. Dublin, 80; Eisler, 73-74.

19. The nature of mill work and the workday.

19. Dublin, 80; Robinson, 31; Lucy Larcom, "Among Lowell Mill Girls: A Reminiscence" (1881;

22

reprinted in <u>Women of Lowell</u>), 602; Eisler,
75-77.

20. See table of mill hours printed in
Eisler, 30. Boarding house curfew is listed in
"Regulations for the Boarding Houses," contained
in illustration on page 10. For a very negative
view of work hours and conditions, see A Citizen
of Lowell, <u>Corporations and Operatives: Being an
Exposition of the Condition [of the] Factory Op-
eratives</u> . . . (1843; reprinted in <u>Women of
Lowell</u>), 15-19.21.

21. Larcom, 599-602; Eisler, 56-66.

22. "Factory Rules from the Handbook to
Lowell, 1848," n.d., <http://www.kentlaw.edu/
ilhs/lowell.htm> (9 August 1996).

23. Dublin, 66, 183, 185; Ware, 239.

24. Ware, 240-42. For teachers' pay see
Eisler, 193.

25. Elisha Bartlett, <u>A Vindication of the
Character and Condition of the Females Employed
in the Lowell Mills</u>, . . . (Lowell, Massachusetts:
Leonard Huntress, Printer, 1841), 21; Dublin,
188.

26. Larcom, 599-600.

27. Eisler, 49-50.

28. Robinson, 91-93; Eisler, 113-32. For
mill rules concerning reading, see Eisler, 31.

29. Robinson, 97-102.

30. Eisler, 33-40; Dublin, 123-24, 129-30;
Robinson, 114-20; Bertha Monica Stearns, "Early
Factory Magazines in New England: The <u>Lowell Of-
fering</u> and Its Contemporaries," <u>Journal of Eco-</u>

*20. Work hours
and free time.*

*21. Favorable
comments on mill
work by the Lowell
mill girls.*

*22. The role of the
overseer. (Example
of a Web cita-
tion.)*

*23. The rate of
women's pay.*

*24. Low alterna-
tive pay for
women.*

*25. Savings
accounts.*

26. Free time.

*27. Leisure time
and wardrobe.*

*28. Reading and
education.*

*29. Women's
writing.*

30. The Lowell
Offering.

23

31. Dickens commenting on the Lowell Offering.

32. The early Lowell setting.

33. The tensions of the 1830s; lowered wages.

34. The 1834 "Turnout."

35. Strikers' petitions.

36. More quotes from petitions.

37. The 1836 "Turnout."

38. Mutual support.

39. Declining working conditions.

40. The workforce after 1845; Irish immigration.

41. Profits for owners.

42. The status of women.

43. Lowell women activists and later movements.

nomic and Business History (August 1930):
690-91, 698.

    31. Dickens is quoted in Robinson, 11. Also see Larcom, 609; Eisler, 41.

    32. Larcom, 598, 609; Eisler, 63-65.

    33. Dublin, 87-90.

    34. Robinson, 84; Dublin, 89-91.

    35. Dublin, 91.

    36. Dublin, 93.

    37. Dublin, 98-99.

    38. Dublin, 44, 82-83, 103.

    39. Dublin, 108, 134; Robinson, 204, 208-09; Eisler, 215.

    40. Dublin, 140, 156, 197. On the decline of Lowell, see Dalzell, 69.

    41. Dalzell, 60-61, 70-73.

    42. Dublin 32; Welter, 151-74. For the contemporary debate about the impact of factory work on women, see the pamphlets: Bartlett, A Vindication of the Character and Condition. . . and A Citizen, Corporations and Operatives. . .

    43. Dublin, 127-29; Ware, 292.

24

Bibliography

Books

Bartlett, Elisha. A Vindication of the Character
and Condition of the Females Employed in the
Lowell Mills, . . . Lowell, Massachusetts:
Leonard Huntress, Printer, 1841. Reprinted
in Women of Lowell. New York: Arno Press,
1974.

Citizen of Lowell, A. Corporations and Operatives: Being an Exposition of the Condition
[of the] Factory Operatives. . . . 1843.
Reprinted in Women of Lowell. New York: Arno
Press, 1974.

Dalzell, Robert F. Enterprising Elite: The Boston
Associates and the World They Made. Cambridge: Harvard University Press, 1987.

Dublin, Thomas. Women at Work: The Transformation
of Work and Community in Lowell, Massachusetts, 1826-1860. New York: Columbia University Press, 1979.

Eisler, Benita, ed. The Lowell Offering: Writings
by New England Mill Women (1840-1845).
Philadelphia: J.B. Lippincott Co., 1977.

Prude, Jonathan. The Coming of Industrial Order:
Town and Factory Life in Rural Massachusetts, 1810-1860. Cambridge: Cambridge University Press, 1983.

Robinson, Harriet H. Loom and Spindle; Or, Life
Among the Early Mill Girls. 1898. Reprinted
in Women of Lowell. New York: Arno Press,
1974.

*Bibliography be-
gins on a new
page.*

*Citations are
listed alphabeti-
cally under each
heading.*

*Second and fol-
lowing lines of
each citation are
indented.*

25

Tucker, Barbara M. Samuel Slater and the Origins
   of the American Textile Industry: 1790-1860.
   Ithaca: Cornell University Press, 1984.
Ware, Caroline F. The Early New England Cotton
   Manufacture. Boston: Houghton Mifflin Com-
   pany, 1931.

Articles

Clark, Christopher. "The Household Economy, Market Exchange, and the Rise of Capitalism in
   the Connecticut Valley, 1800-1860." Journal
   of Social History 13 (winter 1979): 169-89.
Hood, Adrienne D. "The Gender Division of Labor
   in the Production of Textiles in the Eighteenth Century." Journal of Social History
   27. Spring 1994. <http://www.searchbank.com/
   infotrac/session/4/0/82904/3?xrn_7> (9 September 1996).
Kulikoff, Allen. "The Transition to Capitalism in
   Rural America." William and Mary Quarterly
   46 (1989): 120-144.
Larcom, Lucy. "Among Lowell Mill Girls: A Reminiscence." 1881. Reprinted in Women of Lowell. New York: Arno Press, 1974.
Mohanty, Gail Fowler. "Handloom Outwork and Outwork Weaving in Rural Rhode Island,
   1810-1821." American Studies 30 (fall 1989):
   41-68.
Stearns, Bertha Monica. "Early Factory Magazines
   in New England: The Lowell Offering and Its
   Contemporaries." Journal of Economic and
   Business History (Aug. 1930): 685-705.

26

Tucker, Barbara M. "The Family and Industrial
    Discipline in Ante-Bellum New England."
    Labor History 21 (winter 1979-80): 55-74.
Welter, Barbara. "The Cult of True Womanhood."
    American Quarterly 18 (1966): 151-74.

                    Films
Sins of Our Mothers. 58 min. WGBH/WNET/KCET/PBS,
    1988. Videocassette.

                  Documents
"Factory Rules from the Handbook to Lowell,
    1848." N.d. <http://www.kentlaw.edu/ilhs
    .lowell.htm> (9 August 1996).

Basic Reference Sources
for History Study
and Research

Chapter 4, "How to Research a History Topic," describes the ways of searching for information on a history topic in your library and on the Web. This appendix makes that job easier by separating different kinds of reference sources by type so that you know what *kind* of printed or online finding aid will get you where you want to go.

This list of reference sources is especially designed for undergraduate historical research. It contains several kinds of sources: (1) *reference works* (dictionaries, **encyclopedias, atlases, yearbooks**); (2) *guides* to biographies, newspaper articles, **journal** articles, **book reviews,** and government documents; and (3) several hundred **subject bibliographies** arranged according to topic. While reference works contain brief descriptions of aspects of your historical topic, guides and subject bibliographies lead you to specific studies of the topic itself. If, for example, your topic is nineteenth-century Asian immigration to the United States and you are seeking information on the theme "Chinese Immigrant Labor on the Transcontinental Railroad," the section of the subject bibliographies entitled "Asian Immigrant and Ethnic History" is a good place to begin.

Also included in this appendix is a section called "Electronic Reference Sources" (see p. 204). This section includes the rapidly growing world of information sources on the **World Wide Web.** Most of your library's computer terminals will give you access to **CD-ROMs** owned by your library and to the World Wide Web. In the future, more and more historical research is likely to be done online, so it is important that you know your way around the universe of electronic information. For the present, however, more reliable background information on your topic/theme will probably be available in your library's *printed* reference works.

Many of the works cited in this appendix should be available in the reference section of your own library. If your library is small, however, you may not find some of them. On the other hand, if your school's library is large, you will have even more sources available to you.

Printed works in the appendix are listed by title first so that you can more easily spot the work that seems closest to your topic. Following the title is publication information and then the name of the editor or compiler (if available). When looking for one of these works in a catalog, however, first conduct an "author" search under the name of the editor or compiler. If the book does not turn up this way, then search for the work by title. When you have access to more than one edition of a work, it is usually best to use the most recent one. As always, the reference librarian is your best guide to your school's information resources.

Dictionaries, Encyclopedias, Atlases, and Yearbooks

These sources are general reference works. They can help you to define and correctly spell important terms, gather general information on your topic/theme, locate geographical areas, obtain statistical data, and much more. These sources are a good point at which to begin any historical investigation. You can also consult them for specific facts. However, these sources do not contain extensive examinations or interpretations of historical subjects, and therefore you should not depend upon them for the substance of your work.

General Dictionaries

Webster's New International Dictionary

Funk and Wagnall's New Standard Dictionary

The Random House Dictionary of the American Language

Oxford English Dictionary, 2d ed. Oxford: Clarendon Press, 1989. This is the most complete English-language dictionary. If you are studying the historical development of the meaning of a word, it is an essential reference. If, however, you wish to determine the contemporary spelling or definition of a term, the unabridged language dictionaries are better sources. If the term is colloquial or is a recent derivation, be sure to use the most recent edition available.

Historical Dictionaries

Historical dictionaries define only historical terms. Unlike language dictionaries, they briefly describe the origin and general historical context of the term. Some historical dictionaries give extensive explanations of terms and thus are similar to encyclopedias.

Concise Dictionary of American History. New York: Charles Scribner's Sons, 1983. David William Voorhees, ed. This is an abridgment of the eight-volume *Dictionary of American History.*

Macmillan Concise Dictionary of World History. New York: Macmillan, 1986. Bruce Wetterau, comp. and ed.

A Dictionary of Twentieth Century History, 1914–1990. Oxford: Oxford University Press, 1997. Peter Teed, ed.

A Dictionary of Modern History, 1789–1945. Baltimore: Penguin Books, 1994. Alan W. Palmer, ed.

Dictionary of American History. Rev. ed. New York: Scribner's, 1976. James T. Adams and Roy V. Coleman, eds. *Supplement,* 1996.

The Harper Dictionary of Modern Thought. New York: Harper & Row, 1988. Alan Bullock and Stephen Trombley, eds.

A Dictionary of Ancient History. Oxford: Blackwell, 1994.

Oxford Dictionary of Byzantium. 3 vols. Oxford University Press, 1991. Alex P. Kazhdan, ed.

A Dictionary of American History. Oxford: Blackwell, 1995. Thomas L. Purvis, ed.

Dictionary of Contemporary History, 1945 to the Present. Oxford: Blackwell, 1999. Duncan Townson, ed.

Specialized Dictionaries

A Dictionary of the Social Sciences. New York: The Free Press, 1964. J. Gould and W. Kolb, eds.

The New Grove Dictionary of Music and Musicians. 2d ed. 29 vols. New York: Macmillan, 2000. Stanley Sadie, ed.

Baker's Biographical Dictionary of Musicians. 8th ed. New York: Schirmer, 1992. Theodore Baker, comp., Nicolas Slonimsky, ed.

The Oxford Dictionary of Philosophy. Oxford: Oxford University Press, 1994. Simon Blackburn, comp.

Webster's New Geographical Dictionary. Springfield, Mass.: Merriam-Webster, 1988. This is a convenient source for determining the spelling, location, and description of geographical terms.

General Encyclopedias

If your subject is a recent one, or if important new facts and interpretations have arisen in recent years, be sure to obtain the latest edition of whatever encyclopedia you use. If a recent edition is not available, check the annual supplements published by most good encyclopedias. Online versions of encyclopedias may be available to you.

Encyclopaedia Britannica. Chicago: Encyclopaedia Britannica Educational Corporation.
This is one of the best encyclopedias. It is also available on the Web at <britannica.com>.

Encyclopedia Americana. Danbury, Conn.: Grolier Educational Corporation.

Collier's Encyclopedia. New York: Crowell Collier and Macmillan.

The Columbia Encyclopedia. New York: Columbia University Press.

Historical Encyclopedias

The Encyclopedia of Ancient Civilizations of the Near East and Mediterranean. New York: M. E. Sharpe, 1997. John Heywood, ed.

Harper Encyclopedia of the Modern World [1760 to present]. New York: Harper & Row, 1970. Richard B. Morris and Graham W. Irwin, eds.

Encyclopedia of American History. New York: Harper & Row, 1982. Richard B. Morris et al., eds.

The Encyclopedia of the Middle Ages. New York: Viking, 1999. Norman F. Cantor, ed.

Women's Studies Encyclopedia: History, Philosophy, and Religion. Vol. 3. Westport, Conn.: Greenwood Press, 1999. Helen Tierney, ed.

Encyclopedia of World History. New York: Oxford University Press, 1998.

Specialized Encyclopedias

For encyclopedias of particular historical fields, see the subheadings under "Subject Bibliographies."

International Encyclopedia of the Social Sciences. New York: Macmillan, 1968–1991. David L. Sills, ed. If your research takes you into such fields as political science, economics, anthropology, law, sociology, and psychology, this is an important sourcebook for you. (A biographical supplement, published in 1979, includes biographies of famous social scientists.)

Encyclopedia of Philosophy. New York: Macmillan Library Reference, 1996.

Encyclopedia Judaica. 16 vols. Jerusalem: Keter Publishing House, 1972. Geoffrey Wigoder, ed. Reprinted, New York: Coronet Books, 1994.

New Catholic Encyclopedia. Palantine, Ill.: J. Heraty, 1981.

Encyclopedia of Religion. 16 vols. New York: Macmillan, 1993. Mircea Eliade, ed.

Encyclopedia of World Art. New York: McGraw Hill, 1959–1983. Supplements, 1987.

Benet's Reader's Encyclopedia of American Literature. New York: Harper Collins, 1996. George Perkins, ed.

The Concise Encyclopedia of Islam. New York: Harper & Row, 1989. Cyril Glasse, ed.

McGraw-Hill Encyclopedia of Science and Technology. 8th ed. New York: McGraw-Hill, 1997.

Encyclopedia of the United States in the Twentieth Century. 4 vols. New York: Scribner's, 1996. Stanley Kutler, ed.

The New Grove Dictionary of Music and Musicians. 2d ed. 29 vols. New York: Macmillan, 2000. Stanley Sadie, ed.

General Atlases

The Times Atlas of the World: Comprehensive Edition. London: Times Publishing Co., 1999.

National Geographic Atlas of the World. Washington, D.C.: National Geographic Society, 1992.

See also Webster's *New Geographical Dictionary* under "Specialized Dictionaries" on page 172.

Historical Atlases

Muir's Historical Atlas: Ancient, Medieval & Modern. London: George Philips, 1976.

Times Atlas of World History. 4th ed. New York: Hammond, 1993.

Atlas of American History. New York: Scribner's, 1984. Kenneth T. Jackson, ed.

The Atlas of Medieval Man. New York: Crescent Books, 1985. Colin Platt, ed.

The Complete Atlas of World History. 3 vols. New York: M. E. Sharpe, 1997.

Harper Atlas of World History. New York: Harper Collins, 1992.

Times Atlas of European History. New York: Times/Harper Collins, 1994. Thomas Cussans, ed.

Historical Atlas of the United States. Washington, D.C.: National Geographic Society, 1988. Wilbur E. Garrett, ed.

Historical Atlas of Britain. New York: Continuum, 1981. Malcolm Falkus, ed.

Muir's Atlas of Ancient and Classical History. London: George Philips, 1982.

Atlas of World History. Rev. ed. Chicago: Rand McNally, 1995. Robert R. Palmer et al., eds.

Atlas of the Greek World. New York: Facts on File, 1989. Peter Levi, comp.

Atlas of the Roman World. New York: Facts on File, 1982. Tim Cornell and John Matthews, comps.

Yearbooks

Statesman's Yearbook. New York: St. Martin's Press, 1864–present. This and the following yearbooks provide up-to-date political information, especially of a governmental nature.

Political Handbook of the World. New York: McGraw-Hill, 1927–present. Arthur S. Banks and William Overstreet, eds.

United Nations Statistical Yearbook. New York: United Nations Statistical Office, 1949–present. There is also a *United Nations Demographic Yearbook,* which provides world and national population statistics.

Biography Collections

Biography collections consist of short biographies of well-known persons. They contain a general outline of the milestones and accomplishments of individuals who have made notable contributions to the times in which they lived and/or to posterity. These works are useful as a first step in biographical research on persons central to your topic or as a way of identifying characters peripheral to it. Each collection has different criteria for determining which individuals it includes. Take care to select the biography collection that is most likely to include the type of individual on whom you are seeking information. Some are also available on CD-ROM or on the Web.

Guides to Biography Collections

Biography Index: A Cumulative Guide to Biographical Material in Books and Magazines. New York: H. W. Wilson, 1949–present.

Biography and Genealogy Master Index. 8 vols. Detroit: Gale, 1980. Miranda C. Herbert and Barbara McNeil, eds. Supplements issued annually. Also available on CD-ROM.

Biographical Dictionaries Master Index. Detroit: Gale, 1975–. Dennis La Beau and Gary C. Tarbert, eds.

British and Canadian Biography Collections

Dictionary of National Biography. Oxford: Oxford University Press, 1908–present. Leslie Stephen and Sidney Lee, eds. A summary of this large multivolume collection can be found in *A Concise Dictionary of National Biography, from Earliest Times to 1985.*

Who's Who. London: Allen & Unwin, 1849–present. Annual. This volume covers *living* individuals. For historical research, you must choose a year during which your subject was most active, or preferably use the *Who Was Who* collection that follows.

Who Was Who. Vol. 1, 1897–1915; vol. 2, 1916–1928; vol. 3, 1929–1940; vol. 4, 1941–1950; vol. 5, 1951–1960; vol. 6, 1961–1970; vol. 7, 1971–1980. A cumulative index for 1897–1980 was published in 1981. (See annotation to *Who Was Who in America* for further information.)

Canadian Who's Who. 19 vols. Toronto: University of Toronto Press, 1984.

Dictionary of Canadian Biography. Toronto: University of Toronto Press, 1966–present. An index to this multivolume work is listed below.

Dictionary of Canadian Biography: Index. Volumes I to XII, 1000 to 1900. Toronto: University of Toronto Press, 1991.

American Biography Collections

American National Biography. 24 vols. New York: Oxford University Press and The American Council of Learned Societies, 1999. John A. Garraty and Mark C. Carnes, gen. eds. The newest and most extensive collection of U. S. biographies. To be updated online.

Dictionary of American Biography. New York: Scribner's, 1928–1996, including supplements. This collection includes both American citizens and people who lived much of their lives in this country even if they were not citizens. It lists only individuals who are no longer living. As with most biography collections, the date of original publication is the best key to determining who is included. Most of the original volumes were written between 1928 and 1936. If your subject died after 1930, check the numerous supplements. A one-volume work containing shortened versions of these biographies is published under the title *Concise Dictionary of American Biography,* 3d ed., 1980. An index was published in 1990.

Who Was Who in America: Historical Volume, 1607–1896. Chicago: Marquis Who's Who, 1967. If you are uncertain about your subject's death date, check *Who Was Who Index, 1607–1993.*

Who Was Who in America. Vol. 1, 1897–1942; vol. 2, 1943–1950; vol. 3, 1951–1960; vol. 4, 1961–1968; vol. 5, 1969–1973; vol. 6, 1974–1976; vol. 7, 1977–1981; vol. 8, 1982–1985. Chicago: Marquis Who's Who. The years covered in each volume indicate the dates of death for those included in it. For example, if your subject died in 1945, he or she should be included in volume 2. For individuals who died before 1897, see the preceding citation.

Who's Who in America. Chicago: Marquis Who's Who, 1897–present. This volume covers living individuals. For purposes of historical research, you must obtain the older volumes or, preferably, use the *Who Was Who* collections that follow.

Notable American Women 1607–1950: A Bibliographical Dictionary. 3 vols. Cambridge, Mass.: Harvard University Press, 1971. Edward T. James, ed. Supplemented by: *Notable American Women: The Modern Period.* 1980. This volume includes women who died between 1951 and 1975.

Research Guide to American Historical Biography. New York: Beacham, 1988. Robert Muccigrosso, ed.

Biographical Directory of the American Congress, 1774–1989. Washington, D.C.: Government Printing Office, 1989.

Biographical Directory of the United States Executive Branch, 1774–1989. Westport, Conn.: Greenwood Press, 1990.

Who's Who of American Women. Chicago: Marquis Who's Who, 1958–.

Dictionary of American Negro Biography. New York: W. W. Norton, 1982. Rayford W. Logan and Michael Winston, eds.

Biographical Directory of American Labor. Westport, Conn.: Greenwood Press, 1984. Gary M. Fink, ed.

American Men and Women of Science. New York: Bowker, 1906–present.

American Diaries: An Annotated Bibliography of Published American Diaries and Journals. Detroit: Gale, 1983–1987.

The Encyclopedia of American Biography. New York: Harper Collins, 1996. John Garraty and Jerome Sternstein, eds.

International Biography Collections

International biography collections list persons of all national origins.

Current Biography. New York: H. W. Wilson, 1940–present. This covers living persons. Older volumes, however, may list individuals who are now of historical significance. Only useful for historical research for the period since the 1930s. To locate the volume you need, check *Current Biography: Cumulated Index, 1940–1970.*

International Who's Who. London: Europa, 1935–present.

New York Times Obituary Index, 1858–1968, 1969–1980. New York: New York Times, 1970, 1980. Current volumes by Meckler, 1990–.

Who's Who in the World. Chicago: Marquis, 1971–present.

The International Dictionary of Women's Biography. New York: Continuum, 1982. Jennifer S. Uglow, ed.

Dictionary of International Biography. Cambridge: England International Biographical Centre, 1995.

Dictionary of Scientific Biography. 16 vols. New York: Scribner's, 1970–1980. Charles C. Gillispie, ed. Includes index.

National Biography Collections

Most national biography collections deal with contemporary personages. However, such collections may be useful for research into recent history or for obtaining information on the early careers of contemporary figures. Here is a brief selection.

Dictionary of Canadian Biography. Toronto: University of Toronto Press, 1966–present.

Who's Who in Latin America. Chicago: A. N. Marquis, 1946–1951. Percy A. Martin, ed.

Dictionary of African Historical Biography. Berkeley: University of California Press, 1986. Mark R. Lipschultz and R. Kent Rasmusson, eds.

Dictionary of African Biography. New York: Reference Publications, 1977–present. Volumes expected on each African country.

Japan Biographical Encyclopedia and Who's Who. Tokyo: Rengo Press, 1958–present.

Australian Dictionary of Biography. 12 vols. Carlton, Victoria: Melbourne University Press, 1966–1991. Douglas Pike et al., eds.

Newspaper Directories and Indexes

If you determine that a particular newspaper is especially important to your research, the best way to locate back issues is to check a newspaper directory. These directories can tell you in which libraries that newspaper can be found and how complete the collection is. Remember, the newspaper directory is useful only if you know the name of the paper for which you are looking. You might be able to obtain the newspapers you need if they are on microfilm or microfiche. Some newspaper directories and indexes are now available on CD-ROM and on the World Wide Web.

Newspaper Directories

American Newspapers, 1821–1936: A Union List of Files Available in the United States and Canada. New York: H. W. Wilson, 1937. Winifred Gerould, ed. Also available on microfilm. Ann Arbor: University Microfilms, 1966.

Newspapers on Microfilm: A Union Check List. Washington, D.C.: Library of Congress, 1963. George Schwegman Jr., ed. This volume is supplemented by *Newspapers in Microform: United States, 1948–1984.*

African Newspapers in Selected American Libraries. Washington, D.C.: Library of Congress, 1965.

Latin American Newspapers in United States Libraries. Austin: University of Texas Press, 1969. Steven M. Charno, ed.

Newspaper Indexes

Once you have access to a particular newspaper, you must determine which issues contain articles on your theme. If your theme is a specific event, then merely check the issues of the newspaper published at the time of or shortly after the event. However, if you are seeking articles about an event that was not confined to a particular day or week (for example, the stock market crash of 1929), then you will have to check newspaper issues covering many weeks or even months. An indispensable aid in such a task is the newspaper index.

If you know the year in which the event occurred, then a newspaper index can tell you the days in that year when a particular paper contained related articles or editorials. The only problem with newspaper indexes is that so few of them exist. If there is no index to the paper you wish to read, check the index of another newspaper. This will tell you the dates on which that newspaper carried articles on your subject. You can then go back to the newspaper in which you were initially interested and read it for those dates. In most cases, you will find what you need. Some newspaper indexes are now available on the Web at the newspapers' home pages.

New York Times Index. New York: New York Times, 1913–present. This is usually the best source for beginning students. Most libraries have files of the *New York Times,* and the index has been extended back to 1851.

New York Daily Tribune Index. New York: Tribune Association, 1841–1907.

Palmer's Index to The Times [of London] *Newspaper,* 1790–1941. London: 1868–1943.

Official Index to The Times [of London]. London: 1907–present.

Christian Science Monitor Index. Corvallis, Oregon: 1960–present. Because this index goes back only to 1960, it is of limited use for historical research.

Periodical Guides and Indexes

Periodical guides describe the location and general content of **periodicals.** Like newspaper guides, they are most useful if you already know which periodical you need and want to find out where collections of it are located. Many periodical indexes are now available on the World Wide Web. (See "Electronic Reference Sources," pp. 204–11.)

Periodical Guides

Historical Periodicals: An Annotated World List of Historical and Related Serial Publications. Santa Barbara, Cal.: ABC-Clio, 1961. Eric H. Boehm and Lalit Adolphus, eds. This volume is succeeded by the directory that follows.

Historical Periodicals Directory. Vol. 1, United States and Canada, 1981; vol. 2, Europe (West), 1982; vol. 3, Europe (East), 1982; vol. 4, Latin America, 1983. Vol. 5, Australia and New Zealand, 1986. Santa Barbara, Cal.: ABC-Clio. Eric H. Boehm, Barbara H. Pope, and Marie Ensign, eds.

Ulrich's International Periodicals Directory. New York: Bowker, 1985.

Magazines for Libraries. 8th ed. New York: Bowker, 1995. This guide describes each publication and helps to determine which are best for historical research.

General Periodical Indexes

General periodical indexes list articles that have appeared in periodical publications. Usually organized by subject, they contain all of the articles on a given topic that appeared in the periodicals that are indexed. The periodicals covered by a particular index are usually listed. When you choose an index, be sure that it covers the kind of periodical likely to contain articles on your theme and that these articles are written for a serious or scholarly audience. There are also many electronic databases that index periodicals. Be sure to check your library's databases and also the World Wide Web.

Historical Abstracts. Santa Barbara, Cal.: ABC-Clio, 1955–present. Part A: Modern History (1450–1914); Part B: The Twentieth Century (1914–present). Eric H. Bochm, ed. This is the best source for articles in history journals. It covers a wide range of subjects. A brief description of each article is included. After 1964, it does not include articles on United States or Canadian history. Also available in CD-ROM.

America: History and Life: A Guide to Periodical Literature. Santa Barbara, Cal.: ABC-Clio, 1965–present. Supplement, 1980. A brief description of each article is included. It covers the United States and Canada. Also available in CD-ROM and on the Web.

Reader's Guide to Periodical Literature. New York: H. W. Wilson, 1900–present. These volumes cover the twentieth century. Be selective when using them because many of the periodicals included are written for a popular rather than a scholarly audience. However, the magazines listed are valuable as records of popular opinions and interests.

Nineteenth Century Reader's Guide to Periodical Literature. New York: H. W. Wilson, 1944.

Public Affairs Information Service Bulletin. New York: P.A.I.S., 1915–present. This work emphasizes periodicals and other publications in the social sciences and includes many government publications.

The Combined Retrospective Index Set to Journals in History, 1838–1974. Washington, D.C.: Carrollton, 1977. Annadel N. Wile, exec. ed.

Social Science and Humanities Index. New York: H. W. Wilson, 1907–1973.

Poole's Index to Periodical Literature, 1802–1881. Boston: Houghton Mifflin, 1891. There is a supplement covering 1882–1906.

Social Sciences Index. New York: H. W. Wilson, 1974–present. For the period prior to 1974, see *Social Science and Humanities Index.*

Humanities Index. New York: H. W. Wilson, 1974–present. For the period prior to 1974, see *Social Science and Humanities Index.*

Specialized Periodical Indexes

There are many periodical indexes on specialized topics. If your research takes you into a specialized field, the indexes listed here may be worth looking into.

Agricultural Index; Applied Science and Technology Index; Art Index; Business Periodicals Index; Education Index; Index to Legal Periodicals; Index Medicus; Music Index. These and other indexes are also available in database format or on the World Wide Web.

Some specialized periodical indexes of value in historical research are:

American Historical Review: General Index for Volumes XLI–LXX, 1935–1965. New York: Macmillan, 1965.

Guide to the American Historical Review, 1895–1945. Washington, D.C.: Government Printing Office, 1945. Franklin D. Scott and Elaine Tegler, comps. (This work is found in American Historical Association, *Annual Report for the Year 1944*, Vol. I, pt. 2, pp. 65–292.)

Women's Magazines, 1693–1968. London: Michael Joseph, 1970. Cynthia White, comp.

Hispanic American Periodicals Index. Los Angeles: U.C.L.A. Latin American Center Publications, 1974–. Barbara H. Valk, ed.

Foreign Affairs 50-Year Index: Vols. 1–50, 1922–1972. New York: Council on Foreign Relations, 1973. Robert J. Palmer, comp.

The Pacific Historical Review: A Cumulative Index to Volumes I–XLIII, 1932–1974. Berkeley: University of California Press, 1976. Anne M. Hager and Everett Gordon, comps.

Fifty Year Index: Mississippi Valley Historical Review, 1914–1964. Bloomington, Ind.: Organization of American Historians, 1973. Francis J. Krauskopf, comp.

Index to Economic Journals. American Economic Association, 1886–present. Homewood, Ill.: R. D. Irwin.

Guide to the Hispanic American Historical Review: 1918–1945, 1945–1955. Durham, N.C.: Duke University Press, 1956–1975. Durham, N.C.: Duke University Press, 1980. Stanley R. Ross, Wilbur Chaffee, eds.

Index to the Canadian Historical Review. Toronto: University of Toronto Press, 1920–.

Historical Periodicals

Following is a list of some of the best-known historical periodicals published in the United States, Britain, and Canada and written for professional and student researchers. Some of these journals have their own cumulative indexes (like that to the *American Historical Review* listed previously) and thus can be useful places to begin the search for historical material. There are also many highly specialized periodicals in history. For example, most state historical societies publish journals. Be sure to examine periodical indexes that include the journals most closely related to your subject. Many periodicals are becoming available on the World Wide Web. (See "Electronic Reference Sources," pp. 204–11.)

U. S., British, and Canadian Historical Journals

Agricultural History
American Historical Review
American Jewish History
The American Journal of Legal History
American Quarterly
The Americas
Bulletin of the Institute of Historical
  Research
Business History Review
Cambridge Historical Journal
Canadian Historical Review
Canadian Journal of History
Central European History
China Quarterly
Comparative Studies in Society and
  History
Current History
Daedalus
Diplomatic History
Early Medieval History
Economic History Review
Economic Journal
Eighteenth Century Studies
English Historical Review
Ethnohistory
Feminist Studies
Film and History
French Historical Studies
Gender and History
Hispanic American Historical Review
The Historian
Historical Journal
Historical Methods
Historical Research
History
History and Theory
History of Education Quarterly
History of Political Economy
History of Religions
The History Teacher
International Journal of African
  Historical Studies

International Review of Social History
Irish Historical Studies
Isis
Journal of African History
Journal of American History
Journal of American Studies
Journal of Asian Studies
Journal of Black Studies
Journal of British Studies
Journal of Canadian Studies
Journal of Contemporary History
Journal of the Early Republic
Journal of Ecclesiastical History
Journal of Economic History
Journal of the History of Biology
Journal of the History of Ideas
Journal of Imperial and
  Commonwealth History
Journal of Interdisciplinary History
Journal of Japanese Studies
Journal of Latin American History
Journal of Modern History
Journal of Near Eastern Studies
Journal of Negro History
Journal of Political Thought
Journal of Popular Culture
The Journal of Psychohistory
Journal of Religious History
Journal of Social History
Journal of Southern History
Journal of Sports History
Journal of Urban History
Journal of Women's History
Journal of World History
Labor History
Latin American Research Review
Mid-America
Middle East Review
Oral History Review
Pacific Affairs
Pacific Historical Review
Past and Present

Political Studies	*Social History*
The Public Historian	*Social Science History*
Renaissance Quarterly	*Speculum*
Russian History	*Transactions of the Royal*
Scottish History Review	*Historical Society*
Slavic Review	*Western Historical Quarterly*
Slavic Studies	*William and Mary Quarterly*

Book Review Indexes

In addition to articles, historical periodicals usually contain reviews of recently published books on historical subjects. If you wish to know the content of a particular book or to find out what other historians thought of it, you can look up the reviews of it. The indexes in the following list organize book reviews by author, title, and sometimes by subject. They indicate which periodicals reviewed the book and in what issue. If the index is annual, you will need to know the year of publication of the book in which you are interested. Most books are reviewed within one to two years after publication. Book reviews are also available on CD-ROM. (See "Electronic Reference Sources," pp. 204–11.)

Index to Book Reviews in Historical Periodicals. Metuchen, N.J.: Scarecrow, 1974–.

Combined Retrospective Index to Book Reviews in Scholarly Journals, 1886–1974. 15 vols. Arlington, Va.: Carrollton Press, 1982.

Book Review Digest. New York: Wilson, 1905–present. Monthly.

Index to Book Reviews in the Humanities. Detroit: Gale, 1960–present. Annual.

Book Review Digest: Author/Title Index, 1905–1974. 4 vols. New York: Wilson, 1976. Leslie Dunmore-Lieber, ed.

New York Times Book Review Index, 1896–1970. 5 vols. New York: New York Times, 1973.

National Library Service Cumulative Book Review Index, 1905–1974. 6 vols. Princeton: National Library Service Co., 1975.

Book Review Index. Detroit: Gale, 1965–present. Bimonthly.

Book Review Index: A Master Accumulation, 1969–1979. 7 vols. Detroit: Gale, 1980. Gary C. Tarbert, ed.

Government Publications and Public Documents

The works included here are guides to books, pamphlets, speeches, treaties, hearings, reports, and so on, published by public agencies. This list, like most in this appendix, is confined to works in English and is by no means complete. If your research topic is related to governmental affairs at any level, these works can lead you to documents and publications by or about the agencies you are studying. The major publications of the U.S. government are available at many libraries. Many U.S. government documents are also available on the World Wide Web.

International Agencies

Guide to League of Nations Publications: A Bibliographical Survey of the Work of the League, 1920–1947. New York: Columbia University Press, 1951. Hans Aufricht, comp.

United Nations Documents Index. New York: United Nations Library, 1950–1977. These volumes are supplemented by *UNDOC: Current Index*.

Foreign Government Publications

Great Britain, Parliament: Parliamentary Debates. London: 1803–present.

U.S. Government Publications

A great many U. S. government documents are also available at a variety of sites on the World Wide Web.

Introduction to United States Government Information Sources. 5th ed. Englewood: Libraries Unlimited, 1996. Joe Morehead and Mary Fetzer, eds.

Subject Guide to Major United States Government Publications. Chicago: American Library Association, 1987. William J. Wiley, comp.

Guide to United States Government Publications. McLean, Va.: Documents Index, 1985. John L. Andriot, ed. Cumulative bimonthly supplements.

Monthly Catalogue of United States Government Publications. Washington, D.C.: Government Printing Office, 1895–present.

United States Congressional Committee Hearings Index, 1833–1969. Washington, D.C.: CIS, 1981–.

United States Congressional Committee Prints Index from Earliest Publications through 1969. 5 vols. Washington, D.C.: CIS, 1980.

United States Serial Set Indexes: American State Papers . . . 1789–1969. Washington, D.C.: CIS, 1975.

Subject Guide to United States Reference Sources. Littleton, Colo.: Libraries Unlimited, 1985. Judith Schick Robinson, ed.

Annotated Bibliography of Bibliographies on Selected Government Publications and Supplementary Guides to the Superintendent of Documents Classification System. Kalamazoo, Mich.: Western Michigan University, 1967–1990. Alexander C. Body, ed.

(For sources on local U.S. history, see "Sources for Family History Research" on pp. 214–15.)

Subject Bibliographies

A subject bibliography lists printed works on a particular topic. The ones listed here are those that the beginning student is most likely to obtain. Emphasis has been placed on bibliographies that (1) are written especially for students, (2) are of recent publication or republication and therefore likely to be in new library collections, (3) contain predominantly or solely works in the English language, and (4) are general rather than specialized. If the title of a bibliography indicates that it is annotated, this means that it not only *lists* books on a particular topic but also provides a brief description of their contents. (In some instances, helpful sources that are not bibliographies have been included.)

Disciplines Other than History

The following bibliographies list works in fields other than history. If an important aspect of your research topic falls under other major branches of knowledge, then you might find valuable materials in nonhistorical publications.

A Select Bibliography: Asia, Africa, Eastern Europe, Latin America. New York: American University, 1960, plus supplements. These are studies in the social sciences covering the developing countries of the world. For more recent works, see *Cumulative Supplement, 1961–1971* and *1972–1982.*

Sources of Information in the Social Sciences. Chicago: American Library Association, 1986. William H. Webb, ed.

Sources of Information in the Humanities. 3 vols. Chicago: American Library Association, 1982. John F. Wilson, ed.

The Humanities: A Selective Guide to Information Sources. Englewood, Colo.: Libraries Unlimited, 1994. Ron Blazek and Elizabeth Aversa, eds.

Specialized Branches of History

Encyclopedia of Medical History. New York: McGraw-Hill, 1985. Roderick E. McGrew, ed.

Dictionary of the History of Ideas. New York: Scribner's, 1968–1974. Philip P. Wiener, ed.

History of Psychology: A Guide to Information Sources. Detroit: Gale, 1979. Wayne Viney, Michael Wertheimer, and Marilyn Lou Wertheimer, eds.

ISIS Cumulative Bibliography: A Bibliography of the History of Science from Isis Critical Bibliographies. London: History of Science Society, 1971–1975 and 1986–1997.

Bibliography of the History of Medicine. Bethesda, Md.: National Library of Medicine, 1965–. Also available on the World Wide Web.

New Oxford History of Music. 10 vols. Oxford: Oxford University Press, 1954–1985.

The Encyclopedia of Military History: From 3500 B.C. to the Present. New York: Harper & Row, 1993. Ernest R. Dupuy and Trevor N. Dupuy, eds.

The Holocaust: An Annotated Bibliography. Haverford, Pa.: Catholic Libraries Association, 1985. Harry James Cargas, ed.

The New Standard Jewish Encyclopedia. Garden City, N.Y.: Doubleday, 1992. Geoffrey Wigoder, ed.

Psychohistorical Inquiry: A Comprehensive Research Bibliography. New York: Garland, 1984. William J. Gilmore, ed.

Companion Encyclopedia of the History of Medicine. New York: Routledge, 1997.

Encyclopedia of the Holocaust. New York: Macmillan, 1990.

The Cold War, 1945–1991. 3 vols. Detroit: Gale, 1992. Benjamin Frankel, ed.

Dictionary of Concepts in History. New York: Greenwood, 1988. Harry Ritter.

Church History: An Introduction to Research, Reference Works, and Methods. Grand Rapids, Mich.: Wm. B. Erdmans, 1996. James E. Bradley and Richard A. Muller, eds.

General World History

The remainder of this appendix contains the basic source material for historical research — history bibliographies. Once you have chosen your research topic and theme, these bibliographies and the reference collection of your library should be your initial step in finding sources. For the convenience of the beginning student, the list of subject bibliographies is separated according to the chronological period or geographical area that the works cover. The bibliographies themselves break down the topics even further.

Don't expect to find an entire bibliography dedicated to your particular topic. Choose the ones that cover the period or area into which your topic falls. Remember, your library will probably not have all of these books. If the most promising bibliography is not there, try a different work. As with other reference sources, some of these works are available in electronic form.

American Historical Association: A Guide to Historical Literature. Oxford: Oxford University Press, 1995. Mary Beth Norton, ed. This work has chapters on all periods and areas, and on many specialized topics.

Historical Abstracts. Santa Barbara, Cal.: ABC-Clio, 1955–present. Part A: Modern History (1450–1914); Part B: The Twentieth Century (1914–present). Eric H. Boehm, ed. This is the best source for articles in history journals. Also available on CD-ROM and on the World Wide Web.

World Historical Fiction Guide. Metuchen, N.J.: Scarecrow Press, 1973. Daniel McGarry and Sarah White, eds. If you are studying historical novels, this is an important source.

Serial Bibliographies and Abstracts in History: An Annotated Guide. Westport, Conn.: Greenwood Press, 1986. David Henige, ed.

Bibliographies in History. Santa Barbara, Cal.: ABC-Clio, 1988.

Reference Sources in History: An Introductory Guide. Santa Barbara, Cal.: ABC-Clio, 1990. Ronald H. Fritze et al., eds.

World History from Earliest Times to 1800. Oxford: Oxford University Press, 1988. H. Judge, ed.

Encyclopedia of Nationalism. New York: Paragon House, 1990. Louis L. Snyder, ed.

Slavery and Slaving in World History, A Bibliography. New York: M. E. Sharpe, 1997–1998. Joseph C. Miller, ed.

Ancient History

The Encyclopedia of Ancient Civilizations. New York: Mayflower Books, 1980. Arthur Cotterell, ed.

The Cambridge Ancient History. Cambridge: Cambridge University Press, 1923–1939, 1951–1954, 1970–present. This is a multivolume historical work with extensive bibliographies.

The Oxford History of the Classical World. Oxford: Oxford University Press, 1986. John Boardman et al., eds. An excellent bibliography is included.

The Encyclopedia of Ancient Egypt. New York: Gramercy, 1999. Margaret Bunson, ed.

Civilizations of the Ancient Near East. New York: Scribner's, 1995. Jack S. Sasson, ed.

Civilizations of the Ancient Mediterranean: Greece and Rome. New York: Scribner's, 1988. Michael Grant and Paul A. Cimbala, eds.

Encyclopedia of Early Christianity. New York: Garland, 1997. Everett Ferguson et al., eds.

Medieval History

A Guide to the Study of Medieval History. New York: F. S. Crofts & Sons, 1931. Louis J. Paetow. This guide is updated in a supplement by Gray C. Boyce, Medieval Academy of America, 1980, and by:

Literature of Medieval History, 1930–1975. 5 vols. Millwood, N.Y.: Kraus International Publisher, 1981. Gray C. Boyce, ed.

Cambridge Medieval History. Cambridge: Cambridge University Press, 1911–1936.

The New Cambridge Medieval History. New York: Cambridge, 1995. Rosamond McKitterick, ed.

Dictionary of the Middle Ages. New York: Scribner's, 1982–1989. Joseph R. Strayer, ed.

The Middle Ages: A Concise Encyclopedia. New York: Thames and Hudson/Norton, 1989. H. R. Loyn, ed.

Atlas of Medieval Europe. New York: Facts on File, 1983. Donald Matthew, comp.

Dictionary of Medieval Civilization. New York: Macmillan, 1984. Joseph Dahmus, ed.

Early Modern and Modern European History

The Longman Handbook of Modern European History, 1763–1835. New York: Longman, 1987.

Modern European History, 1494–1789: A Select Bibliography. London: Historical Association of London, 1966. Alun Davies, comp.

Modern European History: 1789 to the Present. New York: M. Weiner Publishing, 1986.

The European Powers in the First World War: An Encyclopedia. New York: Garland, 1999. Spencer C. Tucker, ed.

Cambridge Modern History. Cambridge: Cambridge University Press, 1902–1911; reissued, 1970. These history volumes have large bibliographies. *The New Cambridge Modern History,* however, has no bibliography.

A Bibliography of Modern History. Cambridge: Cambridge University Press, 1968. John Roach, ed. This bibliography was created to accompany *The New Cambridge Modern History.*

Renaissance Humanism, 1300–1550: A Bibliography of Materials in English. New York: Garland, 1985. Benjamin Kohl, ed.

Modern European Imperialism: A Bibliography of Books and Articles, 1815–1972. Boston: G. K. Hall, 1974. John P. Halstead, comp.

Women in Western European History: A Select Chronological, Geographical and Topical Bibliography from Antiquity to the French Revolution. Westport, Conn.: Greenwood Press, 1982. Linda Frey, Marsha Frey, and Joanne Schneider, eds.

Women in Western European History: A Select Chronological, Geographical, and Topical Bibliography: The Nineteenth and Twentieth Centuries. Westport, Conn.: Greenwood Press, 1984. Linda Frey and Marsha Frey, eds.

The Columbia Dictionary of European Political History Since 1914. Berkeley: University of California Press, 1992. John Stevenson, gen. ed.

The Oxford Encyclopedia of the Reformation. New York: Oxford, 1996. Hans J. Hillerbrand, ed.

Modern Europe: France, Italy, Spain, Germany, Scandinavia

Historical Dictionary of the French Fourth and Fifth Republics, 1946–1991. Westport, Conn.: Greenwood Press, 1992. Wayne Northcutt, ed.

Dictionary of Modern Italian History. Westport, Conn.: Greenwood Press, 1985. Frank J. Coppa, ed.-in-chief.

Modern Italian History: An Annotated Bibliography. Westport, Conn.: Greenwood Press, 1990. Frank J. Coppa and William Roberts, comps. A companion to *Dictionary of Modern Italian History.*

Historical Dictionary of Modern Spain, 1700–1988. Westport, Conn.: Greenwood Press, 1990. Robert W. Kern, ed.-in-chief.

Nazism, Resistance, and the Holocaust in World War II: A Bibliography. Metuchen, N.J.: Scarecrow Press, 1985. Vera Laska, ed.

Modern Germany: An Encyclopedia of History, People and Culture, 1871–1900. New York: Garland, 1998. Dieter K. Bose, ed.

Historical Dictionary of Germany. Metuchen, N.J.: Scarecrow, 1994. Wayne C. Thompson, Susan L. Thompson, and Juliet S. Thompson, eds.

France. ABC-Clio, 1990. Frances Chambers, ed.

Dictionary of Scandinavian History. Westport, Conn.: Greenwood Press, 1986. Byron J. Nordstrom, ed.

Scandinavian History: 1520–1970. London: Historical Association, 1984.

British History

British History to 1789

A Bibliography of English History to 1485. Oxford: Clarendon Press, 1975. Edgar B. Graves, ed.

The Blackwell Encyclopedia of Anglo-Saxon England. New York: Blackwell, 1999. Michael Lapidge, ed.

Women in Early Modern England, 1500–1700. New York: Garland, 1998. Jacqueline Eales, ed.

Tudor England, 1485–1603: A Bibliographical Handbook. Cambridge: Cambridge University Press, 1968. Mortimer Levine, comp.

A Bibliography of British History, Stuart Period, 1603–1714. Oxford: Clarendon Press, 1970. Mary Keeler, ed.

Early Modern British History, 1485–1760. London: Historical Association of London, 1970. Helen Miller and Aubrey Newman, comps.

A Bibliography of British History, The Eighteenth Century, 1714–1789. Oxford: Clarendon Press, 1951. Stanley Pargellis and D. J. Medley, eds.

The Kings of Medieval England, c. 560–1485: A Survey and Research Guide. Lanham, Md.: Scarecrow Press, 1996. Larry W. Usilton, ed.

British History Since 1789

The Oxford History of England: Consolidated Index. Oxford: Clarendon/Oxford University Press, 1991. Richard Raper, comp.

British History Since 1760: A Select Bibliography. London: Historical Association of London, 1970. Ian R. Christie, comp.

A Bibliography of British History, 1789–1851. Oxford: Clarendon Press, 1977. Lucy Brown and Ian R. Christie, eds.

A Bibliography of British History, 1914–1989. Oxford: Clarendon Press, 1996. Keith Robbins, ed.

Modern England, 1901–1970: A Bibliographical Handbook. Cambridge: Cambridge University Press, 1976. Alfred F. Havighurst, comp.

British Economic and Social History: A Bibliographical Guide. 3d ed. Manchester: Manchester University Press, 1995. W. H. Chaloner and R. C. Richardson, eds.

A Dictionary of British History. New York: Stein and Day, 1983. J. P. Kenyon, ed.

Victorian Britain: An Encyclopedia. New York: Garland, 1988. Sally Mitchell, ed.

The Cambridge Historical Encyclopedia of Great Britain and Ireland. Cambridge: Cambridge University Press, 1985. Christopher Haigh, ed.

Irish, Scottish, and British Empire History

A Dictionary of Irish History Since 1800. Totowa, N.J.: Barnes & Noble, 1980. D. J. Hickey and J. E. Doherty, eds.

A Bibliography of Works Relating to Scotland, 1916–1950. Edinburgh: Edinburgh University Press, 1959–1960. P. D. Hancock, ed.

Cambridge History of the British Empire. Cambridge: Cambridge University Press, 1929–1959. John Rose, Arthur Newton, and Ernest Benians, comps.

A Chronicle of Irish History Since 1500. Savage, Md.: Rowman and Littlefield, 1990. J. E. Doherty and D. J. Hickey, eds.

East European History

The American Bibliography of Slavic and East European Studies. Stanford: American Association for the Advancement of Slavic Studies, 1967–present.

Poland's Past and Present: A Select Bibliography of Works in English. Newtonville, Mass.: Oriental Research Partners, 1977. Norman Davies, ed.

Yugoslavia: A Comprehensive English-Language Bibliography. Wilmington, Del.: Scholarly Resources, 1993. Francine Friedman, ed.

Russian History (and USSR)

A Bibliography of Works in English on Early Russian History to 1800. New York: Barnes & Noble, 1969. Peter A. Crowther, comp.

Books in English on the Soviet Union, 1917–1973: A Bibliography. New York: Garland, 1975. David L. Jones, comp.

The Rise and Fall of the Soviet Union: A Selected Bibliography of Sources in English. Westport, Conn.: Greenwood Press, 1992. Abraham J. Edelheit and Hershel Edelheit, eds.

The American Bibliography of Slavic and East European Studies. Stanford, Cal.: American Association for the Advancement of Slavic Studies, 1967–present.

Russia and the Former Soviet Union: A Bibliographic Guide to English Publications, 1986–1991. Englewood, Colo.: Libraries Unlimited, 1994. Helen F. Sullivan and Robert H. Burger, eds.

An Atlas of Russian History. New Haven: Yale University Press, 1970. Allen F. Chew, ed.

The Modern Encyclopedia of Russian and Soviet History. Gulf Breeze, Fla.: Academic International Press, 1976–. Plus supplements.

The Soviet Union: A Biographical Dictionary. New York: Macmillan, 1991. Archie Brown, ed.

Soviet Foreign Policy, 1918–1945: A Guide to Research and Research Materials. Wilmington, Del.: Scholarly Resources, 1991. Robert H. Johnston, ed.

Dictionary of the Russian Revolution. Westport, Conn.: Greenwood Press, 1989. George Jackson, ed.

The Russian Revolution, 1905–1921: A Bibliographic Guide to the Works in English. Westport, Conn.: Greenwood, 1995. Murray Frame, ed.

Ukraine: A Bibliographic Guide to English Language Publications. Englewood, Colo.: Ukrainian Academic Press, 1990. Bohdan Wynar, ed.

African History[1]

The Encyclopedia of Precolonial Africa. Walnut Creek, Cal.: AltaMira Press, 1997. Joseph O. Vogel, ed.

An Atlas of African History. New York: Africana Publisher, 1978. J. D. Fage, ed.

Cambridge History of Africa. 8 vols. Cambridge University Press, 1975–1986.

Africa South of the Sahara: A Bibliography for Undergraduate Libraries. Williamsport, Pa.: Bro-Dart, 1971. Peter Duignan, ed.

---

[1]For the northern African states that border on the Mediterranean, see Near and Middle Eastern History.

Africa and the World: An Introduction to the History of Sub-Saharan Africa from Antiquity to 1840. San Francisco: Chandler, 1972. Peter Duignan and Lewis H. Gann, eds.

Historical Dictionary of——. Metuchen, N.J.: Scarecrow Press, 1972–. This is a series of historical dictionaries including separate volumes for most African nations.

South African History: A Bibliographic Guide with Special Reference to Territorial Expansion and Colonization. New York: Garland Publishing, 1984. Naomi Musiker, ed.

Dictionary of African Historical Biography. Berkeley: University of California Press, 1986. Mark R. Lipschultz and R. Kent Rasmusson, eds.

African Bibliography. Manchester, Eng.: Manchester University Press, 1984–.

Near and Middle Eastern History

The Islamic Near East and North Africa: An Annotated Guide to Books in English for Non-Specialists. Littleton, Colo.: Libraries Unlimited, 1977. David W. Littlefield, ed.

Books on Asia from the Near East to the Far East: A Guide for General Readers. Toronto: University of Toronto Press, 1981. Eleazir Birnbaum, ed.

Middle East and Islam: A Bibliographical Introduction. Geneva: Inter Documentation, 1979. Derek Hopwood and Diana Grimwood-Jones, eds.

Encyclopedia of Islam. Leiden, Netherlands: E. J. Brill, 1960–present. C. E. Botsworth et al., eds.

The Cambridge Encyclopedia of the Middle East and North Africa. Cambridge: Cambridge University Press, 1988. Trevor Mostyn, exec. ed.

The Oxford Dictionary of Byzantium. Oxford: Oxford University Press, 1991. Alexander P. Kazhdan, ed.

Oxford Encyclopedia of the Modern Islamic World. New York: Oxford, 1995. This covers the eighteenth century to the present.

General Asian History

Encyclopedia of Asian History. New York: Scribner's, 1988. Ainslis T. Embree, ed.

Cumulative Bibliography of Asian Studies, 1941–1965, 1966–1970. Boston: G. K. Hall, 1972.

Bibliography of Asian Studies. Ann Arbor: Association for Asian Studies, 1956–1991.

Historical and Cultural Dictionary of ——. Metuchen, N.J.: Scarecrow Press, 1972–present. This is a series of dictionaries including separate volumes for most Asian nations.

Indian, Pakistani, and Sri Lankan History

India: A Critical Bibliography. Tucson: University of Arizona Press, 1980. J. Michael Mahar, ed.

Cambridge History of India. New York: Macmillan, 1922–1953. See bibliography at end of volumes.

An Historical Atlas of South Asia. New York: Oxford University Press, 1992. Joseph E. Schwartzberg, ed.

A Dictionary of Indian History. New York: Braziller, 1977. Sachchidananda Bhattacharya.

South Asian Civilizations: A Bibliographical Synthesis. Chicago: University of Chicago Press, 1981. Maureen Patterson, ed.

Cambridge Encyclopedia of India, Pakistan, Sri Lanka, Nepal, Bhutan and the Maldives. Cambridge: Cambridge University Press, 1989. Francis Robinson, ed.

Southeast Asian History

Southeast Asia: A Critical Bibliography. Tucson: University of Arizona Press, 1969. Kennedy G. Tregonning, ed.

Vietnam: A Guide to Reference Sources. Boston: G. K. Hall, 1977. Michael Cotter, ed.

The Wars in Vietnam, Cambodia, and Laos, 1945–1982: A Bibliographic Guide. Santa Barbara, Cal.: ABC-Clio, 1984. Richard Dean Burns and Milton Leitenberg, eds.

Vietnam Studies: An Annotated Bibliography. Lanham, Md.: Scarecrow Press, 1997. Carl Singleton, ed.

Chinese History

Modern China: An Encyclopedia of History, Culture, and Nationalism. New York: Garland, 1998. Wang Ke-wen, ed.

Dictionary of Chinese History. London: Frank Cass, 1979. Michael Dillon, ed.

Historical Atlas of China. Chicago: Aldine, 1966. Albert Herrmann, ed.

Chinese History: A Bibliography. New York: Gordon Press, 1978. Leona Rasmussen Phillips, ed.

China Bibliography: A Research Guide to Reference Works about China Past and Present. Honolulu: University of Hawaii Press, 1999. Harriet T. Zurndorfer, ed.

Japanese and Korean History

Japan and Korea: A Critical Bibliography. Westport, Conn.: Greenwood Press, 1982. Bernard Silberman, ed

The Cambridge Dictionary of Japan, Volume 4: Early Modern Japan. Cambridge: Cambridge University Press, 1991. John Whitney Hall, ed.

Japanese History and Culture from Ancient to Modern Times: Seven Basic Bibliographies. New York: Markus Wiener, 1995. John Dower and Timothy George, eds.

Japanese Studies from Pre-History to 1990: A Bibliographical Guide. Manchester, Eng.: Manchester University Press, 1992. Richard Perren, ed.

Japan. Santa Barbara, Cal.: ABC-Clio, 1990. Frank L. Shulman, ed.

Studies on Korea: A Scholar's Guide. Honolulu: University of Hawaii Press, 1980. Han-kyo Kim, ed.

Latin American and Caribbean History

Latin America: A Guide to the Historical Literature. Austin: University of Texas Press, 1971. Charles C. Griffin, ed.

Encyclopedia of Latin American History and Culture. New York: Scribner's, 1995. Barbara Tenenbaum, ed.

A Guide to the History of Brazil, 1500–1822: The Literature in English. Santa Barbara, Cal.: ABC-Clio, 1980. Francis A. Dutra, ed.

Handbook of Latin American Studies. Cambridge, Mass.: Harvard University Press, 1936–1947; and Gainesville: University of Florida Press, 1948–present. Annual volume.

The Complete Caribbeana, 1900–1975: A Bibliographical Guide to the Scholarly Literature. Millwood, N.Y.: KTO Press, 1978. Comitas Lambros, ed.

The Cambridge Encyclopedia of Latin America and the Caribbean. Cambridge: Cambridge University Press, 1992. Simon Collier et al., eds.

Latin America and the Caribbean: A Critical Guide to Research Sources. New York: Greenwood, 1992. Paula H. Covington et al., eds.

Index to Latin American Periodical Literature, 1929–1960. New York: G. K. Hall, 1962. Pan American Union. Updated through 1970 by G. K. Hall, 1980.

Latin America: A Guide to Economic History, 1830–1930. Berkeley: University of California Press, 1977. Stanley Stein and R. Cortés Conde, eds.

Historical Dictionary of ——. Metuchen, N.J.: Scarecrow Press. This is a series of historical dictionaries including separate volumes for most Latin American nations.

Latin American Politics: A Historical Bibliography. Santa Barbara, Cal.: ABC-Clio, 1986.

Canadian History

Encyclopedia Canadiana. Toronto: Grolier, 1977.

Bibliographia Canadiana. Don Mills, Ont.: Longman Canada Limited, 1973. Claude Thibault, comp.

The Oxford Companion to Canadian History and Literature. Toronto: Oxford University Press, 1967, *Supplement,* 1973. Norah Story, comp.

Canadian Reference Sources: A Select Guide. 2nd ed. Ottawa: Canadian Library Association, 1973, *Supplement,* 1981. Dorothy E. Ryder, ed.

Canada Since 1867: A Bibliographical Guide. Toronto: Samuel Stevens, 1977. J. L. Granatstein and Paul Stevens, eds.

Western Canada Since 1870: A Select Bibliography and Guide. Vancouver: University of British Columbia Press, 1978. Alan F. J. Artibise, ed.

Bibliography of Ontario History, 1867–1976: Cultural, Economic, Political and Social. 2 vols. Buffalo: University of Toronto Press, 1980. Olga B. Bishop, ed.

Economic History of Canada: A Guide for Information Sources. Detroit: Gale, 1978. Trevor J. O. Dick, ed.

Historical Atlas of Canada. Toronto: University of Toronto Press, 1987. R. Cole Harris and Donald Kerr, eds.

The Canadian Encyclopedia. Edmonton, Alta.: Hurtig, 1985. James H. March, ed.-in-chief.

U.S. History

In the case of U.S. history, the bibliographies have been arranged by certain topics of special interest to students.

Many of this first group of bibliographies have separate chapters on specialized topics.

Harvard Guide to American History. Rev. ed. Cambridge, Mass.: Harvard University Press, 1979. Oscar Handlin et al., eds. Chapters six through thirty contain detailed reading lists for many periods and topics in U.S. history.

The Reader's Companion to American History. Boston: Houghton Mifflin, 1991. Eric Foner and John A. Garraty, eds.

The American Historical Association's Guide to Historical Literature. 3d ed., 2 vols. Ithaca: Cornell University Press, 1995. Mary Beth Norton, ed. This guide contains a large section on U.S. history.

Writings on American History. Washington, D.C.: American Historical Association, 1956; and Millwood, N.Y.: KTO Press, 1976–present. The original series of volumes covers (with two brief lapses) books and articles written between 1902 and 1961. The new series is now annual and covers only articles written since 1962. Coverage of books is continued in:

Writings on American History, 1962–1973: A Subject Bibliography of Books and Monographs. 10 vols. White Plains, N.Y.: Kraus International Publications, 1985. James R. Masterson, comp.

Writings on American History, 1962–1973: A Subject Bibliography of Articles. 4 vols. Millwood, N.Y.: KTO Press, 1976. James J. Dougherty, ed. This work is continued in:

Writings on American History: A Subject Bibliography of Articles. 1974–1990.

America: History and Life. Santa Barbara, Cal.: ABC-Clio, 1954–present. After 1965, titled *America: History and Life: A Guide to Periodical Literature*. Each volume now has four parts: (1) abstracts of journal articles, (2) an index to book reviews, (3) a bibliography of articles and dissertations, and (4) an annual index. The best source for articles on U.S. history. Also on CD-ROM.

U.S. History: A Bibliography of the New Writings on American History. Manchester, Eng.: Manchester University Press, 1995. Louise Merriam and J. W. Oberly, eds.

Encyclopedia of American History. New York: Harper & Row, 1982. Richard B. Morris, ed.

Dictionary of American History. New York: Scribner's, 1942–1961. James T. Adams and Roy V. Coleman, eds. Revised, 1976. Supplement, 1996.

Concise Dictionary of American History. New York: Scribner's, 1983. David W. Voorhees, ed. This is an abridgement of the *Dictionary of American History*.

Handbook for Research in American History: A Guide to Bibliographies and Other Reference Works. 1994. 2d ed. Lincoln: University of Nebraska Press, Francis Paul Prucha, ed.

A Bibliography of American Autobiographies. Madison: University of Wisconsin Press, 1961. Louis Kaplan et al., comps. An important source if you are researching the life of a historical figure.

American Autobiography, 1945–1980: A Bibliography. Madison: University of Wisconsin, 1982. Mary Louise Briscoe, ed. Companion to Kaplan's *Bibliography.*

Encyclopedia of American Political History: Studies of the Principal Movements and Ideas. 3 vols. New York: Scribner's, 1984. Jack P. Greene, ed.

Recently Published Articles. Washington, D.C.: American Historical Association, 1976–1990.

A Guide to the Study of the United States of America. Washington, D.C.: Library of Congress, 1960. *Supplement,* 1977. This work covers all fields of knowledge. It has several chapters on aspects of U.S. history.

For sources on the U.S. government, see "U.S. Government Publications" on page 183.

Regional, State, County, and Local U.S. History

The sources listed here can be supplemented by the appropriate sections of the *Harvard Guide to American History, Writings on American History,* and *America: History and Life.* For local histories, also see Appendix B, "Sources for Family History Research", pp. 214–15.

Directory of Historical Organizations in the United States and Canada, 1990. Nashville: American Association for State and Local History, 1990. Mary Bray Wheeler, comp. This volume includes the addresses of state and local historical societies. A continuing publication.

Directory of State and Local History Periodicals. Chicago: American Library Association, 1977. Milton Crouch and Hans Raum, comps.

A Bibliography of American County Histories. Baltimore: Genealogical Publishing Co., 1985. P. William Filby.

State Censuses: An Annotated Bibliography to Censuses of Population Taken after 1790 by States and Territories of the United States. New York: Burt Franklin, 1969. Henry J. Dubester, ed.

Encyclopedia of Urban America. Santa Barbara, Cal.: ABC-Clio, 1998. Neil L. Shumsky, ed.

The Encyclopedia of Southern History. Baton Rouge: Louisiana State University, 1979. David C. Roller, ed.

Encyclopedia of Southern Culture. Chapel Hill: University of North Carolina Press, 1989. Charles Reagan Wilson and William Ferris, eds.

United States Local Histories in the Library of Congress: A Bibliography. Baltimore: Magna Carta, 1975. Marion J. Kaminkow, ed.

Genealogical and Local History Books in Print. 4 vols. Washington, D.C.: Genealogical Books in Print, 1996–1997.

Encyclopedia of the American West. New York: Simon and Schuster/Macmillan, 1996.

Encyclopedia of the Confederacy. New York: Scribner's, 1993. Richard N. Current, ed.

Specific Periods

Colonial Wars of North America, 1512–1763: An Encyclopedia. New York: Garland, 1995. Alan Gallay, ed.

The Blackwell Encyclopedia of the American Revolution. Cambridge, Mass.: Basil Blackwell, 1991. Jack P. Greene, ed.

Encyclopedia of the North American Colonies. New York: Scribner's, 1993. Jacob E. Cooke, ed.

The Encyclopedia of Colonial and Revolutionary America. New York: Facts on File, 1989. John Faragher, ed.

The American Revolution, 1775–1783: An Encyclopedia. New York: Garland, 1993.

James Madison and the American Nation, 1751–1836: An Encyclopedia. New York: Scribner's, 1994. Robert A. Rutland, ed.

The United States in the First World War: An Encyclopedia. New York: Garland, 1999. Anne C. Venzon, ed.

Historical Dictionary of the Progressive Era, 1890–1920. Westport, Conn: Greenwood, 1988. John D. Buenker, ed.

Encyclopedia of the United States in the Twentieth Century. 4 vols. New York: Scribner's, 1996. Stanley Kutler, ed.

A Dictionary of Contemporary American History, 1945 to the Present. New York: Meridian, 1996. Stanley Hockman, ed.

Diplomatic History

A large number of U.S. foreign policy documents are available on the World Wide Web.

Foreign Affairs Bibliography: A Selected and Annotated List of Books on International Relations [1919–present]. New York: Harper & Row, 1933, 1943, 1953; and R. R. Bowker, 1964. Vol. 1 covers 1919–1932; vol. 2, 1932–1942; vol. 3, 1942–1952; vol. 4, 1952–1962; vol. 5, 1962–1972.

Foreign Relations of the United States. Washington, D.C.: Government Printing Office, 1861–present. United States Department of State. These volumes are issued regularly and contain actual diplomatic correspondence. These are *primary* sources rather than bibliographies. They are listed because many libraries have them.

Guide to American Foreign Relations Since 1700. Santa Barbara, Cal.: ABC-Clio, 1983. Richard Dean Burns, ed.

Writing About Vietnam: A Bibliography of the Literature of the Vietnam Conflict. Boston: G. K. Hall, 1989. Sandra M. Wittman, ed.

Encyclopedia of United States Foreign Relations. Oxford: Oxford University Press, 1997. Bruce Jentleson and Thomas Patterson, eds.

Cambridge History of American Foreign Relations. 4 vols. New York: Cambridge University Press, 1995. Bradford Perkins et al., eds. Also available on CD-ROM.

A Bibliography of United States–Latin American Relations Since 1810. Lincoln: University of Nebraska Press, 1968. David F. Trask et al., eds. *Supplement,* 1979.

Dictionary of American Diplomatic History. Westport, Conn.: Greenwood Press, 1989. John E. Findling, ed.

Encyclopedia of American Foreign Policy: Studies of the Principal Movements and Ideas. 3 vols. New York: Scribner's, 1978. Alex DeConde, ed.

Origins, Evolution and Nature of the Cold War: An Annotated Bibliography. Santa Barbara, Cal.: ABC-Clio, 1985. J. L. Black, ed.

Labor History

Labor in America: A Historical Bibliography. Santa Barbara, Cal.: ABC-Clio, 1985.

American Working Class History: A Representative Bibliography. New York: R. R. Bowker, 1983. Maurice F. Neufeld, Daniel J. Leab, and Dorothy Swanson.

Biographical Dictionary of American Labor. Rev. ed. Westport, Conn.: Greenwood Press, 1984. Gary Fink, ed.

Labor Unions. Westport, Conn.: Greenwood Press, 1977. Gary M. Fink, ed. Contains a brief history and bibliography for each major union.

Business and Economic History

Gale Encyclopedia of U.S. Economic History. Detroit: Gale Group, 1999. Thomas Carson, ed.

Biographical Dictionary of American Business Leaders. 4 vols. Westport, Conn.: Greenwood Press, 1983. John Ingham, ed.

American Economic History: An Annotated Bibliography. Englewood Cliffs, N.J.: Salem Press, 1994.

Encyclopedia of American Economic History. 3 vols. New York: Scribner's, 1980. Glen Porter, ed.

Dictionary of United States Economic History. Westport, Conn.: Greenwood Press, 1992. James S. Olson, ed.

African American History

Black/White Relations in American History: An Annotated Bibliography. Lanham, Md.: Scarecrow Press, 1998. Leslie V. Tischauser, ed.

A Bibliographic History of Blacks in America Since 1528. New York: McKay, 1971. Edgar A. Toppin, ed.

Encyclopedia of Black America. New York: DaCapo Press, 1988. Augustus Low, ed.

Afro-American History: A Bibliography. Santa Barbara, Cal.: ABC-Clio, 1981. Dwight L. Smith, ed.

Dictionary of American Negro Biography. New York: W. W. Norton, 1982. Rayford W. Logan and Michael Winston, eds.

Dictionary of Afro-American Slavery. New York: Greenwood Press, 1997. Randall M. Miller, ed.

Black Women in America: An Historical Encyclopedia. Bloomington: Indiana University Press, 1994.

Encyclopedia of African-American Culture and History. New York: Simon and Schuster/Macmillan, 1996. Jack Salzman, David L. Smith and Cornel West, eds.

Mexican American History

A Bibliography for Chicano History. Westport, Conn.: Greenwood Press, 1984. Matt S. Meier and Feliciano Rivera, comps.

Bibliography of Mexican-American History. Westport, Conn.: Greenwood Press, 1984. Matt S. Meier, comp.

Dictionary of Mexican American History. Westport, Conn.: Greenwood Press, 1981. Matt S. Meier and Feliciano Rivera, eds.

Puerto Rican History

Puerto Ricans on the United States Mainland. Totowa, N.J.: Rowman and Littlefield, 1972. Francesco Cordasco, ed.

The Puerto Ricans: An Annotated Bibliography. New York: Bowker, 1973. Paquita Vivó, ed.

An Annotated, Selected Puerto Rican Bibliography. New York: Columbia University Press, 1972. Enrique R. Bravo, comp.

Historical Dictionary of Puerto Rico and the United States Virgin Islands. Metuchen, N.J.: Scarecrow Press, 1973. Kenneth Farr, comp.

Women's History

Notable American Women, 1607–1950: A Biographical Dictionary. Cambridge, Mass.: Harvard University Press, 1974. Edward T. James, ed. 3 vols. Supplemented by *Notable American Women: The Modern Period.* 1980. This volume includes women who died between 1951 and 1975.

The American Woman in Colonial and Revolutionary Times, 1565–1800: A Syllabus with Bibliography. Westport, Conn.: Greenwood Press, 1975. Eugenie Leonard et al.

Women's Magazines, 1693–1968. London: Michael Joseph, 1970. Cynthia White, comp.

The Female Experience in Eighteenth- and Nineteenth-Century America: A Guide to the History of American Women. New York: Garland, 1982. Jill Conway, ed.

The Female Experience in Twentieth-Century America: A Guide to the History of American Women. New York: Garland, 1986. Jill Conway, ed.

Women in American History: A Bibliography. Santa Barbara, Cal.: ABC-Clio, 1979. Cynthia E. Harrison, ed.

Women's Studies Encyclopedia: History, Philosophy, and Religion. Vol. III. Westport, Conn.: Greenwood Press, 1991. Helen Tierney, ed.

Handbook of American Women's History. New York: Garland, 1990. Angela Howard Zophy, ed.

General Immigrant and Ethnic History

General immigrant and ethnic history bibliographies are the best to use if you are researching the history of a minority group not listed separately in this appendix or if you are unsure which group you wish to study.

Minority Studies: A Select Annotated Bibliography. Boston: G. K. Hall, 1975. Priscilla Oaks, ed.

A Handbook of American Minorities. New York: New York University Press, 1976. Wayne C. Miller.

Harvard Encyclopedia of American Ethnic Groups. Cambridge: Harvard University Press, 1980. Stephen Thernstrom, ed.

A Comprehensive Bibliography for the Study of American Minorities. 2 vols. New York: New York University Press, 1976. Wayne C. Miller.

Immigration and Ethnicity: A Guide to Information Sources. Detroit: Gale, 1977. John D. Buenker and Nicholas C. Burckel, eds.

Dictionary of American Immigrant History. Metuchen, N.J.: Scarecrow Press, 1990. Francesco Cordasco, ed.

European Immigrant and Ethnic History

European Immigration and Ethnicity in the United States and Canada: A Bibliography. Santa Barbara, Cal.: ABC-Clio, 1983. David L. Brye, ed.

German American History and Life: A Guide to Information Sources. Detroit: Gale, 1980. Michael Kereztesi and Gary Cocozzoli, eds.

Hungarians in the United States and Canada: A Bibliography. Minneapolis: Immigration History Research Center, 1977. Joseph Szeplaki, ed.

The British in America 1578–1970: A Chronology and Fact Book. Dobbs Ferry, N.Y.: Oceana, 1972. Howard B. Furer, ed. Volume covers the English, Scotch, Welsh, and Scotch-Irish.

The ——— in America: A Chronology and Fact Book. Dobbs Ferry, N.Y.: Oceana, 1971–present. This is a series with separate volumes on the Germans, Scandinavians, Italians, Poles, Dutch, Jews, Hungarians, and others.

The Italian-American Experience: An Encyclopedia. New York: Garland, 1999. Salvatore J. LaGumina et al., eds.

Asian Immigrant and Ethnic History

Asian American Studies: An Annotated Bibliography and Research Guide. Westport, Conn.: Greenwood Press, 1989. Hyung-Chan Kim, ed.

Asians in America: A Selected, Annotated Bibliography. Berkeley: University of California Press, 1983. Isao Fujimoto, ed.

Dictionary of Asian American History. Westport, Conn.: Greenwood Press, 1986. Hyung-Chan Kim, ed.

Native American History

Native Americans: An Encyclopedia of History, Culture and Peoples. Santa Barbara, Cal.: ABC-Clio, 1998.

A Bibliographical Guide to the History of Indian-White Relations in the United States. Chicago: University of Chicago Press, 1977. Francis Paul Prucha, ed. Continued in:

Indian-White Relations in the United States: A Bibliography of Works Published 1975–1980. Lincoln: University of Nebraska Press, 1982. Francis Paul Prucha, ed.

Indians of the United States and Canada: A Bibliography. Santa Barbara, Cal.: ABC-Clio, 1974. Dwight L. Smith, ed.

Handbook of American Indians North of Mexico. New York: Rowman and Littlefield, 1979. Frederick W. Hodge et al. This is a reprint of a 1910 work.

Encyclopedia of Native American Tribes. New York: Checkmark Books, 1999. Carl Waldman, ed.

Native American Periodicals and Newspapers, 1828–1982: Bibliography, Publishing

Record, and Holdings. Westport, Conn.: Greenwood Press, 1984. Maureen Hardy, comp.

Ethnographic Bibliography of North America. 5 vols. New Haven, Conn.: HRAF Press, 1975. George P. Murdock and Timothy J. O'Leary, eds.

Handbook of North American Indians. Washington, D.C.: Smithsonian Institution, 1978–1998. William C. Sturtevant, gen. ed.

Guide to Research on North American Indians. Chicago: American Library Association, 1983. Arlene B. Hirschfelder et al., eds.

Cambridge History of the Native Peoples of the Americas. Vol. 1. New York: Cambridge University Press, 1997. Bruce Triggas and Wilcomb Washburn, eds.

Social, Cultural, Intellectual, and Religious History

Social Reform and Reaction in America: An Annotated Bibliography. Santa Barbara, Cal.: ABC-Clio, 1984.

Encyclopedia of American Social History. New York: Scribner's, 1993. Mary K. Cayton, Elliott J. Gorn, Peter W. Williams, eds.

A Dictionary of American Social Change. Malabar, Fla.: Kreiger Publishing Company, 1982. Louis Filler.

Urban America: A Historical Bibliography. Santa Barbara, Cal.: ABC-Clio, 1983. Neil L. Shumsky and Timothy Crimmins, eds.

Urban History. Detroit: Gale, 1981. John D. Buenker, ed.

United States Cultural History: A Guide to Information Sources. Detroit: Gale, 1980. Philip I. Mitterling.

Encyclopedia of Lesbian and Gay Histories and Cultures. New York: Garland, 1999.

Encyclopedia of the American Religious Experience. New York: Scribner's, 1988. Charles H. Lippy, ed.

A Companion to American Thought. Oxford: Blackwell, 1995. Richard W. Fox and James T. Kloppenberg, eds.

Constitutional, Legal, and Military History

Encyclopedia of the American Military. New York: Scribner's, 1994. John E. Jessup, ed.

The Literature of American Legal History. New York: Oceana Pubs., 1985. William E. Nelson and John P. Reid.

Encyclopedia of the American Judicial System. New York: Scribner's, 1987. Robert J. Janosik, ed.

Encyclopedia of the American Constitution. New York: Macmillan, 1990. *Supplement,* 1992. Leonard Levy, ed.-in-chief.

Reference Guide to United States Military History, 1607–1815. New York: Replica Books, 1999. Charles R. Shrader, ed.

Dictionary of the Vietnam War. Westport, Conn.: Greenwood Press, 1988. James S. Olson, ed.

The United States in the First World War: An Encyclopedia. New York: Garland 1999.

Guide to the Sources of United States Military History. Hamden, Conn.: Archon Books, 1975. Robin Higham. *Supplements,* 1981, 1993.

American Naval History: A Guide. Lanham, Md.: Scarecrow Press, 1998. Paolo E. Coletta, ed.

Political History

Political Parties and Elections in the United States: An Encyclopedia. 2 vols. New York: Garland, 1991. L. Sandy Maisel, gen. ed.

Guide to the Presidency. Washington, D.C.: Congressional Quarterly, 1989. Michael Nelson, ed.

Guide to United States Elections. Washington, D.C.: Congressional Quarterly, 1985. John L. Moore, ed.

The American Presidency: A Historical Bibliography. Santa Barbara, Cal.: ABC-Clio, 1984.

Herbert Hoover: A Bibliography of His Times and Presidency. Wilmington, Del.: Scholarly Resources, 1991. Richard D. Burns, comp.

Dwight D. Eisenhower: A Bibliography of His Times and Presidency. Wilmington, Del.: Scholarly Resources, 1991. R. Alton Lee, comp.

Encyclopedia of the American Left. Oxford: Oxford University Press, 1998. Mari Jo Buhle, ed.

Historical Dictionary of the Progressive Era, 1890–1920. Westport, Conn.: Greenwood Press, 1988. John D. Buenker, ed.

American Reform and Reformers: A Biographical Dictionary. Westport, Conn.: Greenwood Press, 1996. Randall M. Miller and Paul A. Cimbala, eds.

Encyclopedia of the American Congress. New York: Simon and Schuster, 1995.

Encyclopedia of the American Presidency. New York: Simon and Schuster, 1994.

Protest, Power and Change: An Encyclopedia of Non-Violent Action. . . . New York: Garland, 1997.

Encyclopedia of American Political History: Studies of the Principal Movements and Ideals. 3 vols. New York: Scribner's, 1984. Jack P. Green, ed.

Miscellaneous Topics in United States History

Dickinson's American Historical Fiction. Metuchen, N.J.: Scarecrow Press, 1986. Virginia B. Gerhardstein.

American Family History: A Historical Bibliography. Santa Barbara, Cal.: ABC-Clio, 1984.

Biographical Dictionary of American Sports. Westport, Conn.: Greenwood Press, 1995. David L. Porter, ed.

Bibliography of North American Folklore and Folksong. New York: Dover Publications, 1961. Charles Haywood, ed.

Encyclopedia of American Agricultural History. Westport, Conn.: Greenwood Press, 1975. Edwin I. Schapsmeier and Frederick H. Schapsmeier.

A Subject Bibliography of the History of American Higher Education. Westport, Conn.: Greenwood Press, 1984. Mark Beach, comp.

The History of Science and Technology in the United States: A Critical and Selective Bibliography. New York: Garland, 1993. Marc Rothenberg, ed.

The Craft of Public History: An Annotated Select Bibliography. Westport, Conn.: Greenwood Press, 1983. David F. Trask and Robert W. Pomeroy III.

History of the Mass Media in the United States: An Encyclopedia. Chicago: Fitzroy Dearborn, 1998. Margaret A. Blanchard, ed.

Sources for Historical Statistics

World Statistical Data

Historical Tables, 58 B.C.–A.D. 1990. New York: Tuttle Publishing, 1991 Sigfrid II. Steinberg.

Statistics Sources 2000. Detroit: Gale, 1999. Steven R. Wasserman.

The International Almanac of Electoral History. Washington, D.C.: Congressional Quarterly, 1991. Thomas Mackie and Richard Rose.

Demographic Yearbook. New York: United Nations Statistical Office, 1949–present. Annual.

Population Index. Princeton, N.J.: Office of Population Research, 1935–present. Also available on the Web.

Statistical Yearbook. New York: United Nations Statistical Office, 1949–present.

European Statistical Data

European Political Facts, 1918–1990. 3d. ed. New York: St. Martin's Press, 1992. Christopher Cook and John Paxton.

The Gallup International Public Opinion Polls. [France: 1939, 1944–1975] New York: Random House, 1976. George H. Gallup.

International Historical Statistics: Europe, 1750–1993. New York: Stockton Press, 1996. B. R. Mitchell, ed.

African, Asian, Latin American, and Middle Eastern Statistical Data

Statistical Abstract of Latin America. Los Angeles: U.C.L.A. Center of Latin American Studies, 1955–present. James W. Wilkie, ed.

The Arab World, Turkey and the Balkans, 1878–1914: A Handbook of Historical Statistics. Boston: G. K. Hall, 1982. Justin McCarthy, ed.

International Historical Statistics: The Americas: 1750–1988. New York: Stockton Press, 1996. B. R. Mitchell, ed.

International Historical Statistics: Africa, Asia and Oceania: 1750–1993. New York: Stockton Press, 1996. B. R. Mitchell, ed.

British Statistical Data

Abstract of British Historical Statistics. Cambridge: Cambridge University Press, 1976. B. R. Mitchell.

Annual Abstract of Statistics. London: Central Statistical Office of Great Britain, 1915/1928–present.

British Labour Statistics: Historical Abstract, 1886–1968. London: Great Britain Department of Employment and Productivity, 1971.

The British Voter: An Atlas and Survey Since 1885. London: Batsford, 1981. M. Kinnear.

British Political Facts, 1900–1979. New York: St. Martin's Press, 1980. David Butler and Ann Sloman.

The Gallup International Public Opinion Polls: Great Britain, 1937–1975. Westport, Conn.: Greenwood Press, 1977. George H. Gallup.

British Historical Statistics. Cambridge: Cambridge University Press, 1988. B. R. Mitchell, ed.

U.S. and Canadian Statistical Data

Historical Statistics of the United States, Colonial Times to 1970. Washington, D.C.: Bureau of the Census, 1976, and Government Printing Office, 1989. Also available on CD-ROM and the Web.

Statistical Abstract of the United States. Washington, D.C.: Government Printing Office, 1878–present. Annual. Also available on the Web.

Historical Statistics of Canada. Ottawa: Statistics Canada, 1983. M. C. Urquhart.

Bureau of the Census Catalog of Publications, 1790–1972. Washington, D.C.: Bureau of the Census, 1974.

American Statistics Index . . . : A Complete Guide and Index to the Statistical Publications of the United States Government. Washington, D.C.: Congressional Information Service, 1973–present.

Federal Population Censuses 1790–1890: A Catalogue of Microfilm Copies of the Schedules. Washington, D.C.: National Archives Trust Fund Board, 1979. Catalogs of the 1900 and 1910 censuses were published in 1978 and 1982.

The Gallup Poll. New York: Random House and Scholarly Resources, 1935–present. George H. Gallup.

The Gallup Poll Cumulative Index: Public Opinion, 1935–1997. Wilmington, Del.: Scholarly Resources, 1999.

Guides to Photographs, Microfilms, Microforms, Movies, Recordings, and Oral History

A large number of the audio and video recordings mentioned in these works are becoming available on the World Wide Web.

Guide to Microforms in Print: Author, Title. Westport, Conn.: Meckler, 1985. Annual since 1961. Also see:

Guide to Microforms in Print: Subject. Westport, Conn.: Meckler, 1985. Annual since 1961. Now published by K. G. Saur Verlag, Munich.

Catalogue of National Archives Microfilm Publications. Washington, D.C.: N.A.R.S., 1974–present.

List of National Archives Microfilm Publications, 1947–1974. Washington, D.C.: N.A.R.S., 1974. Supplemented by:

Supplementary List of National Archives Publications, 1974–1982. Washington, D.C.: N.A.R.S., 1982.

Subject Guide to Microforms in Print. Washington, D.C.: Microcard Editions, 1962–present. Albert J. Diaz, ed.

Library of Congress Catalogue: Music and Phonorecords. Washington, D.C.: Library of Congress, 1953–present. Annual.

The Oral History Collection of Columbia University. New York: Columbia University Oral History Research Office, 1979. Elizabeth Mason and Louis M. Starr.

Oral History in the United States: A Directory. New York: Oral History Association, 1971. Gary L. Shumway, comp. Locates and describes oral history collections.

Oral History Index: An International Directory of Oral History Interviews. London: Meckler, 1990.

Picture Sources. New York: Special Libraries Association, 1983. Ernest H. Robl, ed.

Microform Research Collections. Meckler, 1984. 2d ed. Suzanne Cates Dodson, ed.

Pamphlets in American History: A Bibliographical Guide to the Microfilm Collections. 4 vols. Sanford, N.C.: Microfilming Corp. of America, 1979–1983.

Newspapers on Microfilm: United States, 1948–1983. Washington, D.C.: Library of Congress, 1984.

Directory of Oral History Collections. Phoenix: Oryx, 1988. Allen Smith, ed.

American Periodical Series, 1741–1900. Ann Arbor: University Microfilms, 1946–1978.

American Culture Series, 1493–1875. Ann Arbor: University Microfilms, 1979.

Guides to Dissertations, Archives, and Manuscripts

Dissertation Abstracts International. Ann Arbor: University Microfilms, 1938–present. Annual.

A Guide to Archives and Manuscripts in the United States. New Haven: Yale University Press, 1965. Philip C. Hamer, ed.

Directory of Archives and Manuscript Repositories in the United States. Phoenix: Oryx, 1988. This volume updates Hamer.

Guides to Archives and Manuscript Collections in the United States: An Annotated Bibliography. Westport, Conn.: Greenwood, 1994. Donald L. De Witt, ed.

The National Union Catalog of Manuscript Collections. Washington, D.C.: Library of Congress, 1962.

Electronic Reference Sources

Great changes in technology have created a universe of sources in electronic form for use in historical research. This digital information can be sorted by **search engines,** allowing you to sift through a tremendous amount of historical material from your home or school library. The **home page** or original search page of your library's **online catalog** will indicate how much of this digital material you can access. Some of this material will be in your library while much will be outside of it on the **World Wide Web.** (For an explanation of how to search your library's online catalog, see Chapter 4, pp. 81–86.)

As you already know, the Web is huge. The best researcher using the best search tools is able to explore only a small fraction of the billions of Web pages. Your goal is to use the best search tools and the best search terms in order to find the best material on your theme in a reasonable amount of time. Mentioned in this section are tools for general searching (engines and **directories**), major research sites (gateways), and specialized sites where historical materials are located. Searching can be a frustrating experience. One day the Web will be better organized, but for now there is no substitute for good search skills. It is wise to try several different ways of searching since no one search path will bring you to all of the available material. (For more on search techniques, see Chapter 4, pp. 93–99.) A poor choice of search terms can bring you tons of irrelevant information or none at all. Whenever you *do* get to a promising site, evaluate its usefulness with the "Guidelines for Evaluating Web Sites" on page 103. Always remember to **bookmark** a useful site.

Each of the search engines and each site on the Web has a specific **URL** (Uniform Resource Locator), and you must type it *exactly* in the line of your **Web browser.** *The URLs listed here are current as of May 2000.* URLs can change. If they do, you should reach a message with a forwarding address, though, unfortunately this is not always the case.

Databases on CD-ROM and on the World Wide Web

Until recently, many libraries purchased **CD-ROM** databases on disk. Many major databases are now also available on the World Wide Web. Since it is almost always easier to find what you are looking for if it is in your own library, check with the librarian before you seek databases on the Web.

The databases listed here are those that are still most commonly found on CD-ROM. Some contain statistical information while most refer to journal articles: either the article itself (**full text**) or just a **citation** (where the article can be found). Be sure to check the **date range** of the database. (For more on date range, see p. 85.) In time, most of these databases will probably be on the Web. If a database is listed here with a URL, it is already available on the Web.

Statistics

Historical Statistics of the United States: Colonial Times to 1970.
Statistics Masterfile.

Journal Indexes

Date in brackets indicates earliest coverage of articles.

America: History and Life: United States and Canada [since 1964]. <http://serials.abc-clio.com/>

Articlefirst [since 1990].

Arts and Humanities Citation Search [since 1980].

Biography Index [since 1984]. <http://www.hwwilson.com/>

Expanded Academic Index [since 1980].

Historical Abstracts: World History since 1450 (except United States and Canada) [since 1960]. <http://serials.abc-clio.com/>

Humanities Abstracts [since 1994].

Humanities Index [since 1984].

Index to American Periodicals of the 1700s and 1800s.

Infotrac-Expanded Academic Index. See Expanded Academic Index.

JSTOR. <http://www.jstor.org>

Periodical Abstracts [covers earlier articles, 1961–1991].

Project Muse [full text but covers only recent years].

ProQuest [since 1980].

Reader's Guide Abstracts [since 1994].

Reader's Guide to Periodical Literature [since 1984].

Social Sciences Abstracts [since 1994].

Social Sciences Citation Index [since 1988].

Social Sciences Index [since 1984].

UnCover [since 1988; citations online, full text for a fee]. <http://uncweb.carl.org>

Wilson Select [since 1994; full text].

Search Engines

Search engines provide a line for your search terms. Skill with **keyword** searching is crucial here. (For more on keyword searching, see Chapter 4, pp. 95–99.) One or more of the search engines listed below should be available to you. It is usually best to begin a search with the one(s) built into the browser you are using.

Alta Vista:
<http://www.altavista.com>

Dogpile:
<http://www.dogpile.com>

Excite:
<http://www.excite.com>

Google:
<http://www.google.com/>

Hotbot:
<http://hotbot.lycos.com>

Infoseek:
  <http://infoseek.go.com/>
Kanoodle:
  <http://www.kanoodle.com>
Lycos:
  <http://www.lycos.com>
Metacrawler:
  <http://www.metacrawler.com/>
SavvySearch:
  <http://www.savvysearch.com>
Webcrawler:
  <http://www.webcrawler.com>

Indexes and Directories

These are enormous lists of Web sites organized by subject. Find the category closest to "History." Follow the "History" links, moving from the more general to the more specific. Keep track of your search *path* so that if you get to a site relevant to your topic you can find it again. As always, bookmark relevant sites or write down their URLs.

About.com:
  <http://www.about.com/>
The Argus Clearing House:
  <http://www.clearinghouse.net/>
The English Server:
  <http://english-server.hss.cmu.edu/>
First Search:
  <http://www.oclc.org>
INFOMINE: Scholarly Internet Resource Collections:
  <http://infomine.ucr.edu/>
Librarians' Index to the Internet:
  <http://lii.org>
Magellan, the McKinley Internet Directory:
  <http://magellan.excite.com/>
My Virtual Reference Desk:
  <http://www.refdesk.com>
WWW Virtual Library:
  <http://www.vlib.org>
Yahoo!:
  <http://www.yahoo.com>

Gateway Sites to History Materials

These sites focus on history and have a large number of **links** to specialized history sites. As with the indexes and directories, start with the most general category and then follow the links that lead to subsections of that category until you find a site that by time period, geographical area, or subject is close to your topic. As always, keep track of the path by which you arrived at a particular sight and, if it is a valuable one, bookmark it or simply write down the URL.

Gateway to World History:
<http://www.hartford-hwp.com/gateway/>

Internet History Sourcebooks Project:
<http://www.fordham.edu/halsall/index.html>

Library of Congress:
<http://lcwebloc.gov/>

National Archives and Records Administration:
<http://www.nara.gov>

Organization of American Historians:
<http://www.oah.org/>

Tennessee Tech History Web Site:
<http://www.tntech.edu/www/acad/hist/history.html>

Voice of the Shuttle:
<http://vos.ucsb.edu/shuttle/history.html>

World History Compass:
<http://www.WorldHistoryCompass.com>

WWW-Virtual Library: History:
<http://www.ukans.cdu/history/VL/>

Archives of Texts and Documents

At these sites, specific historical texts (books, articles, primary documents) and, in a few cases, images and sound, are available. These archives have been chosen because online access to them is free, though this is not always the case for downloading or printing. Some of these sites also have links to other history archives.

American Memory: Historical Collections for the National Digital Library:
<http://lcweb2.loc.gov/ammem/ammemhome.html/>

American Studies at the University of Virginia:
<http://xroads.virginia.edu>

American Studies Crossroads Project:
<http://www.georgetown.edu/crossroads/>

The Avalon Project [American History documents, many periods]:
<http://www.yale.edu/lawweb/avalon/>

Berkeley Digital Library SunSITE:
<http://sunsite.berkeley.edu/>

California Digital Library: A Co-Library of the Campuses of the University of California:
<http://www.cdlib.org>

Colorado Digitalization Project:
<http://coloradodigital.coalliance.org>

Columbus and the Age of Discovery:
<http://www.millersv.edu/~columbus/>

Demography and Population Studies:
   <http://demography.anu.edu.au/VirtualLibrary/>

Duke University Rare Book, Manuscript, and Special Collections Library:
   <http://scriptorium.lib.duke.edu>

Early Canadiana Online:
   <http://www.canadiana.org>

Electronic Text Center:
   <http://etext.lib.virginia.edu/>

The English Server: History and Historiography:
   <http://english-server.hss.cmu.edu/history/>

Eurodocs: Primary Historical Documents from Western Europe:
   <http://library.byu.edu/~rdh/eurodocs/>

Everglades Digital Library:
   <http://everglades.fiu.edu/library/index.html>

Hanover Historical Texts Archive:
   <http://history.hanover.edu/project.htm>

History Text Archive:
   <http://www.geocities.com/Athens/Forum/9061/index.html>

Internet History Sourcebooks Project:
   <http://www.fordham.edu/halsall/>

The Internet Public Library:
   <http://www.ipl.org>

National Library of Canada:
   <http://minos.nlc-bnc.ca/index.html>

University of Pennsylvania Digital Library:
   <http://digital.library.upenn.edu>

The British Library:
   <http://portico.bl.uk/diglib/dlp/>

SAGE: Selected Archives at Georgia Tech and Emory Digital Archive Project:
   <http://sage.library.emory.edu>

University of Michigan Documents Center:
   <http://www.lib.umich.edu/libhome/Documents.center/index.html>

The World War One Document Archive:
   <http://www.lib.byu.edu/~rdh/wwi>

Specialized History Sites

These sites are usually dedicated to *particular* historical topics. In most cases, the names describe the area in which they specialize. Here you will find historical documents (primary and secondary, print and nonprint) and also links to similar kinds of sites. Only a small number of the several thousand such sites are listed here. Unless one is close to your theme, begin your search in the directories and gateway sites.

African American Perspectives [1818–1907]:
   <http://memory.loc.gov/ammem/aap/aaphome.html>

Africans in America [African American history since 1450]:
   <http://www.pbs.org/wgbh/aia/>

American Civil War Resources:
<http://scholar2.lib.vt.edu/spec/civwar/cwhp.htm>

American Life Histories: Manuscripts from the Federal Writers' Project, 1936–1940:
<http://lcweb2.loc.gov/ammem/wpaintro/wpahome.html>

Imperialism in the Making of America [1890s to 1901]:
<http://www.boondocksnet.com/moa/index.html>

Britannia History Index: The Age of Empire [Great Britain 1689–1901]:
<http://www.britannia.com/history/h80.html>

Britannia History Index: Reformation and Restoration [England 1486–1689]:
<http://britannia.com/history/h70.html>

Documenting the American South [to 1920]:
<http://metalab.unc.edu/docsouth/index.html>

Documents Relating to American Foreign Policy in Vietnam:
<http://www.mtholyoke.edu/acad/intrel/vietnam.htm>

The Evolution of the Conservative Movement:
<http://memory.loc.gov/ammem/amrvhtml/conshome.html>

First Person Narratives of the American South:
<http://metalab.unc.edu/docsouth/fpn/fpn.html>

The Gilded Page [U.S. 1870–1898]:
<http://www.wm.edu/~srnels/gilded.html>

The Great Chicago Fire:
<http://www.chicagohs.org/fire/intro/gef-index.html>

The Labyrinth: Resources for Medieval Studies:
<http://www.georgetown.edu/labyrinth>

The Making of America [nineteenth century]:
<http://www.umdl.umich.edu/moa/index.html>

Making of America [Nineteenth-century U.S. social history]:
<http://moa.umdl.umich.edu/>

Marriage, Women and the Law, 1815–1914 [U.S.]:
<http://www.rlg.org/strat/projdep.html>

Perry-Castañeda Library Map Collection:
<http://www.lib.utexas.edu/Libs/PCL/Map_collection/Map_collection.html>

Plimoth-on-Web: Plimoth Plantation's Web Page [Colonial U.S. 1620–1692]:
<http://www.plimoth.org>

The Rutgers Oral History Archives of World War II:
<http://history.rutgers.edu/oralhistory/orlhom.htm>

The Sixties Project [U.S. in 1960s]:
<http://lists.village.virginia.edu/sixties/>

Templo Mayor Museum [Ancient Mexico]:
<http://archaeology.la.asu.edu/tm>

The Valley of the Shadow: Two Communities in the American Civil War:
<http://jefferson.village.virginia.edu/vshadow>

Vaudeville and Popular Entertainment, 1870–1920 [U.S.]:
<http://lcweb2.loc.gov/ammem/vshtml/vshome.html>

Electronic History Journals

In addition to finding hundreds of print history journals on the Web (that is, journals that were originally in printed form), there are now a small but growing number of history journals, called e-journals, that are found *only* on the Web. If they are searchable, you can quickly discover if the journal has articles related to your **theme.** A new feature of some e-journals is a discussion list where readers send in their comments on the articles or on other readers' comments. Since most e-journals are new, however, not that many articles have been written for them yet. In some cases, print journals that have moved to the Web make their older issues available online. In either case, the title of the journal can help you decide if it is likely to cover your theme.

American Jewish Quarterly:
    <http://muse.jhu.edu/journals/american_jewish_history/>

American Quarterly:
    <http://muse.jhu.edu/journals/american_quarterly/>

Arachnion: A Journal of Ancient Literature and History:
    <http://www.cisi.unito.it/arachne/arachne.html>

Bulletin of the History of Medicine:
    <http://muse.jhu.edu/journals/bulletin_of_the_history_of_medicine/>

Directory of Electronic Journals, Newsletters and Academic Discussion Lists:
    <http://arl.cni.org/scomm/edir/index.html>

The Early America Review [Eighteenth century]:
    <http://www.earlyamerica.com/review>

Eighteenth-Century Life:
    <http://muse.jhu.edu/journals/eighteenth-century_life/>

Eighteenth-Century Studies [historiography and theory]:
    <http://muse.jhu.edu/journals/eighteenth-century_studies/>

Electronic Antiquity: Communicating the Classics:
    <gopher://info.utas.edu.au:70/11/Publications/>

Electronic Seminars in History [history of education: all periods]:
    <http://www.ihrinfo.ac.uk/ihr/esh/eshmnu.html>

Essays in History [edited by graduate students at the University of Virginia]:
    <http://etext.lib.virginia.edu/journals/EH>

Journal of Asian American Studies:
    <http://muse.jhu.edu/journals/journal_of_asian_american_studies/>

Journal of Early Christian Studies [Christianity from C.E. 100–700]:
    <http://muse.jhu.edu/journals/journal_of_early_christian_studies/>

Journal of the History of Ideas:
    <http://muse.jhu.edu/journals/journal_of_the_history_of_ideas/>

The North Star: A Journal of African-American Religious History:
    <http://cedar.barnard.columbia.edu/~north/>

Renaissance Forum: An Electronic Journal of Early-Modern Literary and Historical Studies:
    <http://www.hull.ac.uk/Hull/EL_Web/renforum/>

Reviews in American History:
    <http://muse.jhu.edu/journals/reviews_in_american_history/>

Sycamore: A Journal of American Culture [interdisciplinary]:
<http://www.unc.edu/sycamore/>

Electronic Discussion Lists in History

If you want to talk online about history to other students or faculty — or anybody who is interested — you should "subscribe" to a discussion list. These are called **listservs.** To subscribe (that is, join) a history discussion list, simply send an email to <listserv@h-net.msu.edu>. Write "sub," the name of the list, your name, and the name of your school. You will receive a confirming e-mail with further instructions.

The home site for history discussion lists as of May 2000 is <http://h-net.msu.edu>. Here are the names and topics of some of the larger discussion groups.

H-Africa [African history and culture]

H-Albion [British history]

H-Amstdy [American studies]

H-ASEH [environmental history]

H-Canada [Canadian history and studies]

H-Diplo [diplomatic history]

H-Ethnic [ethnic and immigration history]

H-Film [scholarly studies of media]

H-Ideas [intellectual history]

H-Labor [labor history]

H-Latam [Latin American history]

H-OIEAHC [colonial and early American history]

H-Pol [U.S. political history]

H-Psychohistory [psychohistory]

H-Russia [Russian history]

H-Sci-Med-Tech [history of science, medicine, and technology]

H-SHGAPE [U.S. Gilded Age and Progressive Era]

H-South [U.S. South]

H-Urban [urban history]

H-West [U.S. western frontiers]

H-Women [women's history]

H-World [world history]

APPENDIX B

Useful Information for the Historian

Historical Sources in Your Own Backyard

Some of the most rewarding kinds of historical research concern people, events, and places that you can almost reach out and touch. The history of your family, of the town you grew up in, or of events that shaped your parents' lives can be uncovered not only in a library but in a nearby museum or in a local history archive filled with old photographs, land deeds, birth registers, and personal correspondence. Every state in the United States and every province in Canada has its own historical society with a library of books, photographs, and documents on the state's history. Every city and most towns, even small ones, have a historical society or a museum where they keep the documents and artifacts (for example, objects like a millstone or a carriage) that tell the story of the town's past.

Wherever your school is located, from downtown Manhattan to rural Nebraska, you are probably not more than a short drive from a local history archive. If your research concerns the town or area where your school is located, look up the address of the local historical society and visit it. One of the most enjoyable aspects of history research is to hold in your hand an actual document or artifact that makes the past come alive — a 150-year-old land deed, a photograph of the center of town in 1890, a record player from 1918, a letter from a mother to her daughter written in 1838.

If you live or go to school in a large city or if you want to research the history of a county or an area of a state, many records are available to you. Each state (each province, in Canada) and each county within that state will have its own archive of historical materials. Each city will have at least one such archive. Cities and towns also have private historical societies. There are thousands of state, county, and local museums and archives. The best way to locate the major archives is to look them up in *Directory of Historical Organizations in the United States and Canada*. This work is published by the American Association for State and Local History, and the most recent volume is edited by Mary Bray Wheeler. This directory lists many hundreds of organizations. It has an index that arranges organizations alphabetically by the name of the place whose history they record. The archives are also listed alphabetically by subject if their collection of documents or artifacts is specialized in some way — say a town that was an important battlefield in the Civil War. The name, address, and telephone number of each organization is listed along with a brief description of the kind of materials it contains.

How to Research Your Family History

One of the most pleasurable kinds of historical research is the composition of your own family's history. Moreover, to research it is to recreate a portion of the historical experience of our nation. Because most of our ancestors came from other nations, a family history also will connect us with the historical experience of other lands. By studying the history of your family, you become aware of your own place within these broader historical experiences. Perhaps most important, knowledge of your family's history and its meaning can give you a strong sense of your cultural roots that will strengthen you throughout your lifetime.

The best sources — and in many cases the only sources — of information on the history of your family are the recollections, understandings, and long-term possessions of your relatives. Researching a family history involves investigating these sources as thoroughly and creatively as possible. This kind of research involves: (1) familiarizing yourself with the general history of the nations and regions, and of the specific times and places, in which your ancestors lived; (2) studying all available family records, such as diaries, photographs, heirlooms; and finally, and most important, (3) interviewing all available family members.

The interview is the core of a family history because, in most instances, it is the only way of uncovering the nature of your family's life. Without the recollections of your relations, you would not be able to discover more than a handful of names, dates, and places — only the barest outline of your family's history.

In preparing for this crucial aspect of family research, you must familiarize yourself with the basic history of your family so that you can place in proper context the information you obtain from the people you interview. You will need to prepare your questions beforehand, focusing on important aspects of family life and of the larger social and political life surrounding the family. Be sure that your questions establish the basics: the names, relationships, and principal home and workplace activities of each member of the family in each generation, going as far down the trunk and out on the limbs of the family tree as possible given the scope of your project and the memories of your relatives. Keep away from trivia (your great-uncle's favorite dessert), and look for information that will enable you to make comparisons between generations of your family and between it and other families. Investigate such topics as the type of dwelling and neighborhood, parent-child and husband-wife relationships, authority and status patterns, income and social mobility. When you come across major family events — immigration, military service, job and residence changes, involvement in political movements — probe the reasons for them, as they will illuminate the ties between your family and the nation's history.

In actually conducting the interview, use your prepared questions, taking care to make them as broad as possible; for example, "What was the neighborhood like when you lived there?" not simply "What was your address in 1936?" When you get an answer that seems to lead in the direction of important material, ignore your prepared questions temporarily and probe further. However, never interrupt an answer, even when the response seems unimportant. Your informants are the experts on their lives, and their self-perceptions — even if illogical or factually incorrect — are essential ingredients of family history. Finally, because the intricate web of your relatives' feelings is as important as the milestones of their lives, it is best to tape-record the interview if possible rather than rely on written notes. Record it all and then collect from your tapes the information which, on the one hand, best reflects your informants' testimony about their lives and, on the other, enables you to say something of importance about those lives and the times in which they were lived.

If there are important pieces missing from the story — your great-grandfather's birthplace, for instance, or the age at which your grandmother married — you can try to supplement your own family's records with official ones. Listed below are the best sources for family history research. Many of them are on the World Wide Web.

Sources for Family History Research

Printed Reference Sources

How to Climb Your Family Tree: Genealogy for Beginners. Baltimore, Md.: Genealogical Publishing Co., 1997.

The Researcher's Guide to American Genealogy. Baltimore, Md.: Genealogical Publishing Co., 1990. Val D. Greenwood, ed.

American Families: A Research Guide and Historical Handbook. Westport, Conn.: Greenwood, 1991.

State Censuses: An Annotated Bibliography of Censuses of Population Taken after 1790 by States and Territories of the United States. New York: Burt Franklin, 1969.

A Bibliography of American County Histories. Baltimore, Md.: American Genealogical Publishing Co., 1985.

Federal Population Censuses: A Catalogue of Microfilm Copies of Schedules [1790–1920]. Washington, D.C.: Library of Congress.

Biography and Genealogy Master Index. Detroit: Gale, 1980. Supplements annually. Now on CD-ROM and the World Wide Web.

Genealogical and Local History Books in Print. 4 vols. Baltimore, Md.: Genealogical Publishing Co., 1996–1997. Marian Hoffman, comp. and ed.

In Search of Your European Roots: A Complete Guide to Tracing Your Ancestors in Every European Country. Baltimore, Md.: Genealogical Publishing Co. 1994. Angus Baxter, ed.

Finding Your Hispanic Roots. Baltimore, Md.: Genealogical Publishing Co., 1997. George Riskamp, ed.

State Census Records. Baltimore, Md.: Genealogical Publishing Co., 1992. Ann S. Lainhart, ed.

American Passenger Arrival Records: A Guide to the Records of Immigrants Arriving at American Ports by Sail and Steam. Baltimore, Md.: Genealogical Publishing Co., 1993. Michael Tepper, ed. (Also see National Archives and Records Administration Web site listed below.)

Guide to Naturalization Records of the United States. Baltimore, Md.: Genealogical Publishing Co., 1997. Christina K. Shaefer, ed.

Electronic Reference Sources

U.S. GOVERNMENT RESOURCES

National Archives and Records Administration's Genealogy Page. This is a very large Web site. It tells you where different kinds of U.S. government records are kept and how you can find information in them. It also contains are large list of genealogical resources on the World Wide Web.
<http://www.nara.gov/genealogy/genindex.html>

GENERAL GENEALOGICAL RESOURCES

Cyndi's List of Genealogy Sites on the Internet. The largest list of sites and links on the Web.
<http://CyndisList.com>

The Church of Jesus Christ of Latter-Day Saints Family Search Genealogy Service:
<http://www.familysearch.org>

The Genealogy Home Page:
<http://www.genhomepage.com>

Gendex: WWW Genealogical Index:
<http://www.gendex.com/gendex>

Grammar and Style Manuals

If you know that your background in grammar and composition is weak, or if you need more specific information concerning report writing, here are a few manuals that should help.

Hacker, Diana. *A Pocket Style Manual.* 3d ed. Boston: Bedford Books/St. Martin's Press, 2000.

Hacker, Diana. *Rules for Writers.* 4th ed. Boston: Bedford Books/St. Martin's Press, 2000.

Lunsford, Andrea and Robert Connors. *The New St. Martin's Handbook.* Boston: Bedford Books/St. Martin's Press, 1999.

Strunk, William Jr. and E. B. White. *Elements of Style.* 3d ed. New York: Macmillan College, 1979.

University of Chicago Press, *The Chicago Manual of Style.* 14th ed. Chicago: University of Chicago Press, 1993.

Common Abbreviations Used in Footnotes, Bibliographies, Catalogs, and Reference Books

anon.	anonymous
app.	appendix
art.	article (plural, arts.)
b.	born
bk.	book (plural, bks.)
c.	copyright
ca.	*circa,* about, approximately. Used with approximate dates, e.g., "ca. 1804."
cf.	*confer,* compare. Used only when the writer wishes the reader to compare two or more works.
col.	column (plural, cols.)
comp.	compiler (plural, comps.)
d.	died
diss.	dissertation
ed.	edition, editor (plural eds.)
e.g.	*exempli gratia,* for example
et al.	*et alia,* and others
et seq.	*et sequens,* and the following
fig.	figure (plural, figs.)
ibid.	*ibidem,* in the same place
i.e.	*id est,* that is
ill.	illustrated, illustration
l. or ll.	line(s)
loc. cit.	*loco citato,* in the place cited (referring to the same passage cited in an immediately previous footnote)
MS	manuscript (plural, MSS)
n.	note, footnote (plural, nn.)
n.d.	no date (of publication is given)
n.p.	no place (of publication) or no publisher (is given)
o.p.	out of print
op. cit.	*opere citato,* in the work cited
passim	here and there (throughout the work cited)
pseud.	pseudonym
q.v.	*quod vide,* which see
rev.	revised
sic	so, thus (enclosed in brackets to indicate an error or unusual statement in a quotation)
supp.	supplement (plural, supps.)
trans.	translator
v. or vol.	volume (plural, vols.)

Glossary

Archive: A place in which public records or historical documents are preserved. On the Web: a site where historical documents are available in digital form.

Atlas: A bound collection of maps, often including illustrations, informative tables, or textual matter.

Bias: An author's attitude toward the subject being studied that influences the way in which the subject is interpreted.

Bibliography: A list, often with descriptive or critical notes, of works relating to a particular subject, period, or author; in student papers, a list of the works referred to or consulted.

Biography: A written history of a person's life.

Bookmark: A place on your browser (usually near the top) where you can click on any Web site that is on your screen and record the URL for future use.

Book review: An essay that comments on a particular work or a series of works on a single subject.

Browser: *See* Web browser.

Call number: A combination of characters assigned to a library book to indicate its place on a shelf.

Catalog: A complete listing of items, such as books, arranged systematically with descriptive details. *See also* Library catalog.

CD-ROM: A compact disc capable of containing a large amount of data that is read by a computer. May contain text, statistics, pictures, audio and video files.

Chart: A visual display of quantitative information. Common examples are bar charts and pie charts.

Chatroom: An open forum on the Web, a place where you or anyone can comment on current messages. Older messages are not preserved. To take part in a more organized and recorded discussion, subscribe to a *Listserv*.

Cheating: *See* Plagiarism.

Citation: A reference to a source of information used in preparing a written assignment; usually takes the form of a footnote/endnote. *See also* Documentation.

Conclusion: The last section of a written document. It sums up findings and interpretations.

Continuity: As a component of writing, continuity is the coherent flow of the author's arguments as the author moves from one point to another.

Cyclical school: School of historical thought that believes history repeats itself. According to this school, essential forces of nature and human nature are changeless, causing past patterns of events to repeat themselves endlessly.

Database: A large collection of data organized for rapid search and retrieval, as by a computer.

Date range: It indicates the time period covered by a large collection of documents (books, articles, newspapers, etc.)

Directory: On a computer, an organized list of files and folders. On the Web, a kind of search engine. *See also* Search engine and Subject index.

Dissertation: An extended, usually written, treatment of a subject; specifically one submitted for a doctorate.

Documentation: The use of historical or other evidence to support a statement or argument; usually takes the form of footnotes/endnotes or material such as pictures, graphs, tables, or copies of documents.

Draft: A preliminary sketch, outline, or version of an essay or paper.

Ellipsis: In a long quotation, the omission of words that are not necessary to the point being made; also, the punctuation (. . .) that appears in place of the omitted words.

Encyclopedia: A work that contains information on all branches of knowledge or that comprehensively treats a particular branch of knowledge; usually comprised of articles arranged alphabetically by subject. Some encyclopedias are online and can be searched electronically.

Endnote: A note of reference, explanation, or comment placed at the end of an essay or paper. *See also* Documentation.

Evidence: *See* Primary document; Secondary source.

Essay exam: A test that requires a complete, well-organized written answer on a particular topic.

Footnote: A note of reference, explanation, or comment placed below the text on a printed page. *See also* Documentation.

Full text: Refers to electronic databases that contain all of the text of a written source rather than merely information for finding the source.

Graph: A precise drawing, usually taking the form of a series of points and lines that make visual the numerical changes in the relationship between two or more things.

Historian: A student or writer of history, especially one who produces a scholarly examination of a historical topic.

Historical novel: A work of fiction based on actual events and people.

Historiography: The study of changes in the methods, interpretations, and conclusions of historians over time.

Home page: The first page of a Web site, with links to other parts of the site and/or to other sites.

Hyperlink: A one-step connection between two different pages on the World Wide Web. They appear on your screen as click-on boxes or icons or as highlighted or underlined text.

Identification question: A test question requiring the identification of a person, place, object, or event and an explanation of its importance in history.

Index: An alphabetical list of persons and subjects and the page numbers where they are discussed in a book. For electronic indexes, *see* Subject index.

Interlibrary loan: The loaning of a book by one library to another.

Internet: A worldwide network of computers that can transfer information back and forth. *See also* World Wide Web.

Introduction: The beginning section of a multipage paper. It sets out the theme (or thesis) of the paper.

Journal: A daily newspaper; a periodical dealing with matters of current interest. For students: a written record, created by the student, of some aspect of a course.

Keyword: A word or words that represent a core aspect of a subject to be researched. Used in searching online catalogs and electronic databases found in libraries and on the World Wide Web.

Library catalog: A system that organizes all the holdings of a library; most are now electronic and can be searched by title, author, or keyword.

Library stacks: Shelves on which a library's books and journals are stored.

Link: *See* Hyperlink.

Linking paragraph: A paragraph that describes to the reader how an essay is moving from one important point to another.

Linking sentence: A sentence that ties together the points made in two paragraphs. It almost always comes at the end of one paragraph or at the beginning of the very next one.

Listserv: Like e-mail but confined to subscribers who have a special interest in the topic of the list. Many thousands of listservs are on the Web. Many are moderated: Someone organizes the messages coming in by date and topic. These messages are preserved so that you can read previous exchanges between subscribers.

Microfiche: A sheet of microfilm containing pages of printed matter in reduced form.

Microfilm: A film bearing a photographic record on a reduced scale of printed or other graphic matter.

Monograph: A scholarly study of a specific topic.

Multiple choice exam: A test made up of questions with several possible answers, one of which is the correct or best answer.

Note cards: Small pieces of paper (3" × 5" or 4" × 6") that are convenient for notes and the indexing of those notes when researching.

Objective exam: A test made up of factual questions for which there is only one correct answer for each question.

Online catalog: An electronic catalog that enables the user to search the holdings of a library, and possibly other libraries and databases, from a computer.

Paraphrase: A restatement of a passage, idea, or work giving the meaning in different words. Paraphrases of original work, like direct quotations, require proper documentation. *See also* Plagiarism.

Peer editing: *See* Peer reviewing.

Peer reviewing: Examining the work (usually written work) of another student in your class. The purpose is to respond constructively to the student so that the work can be improved.

Periodical: A publication with a fixed interval between issues.

Periodical database: A large collection of articles from journals, magazines, or newspapers in electronic, searchable form.

Plagiarism: To steal and present the ideas or words of another as one's own; to use material without crediting its source; to present as new and original an idea or product derived from an existing source. Plagiarism is a serious act of academic dishonesty. *See also* Paraphrase; Quotation.

Plug-ins: Computer software that enhances the capability of a browser or other program.

Primary document, primary source: Firsthand evidence that records the words of someone who participated in or witnessed the events described or of someone who received his or her information from direct participants.

Progressive school: School of historical thought that believes human history illustrates neither endless cycles nor divine intervention but continual progress. According to this school, the situation of humanity is constantly improving.

Proofreading: A careful rereading of your own (or someone else's) written work to correct any errors of style or grammar.

Providential school: School of historical thought that believes that the course of history is determined by God and that the flow of historical events represents struggles between forces of good and evil.

Quotation: A statement that repeats exactly the words of a source. Such a statement must be enclosed within quotation marks and properly documented. *See also* Plagiarism.

Reference book: A work, such as a dictionary or encyclopedia, containing useful facts or information.

Research bibliography: A list of sources that may be needed to research a topic/theme for a formal paper; includes publication information and location of the materials.

Research outline: A list of the parts of your topic/theme that need to be researched and a tentative ordering of these parts.

Research paper: A formal writing assignment on a specific theme that requires the reading and synthesis of primary and secondary sources; also requires documentation such as footnotes/endnotes and a bibliography.

Revise: To look over again in order to correct or improve; to make a new, amended, improved, or up-to-date version of an essay or paper.

Rough draft: First version of a written assignment which is polished and revised in later drafts.

Search engine: A computer program that allows the user to locate World Wide Web sites, usually by keyword or subject.

Secondary source: Records the findings of someone who did not observe a historical event but who investigated primary evidence of it.

Short-answer exam: Test that requires brief written answers to factual questions.

Stacks: *See* Library Stacks.

Statistics: A branch of mathematics dealing with the collection, analysis, interpretation, and presentation of numerical data; a collection of quantitative data.

Subject bibliographies: Lists of books, articles, and other material according to subject.

Subject directory: *See* Subject index.

Subject headings: Terms used in catalogs, such as the *Library of Congress Subject Headings,* to describe the contents of a library's or a Web site's materials.

Subject index: On the World Wide Web, an organized list of links to Web sites according to subject.

Table: A systematic arrangement of data, usually in rows and columns for ready reference; a condensed enumeration.

Take-home exams: Tests usually consisting of one or more short essays that are prepared outside of class.

Textbook: Often the principal reading in an introductory course; usually supplemented by other, more specialized materials.

Theme: A narrow part of a **topic** that you have chosen or been assigned for research. A theme sets limits on the area to be investigated and also suggests the kinds of questions that will be answered and the points that will be made.

Topic: A subject area chosen or assigned for research.

URL: Stands for "Uniform Resource Locator." A URL is the electronic address of a Web site or Web page.

Web browser: Software that interprets hypertext markup language (HTML) and displays embedded graphics and multimedia; allows the user to view a variety of content on World Wide Web sites.

Word processing: The production of typewritten documents, such as course assignments, by computer programs that allow great flexibility in editing.

World Wide Web: Part of the Internet that uses hypertext markup language (HTML) to connect texts, including images and sound, by means of embedded links.

Writing outline: Framework for a research paper that lists thoughts and ideas in an organized manner and acts as a guide for writing the rough draft of a formal paper.

Yearbook: A book published yearly containing a report or summary of statistics or facts.

Acknowledgments (continued from p. iv)

The Massacre in the Main Temple (Codex Duran) from *The Broken Spears* by Miguel Leon-Portilla. © 1962, 1990 by Miguel Leon-Portilla. Expanded and Updated Edition © 1992 by Miguel Leon-Portilla. Reprinted by permission of Beacon Press, Boston.

Metacrawler.com search results. Reprinted with the express consent of GO2Net, Inc. All rights reserved.

Middlesex Company Boarding House Regulations of the Middlesex Company, c. 1850. The American Textile History Museum, Lowell, Mass.

Excerpt from *Narrative of the Life of Frederick Douglass, An American Slave, Written by Himself,* edited with an introduction by David W. Blight. Copyright © 1993 by Bedford/St. Martin's.

From *Rise to Globalism* by Stephen E. Ambrose, copyright 1971, 1976, 1980, 1983, 1985, 1988 by Stephen E. Ambrose. Used by permission of Viking Penguin, a division of Penguin Putnam Inc.

From *World Civilizations,* Eighth Edition, Volume I by Philip Lee Ralph, et al. Copyright 1991, 1986, 1982, 1974, 1969, 1964, 1958, 1955 by W. W. Norton & Company, Inc. Used by permission of W. W. Norton & Company, Inc.

The World since 1500: A Global History, Fourth Edition, by L. S. Stavrianos, 1976. Reprinted by permission of Prentice Hall, Inc., Upper Saddle River, N.J.

Index

223